J. Whittall

D1486255

A CRITICAL INTRODUCTION
TO THE NEW TESTAMENT

A CRITICAL INTRODUCTION TO THE NEW TESTAMENT

by

REGINALD H. FULLER

Professor of New Testament
Union Theological Seminary, New York

GERALD DUCKWORTH & CO. LTD.
3 Henrietta Street, London, W.C.2

First published 1966

© 1966 by Reginald H. Fuller

Printed in Great Britain
by T. and A. Constable Ltd., Hopetoun Street
Printers to the University of Edinburgh

DEDICATED
TO MY WIFE

PREFACE

IT was an honour to be invited by Dr Micklem to write a companion volume to G. W. Anderson's *A Critical Introduction to the Old Testament*, published in this series in 1959. Like its companion, it replaces an earlier volume of the same title, that by A. S. Peake (1919).

This book has grown so gradually out of lectures delivered each year since 1950, first at St David's College, Lampeter, and subsequently at this Seminary, that it is impossible to thank all the scholars to whom I have been indebted. Some are acknowledged in the footnotes.

Most immediately, however, my thanks are due to one of my students, Miss Margaret Jackson, who transcribed in shorthand the lectures as they were given in 1964–65, and by making her notes available to me made my task much easier to accomplish as well as expediting the publication.

REGINALD H. FULLER

Seabury-Western Theological Seminary
Evanston, Illinois
Feast of the Presentation of Christ in the Temple, 1966

CONTENTS

I.—NEW TESTAMENT INTRODUCTION
AS A DISCIPLINE

THE modern study of the New Testament is divided into three main disciplines: Introduction, Exegesis, and the Theology of the New Testament. Introduction, in turn, is divided (cf. G. W. Anderson, *A Critical Introduction to the Old Testament*, p. 1) into general introduction (the history of the text and Canon) and special introduction. The history of the Canon deals with the question, how, when and why were these 27 books selected for inclusion in the New Testament? This will be touched upon briefly in Chapter VII. The study of the history of the text seeks to recover the earliest possible working of the Greek text. Like Dr Anderson we shall omit this aspect here. Special introduction deals with the history of the individual NT books, their sources (if any), the history of those sources before they were used in the particular book, the date the book was written, the place of its writing, the identity of its author and its intended readers, the question of its integrity (i.e. the history of the book between its first writing and its inclusion in the New Testament), the occasion of its writing (what need was it meeting?) and the content of the book.

Introduction is preparatory work for exegesis, which seeks to interpret the text as the author intended it to be understood in the concrete situation for which it was written. Exegesis must be distinguished from exposition, which seeks to determine from the exegesis what the text means for today. Hence, New Testament Introduction is preparatory work for preaching.

New Testament theology has a somewhat questionable place in NT study, and some people question whether it is possible at all. But it does seem to be necessary to gather the doctrinal affirmations of the NT whether we arrange them topically or historically before handing our results over to the dogmatic and systematic theologian.

Chapters II–VI will deal with special introduction.

NT introduction is a fairly modern discipline. In the primitive church there was for a time an interest in dates and authorships, especially in the second century, when the church was concerned with question of apostolic authorship and dating as criteria for inclusion of books within the Canon or for their exclusion (cf. Papias, Marcion and the Anti-Marcionite prologues). But once the NT books were safely included in the Canon, interest was lost in introductory questions, and the works of the Church Fathers on scripture are entirely of the nature of expositions and homilies.

As with the Old Testament (Anderson, p. 2) it was the Reformation and the Renaissance which gave rise to the scientific study of introductory questions. Luther realized the importance of such questions for exegesis, but lacked the tools for dealing with them systematically. It was with the Enlightenment that introduction was firmly established as a scientific discipline, though curiously enough it was a French Roman Catholic (Richard Simon, 1638–1712) who pioneered it.

It was the eighteenth-century German rationalist scholars, beginning with J. D. Michaelis (1717–91), who did the early substantial work. It was they who formulated the right questions to ask, such as: What was the original language of Matthew? Why did Luke write his gospel when Matthew and Mark were written already? Who wrote Hebrews? And it was they and their successors who worked out many of the answers which are commonly accepted today.

The rationalists insisted that the NT must be treated like any other ancient work, with the same historical and critical methods that were being used by their classical colleagues on the literature of Ancient Greece and Rome. But it is important to realize that although NT criticism began with rationalism, the use of critical methods does not commit us to rationalism itself.

This is indicated by the fact that the critical methods first introduced by the rationalists were subsequently continued by representatives of very different schools, by F. D. E. Schleiermacher (1768–1834) who combined rationalism with pietism; by the Hegelian idealists of the Tübingen school, such as F. C. Baur (1792–1860) and D. F. Strauss (1808–74); by their more moderate successors, such as H. J. Holtzmann (1832–1910); by the Ritschlian liberals, such as A. von Harnack (1851–1930); by Karl Barth and the neo-orthodox scholars, and finally by the Bultmann school in Germany.

But why should we pursue historical criticism? And what relevance has it for Christian faith? The answer is, the NT consists of historical documents. They are historical in two different ways. First, they proclaim that God has decisively acted in history, the history of Jesus of Nazareth. If God has so condescended to act, it means that He has exposed His action to all the risks of historical criticism. It is true that the historian can never disclose the revelatory content of that history, but it is his preliminary task to demonstrate that that history was of such a kind that it could be the vehicle of that revelatory content.[1] Secondly, the NT writings are the proclamation *in history* of the history of Jesus as the saving act of God. They were proclamations of Jesus as Christ in concrete historical situations of the past. Thus the earliest church's proclamation of Jesus as the Christ differed from that of the Hellenistic Jewish Christians, and this in turn from that of the Gentile Mission and that of Paul. The proclamation of the sub-apostolic age was different again. All these varying types of proclamation are found within the pages of the New Testament. That is why, if we are to understand what the NT texts were meant to say by the authors when they were first written (which we have to determine before we can know what they say—and do not say—to us), we must first understand the historical situation in which they were first written. Hence the

---

[1] See the present writer's observations in *The Mission and Achievement of Jesus*, 1954, pp. 13–15. It is gratifying to discover that since those words were written, the same concern has become manifest among Bultmann's disciples.

importance of NT introduction alike for exegesis and for preaching.

It is because the NT contains documents emanating from all the periods and environments indicated in the preceding paragraph—because it gives us the proclamation of Jesus as the Christ in these successive periods and environments, that we will treat the NT books, not in their order in the Canon, but so far as possible according to their historical order. Often this entails critical decisions, the reason for which will only become apparent in the discussion.

The problems posed by the various NT writings are extremely varied, and fifteen years of teaching experience has shown that each book must be approached differently. Hence there is no uniformity of arrangement in the treatment of the separate books. Sometimes questions of date and authorship need to be treated first, sometimes the use of sources, sometimes the integrity, sometimes the milieu in which the author wrote. Some attempt has been made to date each writing, and to assign it to a specific place of origin. But the answers to such questions are usually (with the exception of the genuine Pauline letters) highly speculative, and are meant to be no more than rough suggestions. It is far more important to assign each book to its rightful place in the history of the NT tradition, and more attention has been paid to finding an answer to that question.

II.—THE LETTERS OF PAUL

I. The Problem of Authenticity

RSV and NEB contain thirteen letters ascribed to the Apostle Paul. Of these, the Pastorals (Past) are quite certainly later than Paul (though there are a few scholars who still[1] argue for their Pauline authorship). Hebrews, which AV (KJV) understandably, and ERV unforgivably, still ascribed to Paul, is almost universally (even by reputable scholars in the Roman Church, despite the anathema of the Council of Trent) acknowledged to be the work of a different author. Of the remaining letters, the Pauline authorship of 2 Thess, Col and Eph (especially the latter) is widely questioned, and so they will be considered separately as 'disputed letters'. There remain 1 Thess, Gal, Phil, 1 and 2 Cor, Philem, and Rom. Unless we are persuaded by A. Q. Morton and his computer[2] that only Gal, Philem, 1 and 2 Cor and Rom are authentic to Paul, we shall be able confidently to accept all seven as definitely the work of the Apostle.

It is important to be able to place these letters in some sort of relative order. This has a bearing on their exegesis, for then we can detect possible developments in Pauline thought, and thus be able to give a better exegesis of the letters. Also, it is important, as we saw in Chapter I, to reconstruct as far as we can the concrete situations in which the letters were written. To achieve these two tasks, it will be very helpful if we can construct a chronology of Paul's life, or at least that part of it covered by the letters.

[1] We leave open for the time being the possibility that 2 Tim is based on a farewell letter of Paul written shortly before his martyrdom in Rome.

[2] *Christianity in the Computer Age*, 1964.

Pauline Chronology

Most attempts to construct a chronology of Paul's life start from the data in Acts. This procedure is tempting, because only Acts offers a consecutive narrative of Paul's movements, even though it is often vague in its chronological data ('after some time' is one of Luke's favourite chronological indications!) and often leaves gaps (e.g. the 'hidden years' at Tarsus or the important $2\frac{1}{2}$ years' residence at Ephesus). Acts is also written at a distance from the events it narrates, and has often unwittingly telescoped accounts of different events into one (e.g., in Acts 15, the Jerusalem Conference and the promulgation of the apostolic decrees). But recent study of Acts has raised much more serious questions than the mere deficiencies of its chronological data or in information covering certain periods of Paul's career. Acts (see below, pp. 122–132) must now be regarded primarily as a theological reconstruction of early church history from the standpoint of the sub-apostolic church. It tells us more about the theological outlook of the sub-apostolic church than it does about the history of the apostolic age. Thus the recent study of Acts (see below, pp. 122ff) has led to the following important methodological conclusions. In Pauline studies the genuine letters of Paul are our primary sources. Where Paul and Acts contradict each other, Paul must be followed rather than Acts. Acts can be confidently used only when: (1) it tallies with the Pauline data; (2) it offers supplementary data which are otherwise compatible with the Pauline information.

This modern assessment of the relative value of Acts and Paul has consequences for construction of Pauline chronology which are not always realized. The only legitimate procedure today is the reverse of the usual order: to start from the data of Paul, and then fit the data of Acts, after critical assessment, into the Pauline scheme. This method is adopted by J. Knox[1] and by W. Marxsen.[2]

[1] J. Knox, *Chapters in a Life of Paul*, 1954.
[2] W. Marxsen, *Einleitung in das Neue Testament*, 1963.

Pauline Data

Period I

For the early part of Paul's Christian career Gal 1:13–2:14 yields the following data:

(i) Conversion in the neighbourhood of Damascus, inferred from 1:17, whence it appears ('returned') that Paul had been in Damascus prior to his conversion.

(ii) To Arabia Nabatea, and back to Damascus.

(iii) (Two years[1] after conversion): first visit to Jerusalem.

(iv) Activity in Syria and Cilicia (13 years).[2]

(v) Second (conference) visit to Jerusalem.

(vi) Paul's return to Antioch and clash with Peter.

Period II

(i) Paul leaves Philippi for Thessalonica[3] (1 Thess 2:2).

(ii) From Thessalonica to Athens: Timothy sent from Athens to Thessalonica (1 Thess 3:1f, 6).

Period III

(i) Prior to the writing of 1 Cor churches had been established in Galatia (16:1) and Asia Minor (16:19).

(ii) Paul writes 1 Cor from Ephesus (16:8). He announces his future plans. He will stay at Ephesus until Pentecost, then will travel *via* Macedonia to Corinth to

---

[1] The ancients frequently reckoned inclusively counting both first and last years of a series. Also, a fraction of a year counted as a whole year.

[2] Some reckon the thirteen years from the conversion. But the words 'after this' which introduce each visit to Jerusalem indicate that Paul is presenting his movements *seriatim*. It would also, as will become apparent, make the interval between the Apostolic conference and Paul's arrival at Corinth too long.

[3] This journey cannot be identical with that implied in Period III (i.e. the collection journey), for the collection indicates established churches. In 1 Thess Paul is speaking of the journey on which the churches at Philippi and Thessalonica were founded.

arrange the collection, winter there and possibly go to
Jerusalem to superintend its delivery (16:5f).

(iii) When 2 Cor was written Paul had visited Corinth twice
(12 : 14, 13 : 1).

(iv) Rom 15 indicates that this letter was written from
Corinth. At this point Paul plans to go to Jerusalem,
and thence *via* Rome to Spain.

In none of these three periods does Paul furnish any
absolute chronological data. The nearest he comes to it is in
the statement in 2 Cor 11:32 that he fled from Damascus at the
end of his post-conversion (cf. Acts 9:23ff) residence there in
order to escape arrest by Aretas, King of Nabatea (cf. Acts
9:24f). Aretas died in the year 40. Therefore Paul's conversion
must have taken place prior to 40.

ACTS

Period I

This is covered by Acts 9:1–29 (Paul's conversion, post-
conversion residence in Damascus, and first visit to Jerusalem).
Acts omits any reference to Arabia Nabatea, blames Paul's
flight on the 'Jews' (an invariable trait in Acts) and gives a
totally different picture of Paul's relations with the Jerusalem
church on this visit. Gal is to be preferred here.

The thirteen years in Syria and Cilicia are covered by
Acts 9:30 (Paul in Caesarea and Tarsus); 11:25f (Barnabas
brings Paul from Tarsus to Antioch where he resides for a
whole year); 11:27–30, 12:25 (Paul and Barnabas sent to
Jerusalem with famine relief). This visit is impossible to
reconcile with the account in Gal, according to which Paul's
second post-conversion visit was for the Jerusalem conference,
although many (especially British) scholars have made this
identification. We must assume that the author of Acts had
an undated notice of a visit of Paul and Barnabas to Jerusalem to deliver a collection from Antioch. This cannot have
been the third and final visit with the collection from Macedonia and Achaea. Note that since the point of departure and

the personnel involved are identical with Gal 2:1f, the visit
of Acts 11 and 12 must be identified with the conference visit
of Gal 2:1ff, and of Acts 15:1ff. The author of Acts has here
produced a doublet.

The author of Acts further includes the so-called 'first
missionary journey' (Acts 13–14) in this period. It proceeds
from Antioch *via* Cyprus to Pamphylia, Pisidia, South
Galatia and Antioch. The status of this journey has become
highly dubious for recent scholars. Haenchen and Marxsen
think it is a 'model journey' constructed by the author of Acts.
Their suspicions are based on the sub-apostolic theology in
these chapters (the natural theology of Acts 14:15ff and the
appointment of presbyters by Paul and Barnabas in 14:23).
But there is similar theology in Paul's speech at the Areopagus
in Acts 17:22ff. This is in the second missionary journey, which
is basically authentic. So the author could certainly have
inserted this theology into an already existing source. But
there is a more pertinent reason for suspecting the first
missionary journey. This is that a visit to Pisidia, etc., is
difficult to square with Gal 1:21, which speaks of activity only
in Syria and Cilicia during this period. The question is not
unimportant, for it has some bearing on the question of both
the date and the recipients of Galatians (see below, pp. 23–31).
And if, as we think, Galatians was written to the South
Galatians, it is surprising that Paul should have omitted any
reference to his *first* visit at Gal 1:21. Perhaps the best solution
is to suppose that for Acts 13–14 the author of Acts got hold of
an itinerary or travel diary which was in fact a doublet of the
first part of the second missionary journey in 15:40–16:6.[1]
Consequently, we follow Paul rather than Acts for the whole
period between the first and second visits to Jerusalem.

At the conclusion of this thirteen year period (i.e. eliminat-
ing the famine visit of Acts 11 and the first missionary journey
of Acts 13–14) Acts begins again to tally with Gal. Paul and
Barnabas are chosen to represent the church of Antioch at

[1] In which case he wrongly inferred that Paul went with Barnabas
to Cyprus, and that Barnabas then accompanied Paul to South Galatia.

the Jerusalem conference (15:1ff) and, if our argument above, pp. 8f was correct, to bring the famine relief as well. The discrepancies between Acts 15:4–29 and Gal 2–10 need not detain us here (see below, p. 25).

Period II

Here Acts gives its second Missionary journey, following upon the Jerusalem conference (Acts 15:36–18:22). Starting from Antioch, Paul travels *via* South Galatia and Asia Minor to Macedonia, Athens and Corinth, where he stays for a year and a half (18:11) plus 'many days longer' (Acts 18:18, RSV). He then returns to Antioch *via* Ephesus, Caesarea (and Jerusalem?—depending on the meaning of 'church' in 18:22). The Pauline data in Period II fit in here, except for the slight discrepancy over the movements of Timothy.[1] It is also difficult to suppose that Paul actually went to Jerusalem (Acts 18:22) prior to his settling at Ephesus, since Gal, which is concerned to relate *all* of Paul's contacts with Jerusalem, is silent about it.[2]

Period III

Acts here gives its third missionary journey (Acts 18:23, 19:1–21:15). This takes Paul from Antioch *via* South Galatia to Ephesus, where he stays three months (19:8) plus two years (19:10) (cf. 20:31, 'three years' = a round number). While at Ephesus, he announces (19:21) his plan eventually to visit Rome (as in Rom 15:25) and departs for Macedonia and Greece, staying two months at Corinth (20:3). Then he travels back through Macedonia (Philippi) and thence by ship, stopping off at Troas, etc., to Miletus, then to Caesarea, where he disembarks and goes up to Jerusalem.

For this third missionary journey Acts appears to be follow-

---

[1] See below, pp. 20f.
[2] We reject the view that Gal was the earliest of the letters, written prior to the Jerusalem council and the so-called second missionary journey. See below, pp. 23–26.

ing a reliable itinerary, though its sub-apostolic theology is again detectable in the Areopagus speech (17:21–31), and in the speech to the Ephesian elders (20:17–35). The Pauline data confirm the first part of the journey from Ephesus to Corinth, and also, by implication, the second part, from Corinth to Jerusalem. But there are gaps in Acts. There is no mention of Paul's troubles at Corinth (1, 2 Cor) or of his interim visit (2 Cor 2:1, etc.) between the first and final visits. Nor is anything said of the troubles in Galatia, which in our opinion coincided with the Ephesian residence.

Paul's subsequent activities in Acts (21:17–end: arrest at Jerusalem, Caesarean imprisonment, journey to Rome, two years in protective custody) are not covered in the letters—save by his declared intention to visit Rome on the way to Spain, but under very different circumstances. If we think that the captivity epistles (Col, Philem, Eph, and Phil) were written during the Roman imprisonment, there would be further overlapping of data here. In our opinion, however, Eph is almost certainly deutero-Pauline, and the authenticity and date of Colossians are problematic. Phil, Philem were more likely written during the Ephesian residence (see below).

Absolute Chronology in Acts

Acts provides one firm piece of information that enables us to pinpoint an absolute date. This is the statement (18:12) that during his first Corinthian residence Paul was brought before Gallio, the proconsul of Achaea. Now in 1905 there was discovered at Delphi an inscription[1] which enables us to date Gallio's proconsulship from June 51 to May 52.[2]

We cannot be quite sure at what stage of Paul's first residence at Corinth Gallio took up office. But Paul must by

[1] For the text (in translation) see C. K. Barrett, *The New Testament Background: Selected Documents*, 1958 pp. 48f.

[2] So Marxsen. It is just possible that the period was from June 52 to June 53 (so Haenchen, though he considers this less likely), also that Gallio held office for two years (considered possible by Barrett, who however agrees that 51 is more likely date for Gallio's inauguration).

then have worked there long enough to have been reported to
Gallio as a trouble-maker. It is reasonable to suppose that
Paul arrived in Corinth in the autumn of 49 and left in the
summer of 51.

In Acts 18:2 we are told that when Paul first arrived at
Corinth he met Aquila and Priscilla, who had 'lately come
from Italy . . . because Claudius had commanded all the Jews
to leave Rome'. The association of this couple with Paul
during this period is clinched by 1 Cor 16:19 and Rom 16:3–5.
By the time these letters were written, however, they had
moved on to Ephesus (cf. Acts 18:18). But they were clearly
known to the church at Corinth, otherwise Paul would not
have sent a greeting to the Corinthians from them. The
expulsion of the Jews from Rome is noted by Suetonius, *Life
of Claudius* 25: 'Since the Jews constantly made disturbances
at the instigation of Chrestus (widely taken to be a bowdlerize
reference to Christians), he expelled them from Rome'. A late
Latin historian, Orosius (*c.* 400) gives[1] the date of this expulsion of the Jews as 49, which ties in perfectly with our conclusion
that Paul arrived in Corinth in the autumn of 49.

It is reasonable to infer that the so-called second missionary
journey began in the spring of 49. This leaves time for Paul
to found (*sic*, since we regard the first missionary journey as a
doublet of the first part of the second) the churches in South
Galatia.

If Paul's second visit for the Jerusalem conference coincided
with the famine visit, this may help us to date the conference.
Acts 11:28 states that a world-wide famine occurred during
the reign of Claudius (41–54). 'But there never was such a
world-wide famine' (Haenchen)—only partial famines during
Claudius' reign. Josephus (*Ant* XX, 101) tells us that conditions were particularly bad in Palestine in 46–48. For this
reason, 48 is a widely favoured date for the conference. Any
earlier date would run Paul's conversion too close to the
crucifixion.[2] However, the year 49 would be just as possible.

[1] *Historia contra paganos*, VII, 6, 17f. (Reference in Haenchen.)
[2] For which the favoured date today is April, A.D. 30.

From the conference we can easily work backwards to Paul's conversion. The thirteen years' activity in Syria and Cilicia cover 35–48 (or 36–49). Paul's first post-conversion visit to Jerusalem was then in 35 (or 36), his two years in Arabia and Damascus 33–35 (34–36), and his conversion in 33 (34).

Now we return to Paul's first residence in Corinth and try to work forwards. This, however, is much more difficult, owing to the vagueness of the chronological data both in the letters and in Acts, and the lack of any certain external checks.

If Paul arrived in Corinth in the late autumn of 49, he must have left there in the summer of 51, since his residence there lasted eighteen months plus 'many days' (see above, p. 10). The next difficulty is to date the beginning of Paul's residence in Ephesus. Time has to be allowed for him to travel from Corinth *via* Cenchreae to Ephesus and back to Antioch, then to begin the so-called third missionary journey from Antioch *via* South Galatia to Ephesus. Acts gives no chronological information, so we can only conjecture when Paul's Ephesian ministry began. This is one of the major lacunae in Pauline chronology, and it is no wonder that opinions are divided. Haenchen (p. 60) for instance gives 52, while Dodd places it at 54.[1] This latter date seems too long after the latest possible date. We may agree with Haenchen that Paul departed from Corinth and arrived at Ephesus in the summer of 52. Then the Ephesian residence will end in the fall of 54, and Paul spent the winter of 54–55 in Corinth. He is in Philippi for the passover of 55, and appears at Jerusalem with the collection at Pentecost that year. Paul is then arrested and brought to Caesarea, in the summer of 55. According to Acts 24:27 he spent two years in prison in Caesarea. Haenchen, however, thinks that in the source followed by Acts the two years applied to the duration of Felix' procuratorship, and that the author of Acts mistakenly transferred the two years to Paul's imprisonment. Connected with this is the contro-verted problem of the date of Felix' removal and the installa-tion of Festus as his successor. Dodd puts it at 59 or 61. But

[1] *Oxford Helps to the Study of the Bible*, 1931, p. 196.

according to Haenchen, it was much earlier. In *Ant* XX, 182, Josephus relates how the Jews of Caesarea complained to Nero of Felix' misgovernment. Nero dismissed the charge against Felix at the instance of Festus' brother, Pallas. This could only have happened before the end of 55, when Pallas himself fell from grace. Accordingly, Haenchen sets the fall of Felix in the summer of 55, and his two years procuratorship 53–55. This fits in quite well with the dating of Paul's arrest at Pentecost 55.

Festus then sent Paul to Rome. This journey began early in the fall of 55 (cf. the mention of the 'fast', i.e. the day of the Atonement, in 27:9: this falls on 10 Tishri, in September–October). After the shipwreck the three winter months (28:11) were spent in Malta, so that Paul arrived at Rome in the early part of 56. The 'two years' of Acts 28:30 brings us down to 58.

Proposed Pauline Chronology

33 (34). Conversion.

33–35 (34–36). Paul in Arabia Nabatea and Damascus.

35 (36). First post-conversion visit to Jerusalem.

35–48 (36–49). Activity in Syria, Cilicia and Antioch.

48 (49). Second (conference) visit to Jerusalem.

49 (spring to autumn). Paul at Antioch. Foundation of churches in South Galatia. Journey through Asia Minor to Macedonia. Foundation of churches at Philippi and Thessalonica.

49 (autumn)–51 (summer). Paul at Corinth. *I Thess.* (? *II Thess.*)

51 (summer). Paul travels from Corinth *via* Caesarea to Antioch.

52. Second visit to S. Galatian churches.

52 (summer)–54. Residence at Ephesus. *Galatians* (written to the churches of South Galatia); *Corinthian letters*; (?) *Philippian correspondence*; (?) *Philemon.*

54. Paul travels *via* Troas to Macedonia to Corinth.

54–55. Three months in Corinth. *Romans.*

55. Paul travels from Corinth to Jerusalem.
  (Pentecost). Arrest at Jerusalem.
  Imprisonment at Caesarea.
  (Autumn). Paul's journey to Rome. Winter in Malta.
56 (early spring). Arrival in Rome.
56–58. Protective custody in Rome. (?) *Philippians*; (?) *Colossians* and (?) *Philemon*. (?) Farewell letter to *Timothy* = nucleus of 2 Tim.)

This chronology makes no claims to infallability. It is meant simply to serve as a working hypothesis, for the study of Acts and as an aid to the exegesis of the Pauline letters.

The Undisputed Pauline Letters

Prior to Paul's letters there was, so far as we know, no literary production on the part of Christians. Mark's gospel is later by a decade or so (65–70) than the latest of the genuine Pauline epistles.

There were three reasons for this. One was *cultural*. The Palestinian Christians were not sufficiently educated to indulge in literary activity. Secondly, the Greek-speaking missionaries before Paul, though probably more educated than the earliest Palestinian Christians, also left no written documents because they lacked the occasion for literary production. Such an occasion first arose through the need of Paul, with his far-flung missionary work, to keep in touch with the communities he had established. Thirdly there was the expectation of the imminent parousia. No early Christian— and this applies equally to Paul who shared the imminent parousia hope, though he came to modify it—could have had any idea of writing for posterity when it was thought that the end would end in this generation (Mk 9:1, 13:30; Mt 10:23).

What has been said already implies an important fact about Paul's letters. They are strictly *occasional* in character, not systematic theological treatises. They arise out of concrete situations, and that is why the questions of date, place of writing, and the circumstances which gave rise to each of the

letters are so important for their exegesis, and why we began
with a tentative reconstruction of Pauline chronology.

Adolf Deissmann[1] drew a distinction between the 'letter'
and the 'epistle' as literary forms. The letter emerges from a
concrete situation and is addressed to specific readers. The
epistle, on the other hand, is a theological treatise availing
itself of the letter form. Although the Greek NT makes no
such distinction, but applies the term epistle to all the NT
writings between Acts and Revelation, the distinction is a
convenient one, and has been widely adopted. If this distinction is accepted, all of the unquestionably genuine Pauline
documents are letters rather than epistles.

This leads to the next point, the letter form. Today convention requires that we observe certain forms in writing a
letter. We put our address and the date at the top right-hand
corner of the letter, the name and address of the recipient
below on the left, either at the beginning or the end. We begin
'Dear Sir' and end 'Yours faithfully' or 'sincerely', and append
our signature. In antiquity there were also conventions but
they were different from ours. The ancient letter began, 'A to B
greetings', with the writer's name in the nominative and the
recipient's in the dative. Next followed usually some com-
plementary remarks to the recipient before the main matter
of the letter began. Then at the end came a final greeting and
farewell.

Paul employs these ancient epistolary conventions, but
with a distinctive Christian twist. To his name he adds (from
Galatians on, when his apostolic authority was under attack)
some description of his Christian status, such as 'Paul, an
apostle of Jesus Christ'. To his recipients he also gives a
reminder of *their* Christian status: e.g. 'To the church of God
which is at Corinth'. The greeting also takes on the form of a
Christian blessing: 'grace be unto you and peace'.

Then, instead of the conventional complimentary remarks,
he offers a prayer of thanksgiving and intercession for his

[1] *Bible Studies*, 1909[2], pp. 3ff; *Light from the Ancient East*, 1911[2]
pp. 218ff.

recipients. In Gal—where Paul is angry at their backsliding—this thanksgiving is significantly absent.

Similarly, at the conclusion of the letter, the farewell is Christianized into a kind of churchly blessing. The end of 2 Cor is the most striking example of this: 'The grace of our Lord Jesus Christ, and the love of God and the fellowship of the Holy Spirit be with you all'. It seems also, especially at the end of 1 Cor, that Paul deliberately styles his ending to gear into the eucharistic Lord's Supper: 'greet one another with a holy kiss' (the kiss of peace) (16:20). 'If anyone does not love the Lord, let him be anathema' (excluded from the Lord's Supper). 'Come, Lord' (the invocation to the Lord to come at the eucharist in anticipation of the parousia).[1] Paul's letter thus forms the junction between the service of the word and the Lord's Supper. This is an important reminder that the Pauline letters were originally intended to be read in the liturgy.

Since Paul's letters deal with specific situations, the bulk of their content is the result of extemporary composition. But he does incorporate traditional material. Thus to some extent the question of sources, which will engage us much more when we come to the gospels, comes up already in connection with the Pauline letters. It is hardly likely, in view of what was said above (p. 15), that Paul used any written sources (contrast Mt, Lk). But by applying form[2] and style criticism we can detect the presence of traditional material.

These traditional materials fall into two main classes, kerygmatic or doctrinal; and hortatory or catechetical. The best known example of a kerygmatic formula is 1 Cor 15:3ff, which Paul explicitly states he had 'received' from his predecessors and handed on to his converts. The words for 'receiving' and 'handing on' are Greek translations of technical Hebrew terms used by the rabbis for the transmission of tradition. Style criticism on this formula, such as has been

---

[1] Cf. O. Cullmann, *The Christology of the New Testament*, 1963[2], p. 209.

[2] On form criticism see below, pp. 81–94.

done by J. Jeremias[1] shows beyond all doubt that this formula
is non-Pauline, and of Semitic origin. Other such formulae are
found in Rom 1:3ff, where Paul sets out the gospel in terms
clearly non- and pre-Pauline[2], and in Rom 4:25.

E. Stauffer[3] has given us twelve criteria for identifying
formulae of this kind. Often they begin with a relative pro-
noun, 'who . . .'. Often the verbs are in participial form.
Frequently such passages have a rhythmic form, suggesting a
hymn. Invariably they are concerned with the basic kerygmatic affirmations about the incarnation, death, resurrection
and exaltation of Jesus Christ. The language is frequently
different in style and vocabulary from the writer's own. Also,
there is a tendency to go on quoting the hymn or formula after
the immediate point has been made. One of the best examples
is the christological hymn, Phil 2:6ff. Col 1:15–20 also has good
claims to be regarded as a christological hymn.

As for the catechetical material, the most famous example
is the Supper tradition in 1 Cor 11:23–25, where Paul again
explicitly states that this is a tradition which he has 'received'
and is 'passing on'. There is no doubt that this is a pre-Pauline
formula.[4]

Paul also employs catalogues of vices to avoid and virtues
to pursue. See e.g. Rom 1:29–31, 13:13; 1 Cor 5:11, 6:9f;
2 Cor 12:20; Gal 5:19–22 (the works of the flesh and the
fruit of the Spirit); Phil 4:8 (a typically Stoic catalogue).
Archbishop Carrington[5] has discovered certain constantly
recurring patterns of catechetical teaching in the hortatory
parts of the Pauline and later letters, compiled under the
themes of renunciation, resistance and subjection. Beginning
with Col and continuing through Eph, 1 Pet and Past we get
the so-called household codes, comprising class lists and
corresponding duties—masters, servants, husbands, wives,

---

[1] *Eucharistic Words of Jesus*, 1966 ², pp. 101–103.
[2] For a study of the history of this tradition see R. H. Fuller, *The
Foundations of New Testament Christology*, 1965, pp. 165f, 187.
[3] *New Testament Theology*, 1955, pp. 338f.
[4] Jeremias, *op. cit.*, pp. 103f.
[5] P. Carrington, *The Primitive Christian Catechism*, 1940.

parents, children. Perhaps (if Col is Pauline) Paul began the use of these, though they are more characteristic of the deutero-Pauline letters. By that time the delay in the parousia was forcing the church to settle down in the world.

In a class by themselves are apocalyptic formulae, like 1 Thess 4:16f, quoted as a 'word of the Lord', i.e. probably the utterance of a Christian prophet conveyed as a saying of the risen Lord like the sayings in Revelation rather than a logion of the historical Jesus. Similar passages occur in 1 Cor 15.

Another body of material which is pre-Pauline is the OT quotations, generally from the LXX. Not infrequently the passages Paul quotes are also used by other NT writers, including the synoptists. These quotations are so to speak the common property of the early Christian church, drawn apparently from a kind of treasury of OT quotations with a recognized Christian application.[1] A good example is the quotations applied by Paul in Rom 9–11 to the failure of the Jewish mission. Note especially the passage from Isa 8:14, 28:16 about the rejection of the 'stone' in Rom 9:33. This testimony is used in a similar context in Matt 21:42 and 1 Pet 2:6. It can hardly have been Paul who first applied that combined text in this way.

A few dominical sayings (i.e. sayings attributed to Jesus) occur in Paul. There are some in 1 Cor 7 on marriage and the prohibition of divorce ('Not I, but the Lord said'), and the saying about the payment of ministers for their preaching alluded to in 9:14. Also, while direct quotations are remarkably rare, there are numerous echoes of dominical sayings in Rom 12 from the Sermon on the Mount, also the second half of the summary of the law in Rom 13:9.

(a) 1 THESSALONIANS

The foundation of the church at Thessalonica is related in Acts 17. Paul preached in the local synagogue on three successive Sabbaths, whereupon the Jews stirred up a riot

[1] On the subject see C. H. Dodd, *According to the Scriptures*, 1953.

and hounded him out of the city (c. 49). This account is somewhat questionable for three reasons: (1) The development of
events is stereotyped according to a regular Lucan scheme:
Paul preaches in the synagogue, makes some converts, pro-
vokes Jewish opposition, and is forced to leave. (2) It occurs
outside of the 'we sections'.[1] (3) 1 Thess implies that Paul
stayed at Thessalonica longer than two weeks. In 2:7ff he says
that while at Thessalonica he worked with his own hands so
as not to be a burden to his converts. Again Phil 4:16 states
that while Paul was there the Philippians sent him two 'care
parcels', and two in a fortnight is rather a lot! So a longer stay
than Acts allows is probable.

It is curious, too, that Paul says nothing in 1 Thess about
any local Jewish opposition to the church. It appears that the
Thessalonians converts were mainly, if not exclusively, Gentile
(1 Thess 1:9), and the persecution from which the Thessalonians are suffering is from their 'fellow countrymen' (2:14).

Occasion and Date

It is generally agreed that 1 Thess was written during the
so-called second missionary journey, i.e. soon after the community was established at Thessalonica. It was written from
Athens or Corinth (more likely from Corinth). The date is
50.

According to 1 Thess 3:1, Paul was anxious about the
Thessalonians, and sent Timothy from Athens to Thessalonica
on an inspection visit. Timothy then returned to where Paul
was (either at Athens, or by this time at Corinth) with news
which led him to write our letter. This account tallies partly,
but not completely, with Acts. According to Acts 17:15
Timothy and Silas (Silvanus, mentioned in 1 Thess 1:1 as the
co-author with Paul and Timothy of our letter) were left
behind at Beroea, and subsequently rejoined Paul in Corinth
(Acts 18:5). While Acts is almost certainly misinformed about
Timothy's (and Silas') movements in 17:15, its statement that

---

[1] For the meaning of this see below, pp. 123ff.

it was at Corinth that they rejoined Paul may be accepted, as it does not contradict the statements of Paul himself.[1]

From the content of 1 Thess we may infer that Timothy reported on two main problems at Thessalonica. The first is the persecution which the young community was suffering at the hands of its pagan neighbours (1 Thess 2:14). Second, the shock occasioned by the death of one or more members of the Thessalonian congregation (4:13). There may be some connection between these two problems—if the deaths in question were the result of persecution—but there is no need to assume this. Apparently the Thessalonians had been led to expect that all the baptized would live until the parousia (1 Thess 4:15). They were anxious to have a visit from Paul (3:6), but owing to the apostle's preoccupations at Corinth, he writes them this letter (apparently the first letter he ever wrote).[2] Paul would like to have visited his converts (3:6, 10) but being prevented, he did the next best thing and wrote them our letter.

Summary of Contents

Part I

1:1. Opening address.

1:2–10. Thanksgiving for the Thessalonians' eager acceptance of the gospel.

2:1–12. Reminder to the Thessalonians of Paul's own behaviour while he was among them.

2:13–16. Renewed thanksgiving for the Thessalonians'

---

[1] For the important methodological principle here invoked see above, p. 6 and below, pp. 128ff.

[2] It is interesting, and probably significant, that Paul wrote what was apparently his first letter on the so-called second missionary journey, i.e. when he launched out on his own. Previously he had confined his work to Damascus, Arabia Nabatea, Syria and Cilicia (Gal 1:17–2:10) working in collaboration with Barnabas and in close association with the community at Antioch. After the fracas at Antioch he broke with Barnabas and embarked on an independent mission. Such is the course of affairs indicated by Gal. Acts gives a very different account, including the problematical so-called first missionary journey.

acceptance of the gospel, and exhortation to constancy under persecution.

2:17–3:13. Paul's relations with the community at Thessalonica after his departure. His inability to return to them, and consequent mission of Timothy. The news brought back by Timothy leads first to renewed thanksgiving and prayer, and then to Part II.

Part II

(This deals with the problems brought back by Timothy.)

4:1–12. Exhortation to the Thessalonians to Christian living in accordance with the halakha ('walking' = ethics) Paul had delivered to them. The exhortation touches on (*a*) sexual ethics (vv. 3–8); (*b*) love of the brethren (9–10a); (*c*) the necessity of work (10b–12). This last exhortation was probably occasioned by the eschatological excitement aroused at Thessalonica by Paul's preaching. The Thessalonians supposed that since the end was so near there was no need for them to work.

4:13–18. Paul turns at last to concrete doctrinal problems. Some members of the church had died. Did that deprive them of participation in the parousia? Paul answers by quoting a 'word of the Lord' (see above, p. 19) (vv. 16f). The departed will be specially raised to take part in the parousia. This passage shows clearly that at this time Paul believed that the parousia would occur in his own life time ('*we* who are alive', v. 15).

5:1–11. The suddenness of the end (note the use of the parable of the thief in the night, from the gospel tradition), leading into further (eschatologically oriented) ethical exhortation (6–11).

5:12–28. Detailed ethical injunctions. Verse 12 is especially important evidence for 'the ministry at Thessalonica. There were (probably charismatic) men who 'laboured, presided and admonished' the community. There is no evidence that Paul ordained presbyters or bishops for the Thessalonian congregation.

The Importance of 1 Thessalonians

1 Thess gives a good insight into Paul's missionary preaching, his kerygma, as opposed to his didache, elaborated in the letters themselves (see esp. 1:9f). It shows the apocalyptic framework of that preaching. The decisive event of salvation has occurred in Jesus Christ, but it awaits consummation in the (near) future. Meanwhile, there is a tradition of ethical teaching for Christian behaviour during the interim (4:1–12, 5:6–11).

(b) GALATIANS

1. Date

There are many, especially in Britain, who regard Gal as the earliest letter, prior to 1 Thess, and to the Jerusalem conference.

The relevant passages are: Gal 1:6, 'I marvel that you are *so quickly* departing from the gospel'; and 4:13, 'you know that it was through the weakness of the flesh that I preached the gospel to you *at first*'. The Gk 'at first' (τὸ πρότερον) could mean either 'on the former occasion', implying two visits before the writing of Gal thus far, or 'on the first occasion', implying that Paul had visited the Gal only once, i.e. when he founded the churches. The latter interpretation appears to have the *prima facie* support of 1:6 ('so quickly'), and is maintained by those who think Gal is the earliest letter.

At this point it is necessary to inquire into the identity of the recipients. Were they inhabitants of South or of North Galatia? The South Galatian view holds that the recipients of Gal were Galatians not in the ethnic sense, but as residents of the Roman province of Galatia, which extended southward from the old Celtic kingdom of Galatia (centred around Ancyra = modern Angora) to include Lycaonia and the southern part of Phrygia. In that case the churches of Gal will be

B

those of Derbe, Lystra and Iconium, whose foundation Acts 14 places in the so-called first missionary journey. Gal (interpreting τὸ πρότερον = the first time) can then be dated after the events of Acts 14, but prior to the Apostolic Council of Acts 15, i.e. not later than 48, two years earlier than 1 Thess.

This view has the advantage of avoiding any discrepancy between Acts and Gal over the number of visits paid by Paul to Jerusalem after his conversion and prior to the council visit. Gal 2:1ff makes the conference visit the second post-conversion visit, Acts makes the council visit the third: Acts 9:26 Gal 1:18f = first visit; Acts 11:30/12:25 Gal 2:1ff = second visit. (This view also avoids the discrepancies which arise between Acts 15 and Gal 2 over the nature and result of the meeting if the conference of Gal 2 is equated with the council of Acts 15.)

The South Galatian view has other advantages. (1) There is no explicit mention in Acts that Paul was ever in North Galatia. The North Galatianists argue that such a visit is covered by the phrase 'the region of Phrygia and Galatia' (Acts 16:6) and 'the region of Galatia and Phrygia' (Acts 18:23). But, rejoin the South Galatianists, these phrases require interpretation anyhow. And since Acts 16:6 makes no mention of missionary preaching in this region the most natural interpretation of that verse is that it is merely resumptive of 16:1–5 and thus covers South Galatia. (2) Only South Galatians are mentioned among the delegates from the Pauline churches bearing the collection to Jerusalem in Acts 20:4. (3) Gal 2:13 indicates that Barnabas was known to the Galatians, and we know from Acts 14 that he was in South Galatia during the first missionary journey.

In view of all this, the South Galatianists usually conclude that Gal is not only addressed to the South Galatians, but is also the earliest of Paul's letters, written c. 48, prior to the Apostolic Council.

The North Galatianists, as we have seen, argue that Paul invariably uses the term 'Galatia' (Gal 1:2; 1 Cor 16:1) and 'Galatians' (Gal 3:1) in the ethnic sense, corresponding to the old Celtic kingdom of Galatia. These churches were founded, they contend, in Acts 16:6 and revisited in Acts 18:23. Gal was then written 'soon' (Gal 1:6) after this second visit (τὸ πρότερον Gal 4:13—the former of two visits), i.e. during the period of Paul's residence in Ephesus, which we have dated 52–54. Luke's silence about missionary preaching or the foundation of churches in 16:6 is not decisive, since Acts (outside of the travel diary) is often tantalizingly vague, and has many lacunae owing to the paucity of sources.

What then of the discrepancies between Gal 1–2 and Acts 11, 12 and 15? Contemporary North Galatianists (mostly German) meet these by a more critical treatment of Acts. They commonly hold that Acts has (1) duplicated Paul's second (conference) visit to Jerusalem, so that Acts 11 = 15 = Gal 2); (2) Acts 15 has combined two different occasions, a private conference between Paul and the pillars, as in Gal 2, with a later council of the Jerusalem church at which the apostolic decrees were promulgated (cf. Acts 21:25, where James communicates the text of the decrees to Paul, apparently for the first time, despite Paul's presence at their promulgation in Acts 15).

The motive, conscious or unconscious, behind the North Galatian theory seems to be the desire to avoid making Gal the earliest Pauline letter. For 1 Thess presents a less developed Pauline theology than Gal, esp. on the imminence of the parousia: it is far less imminent and central in Gal. Also, Gal has marked affinities with the controversial letters, esp. with 2 Cor 10–13 (see below, pp. 46–49), and is better placed in the period where these were written.

The strength of the South Galatian view is its identification of the recipients of Gal with churches where we know Paul founded. It is most unlikely that he ever penetrated so far as Ancyra in North Galatia. The strength of the North Galatianist position is in its dating of Gal later than 1 Thess and during the controversial period, close to 2 Cor 10–13. Is it possible to combine the strengths of each view and avoid their weaknesses?

Recent study of Acts has thrown doubt not only on the question of the relation between Acts 11, 15 and Gal 2, but also on the whole conception of the first missionary journey (see above, p. 9). If this journey is by and large a doublet of the second, the South Galatian churches must have been founded on the *second* missionary journey of Acts, i.e. *after* the apostolic conference. *This* then will be the visit referred to in Gal 4:13. The second visit implied here (τὸ πρότερον = 'first of two'), will then have occurred on the so-called third missionary journey (Acts 18:23), i.e. immediately before Paul's residence in Ephesus. This visit will be the occasion when Paul ascertained that the Galatians were 'running well' (5:7). And it was 'so quickly' (1:6) after this second visit that the troubles in Galatia will have set in. Paul therefore writes Gal after hearing of these troubles, i.e. during his Ephesian residence, 52–54. The view that it was written about the time of the Corinthian correspondence has much to commend it, and adds force to Paul's statement in 2 Cor 11:28 about his 'anxiety for all the churches'. Another consideration is that such a dating brings Gal much closer to Rom with which again it has marked affinities.

The Recipients

Having already decided in favour of the South Galatian view, we now ask, what kind of communities were they, Jewish, Gentile, or mixed? The answer is clear from 4:8, 'But at that time, not knowing God, you were slaves to beings that were not gods'. In the following verse Paul says they are now returning to the cosmic powers. The Galatians were Gentiles.

The Opponents of Paul

The Galatians were forsaking the Pauline gospel and going over to some perverted form of the gospel (1:6). 'Certain men' (τινές, v. 7) were causing trouble among them. Paul does not directly identify his opponents, but only indirectly by the arguments he marshalls against them. In chs. 1–2 he emphasizes the independence of his apostolic authority. It is, 'not derived from men nor conferred by human agency' (1:1). The gospel he preaches he likewise did not receive *via* human tradition, but directly, through revelation from Jesus Christ (1:12, 16). He carefully traces his relationship with the Jerusalem church in order to demonstrate that his contacts with the original apostles were minimal and in no way involved his authorization as an apostle. They simply recognized his apostleship (1:16b–2:10). It is clear that the 'certain people' attacked Paul's authority as an apostle and maintained that his gospel was second-hand.

Further, these opponents were persuading the Gentile Christian Galatians to submit to circumcision: 'as many as want to make a fair show in the flesh are forcing you to be circumcised' (6:12); 'I say that if you are circumcised, Christ will be of no profit to you at all' (5:2). The demand for circumcision is hardly a wholly different gospel, but is undoubtedly a perversion of the true one (1:6–9). The theological argument of the central section (3:1–5:12) is directed against this position. The perversion of the gospel consists in the offer of salvation through the works of the law rather than through faith in Christ (see esp. 3:2–4:31). But circumcision is not the sole point at issue. By succumbing to the false teachers, the Galatians are reverting to slavery under the 'beings that by nature are no gods' (4:8), under 'the weak and beggerly elemental spirits' (4:9). The false teachers were also imposing certain observances: 'You observe days, and months, and seasons, and years' (4:10).

In 5:16–6:10 Paul exhorts the Galatians against moral laxity (the works of the flesh, see esp. 5:13, 16f, 19–21). This too may have something to do with the false teaching.

Since F. C. Baur and the Tübingen school the commonly accepted view has been that Paul's opponents were 'Judaizers'. Baur himself equated them with the original Jerusalem Christians, including Peter, and James the brother of the Lord. He identified the 'certain men from James' who turned up earlier at Antioch (2:12) with the 'certain men' of 1:7. These men, according to Baur, dogged Paul's steps not only in Galatia but in every community he founded.

Few today would accept Baur's view *in toto*. Yet it remains true that, at any rate until very recently, most scholars have accepted the view that Paul's opponents in Galatia were 'Judaizers', i.e. Jewish Christians who wished to force Gentile converts to submit to the whole Jewish law.[1]

But there are difficulties in the way of this view. (1) The identification of the 'certain men from James' of 2:12 with the Galatian trouble makers is pure inference. (2) The point at issue in the Antioch fracas was different from the troubles in Galatia. It concerned the Jewish food laws and integrated (Jewish-Gentile) Lord's Suppers (2:12), not circumcision. *That* question had already been settled at the apostolic conference so far as the Jerusalem authorities were concerned (2:6). (3) In 5:3 Paul has to remind the Galatians, what apparently they did not realize, that circumcision involved the observance of the *whole* Jewish law—a fact of which any Judaizer would surely be aware.

There are other features in the Galatian situation which do not at all square with the view that Paul's opponents were Judaizers, viz. the reference to the cosmic powers ('weak and beggerly elemental spirits', 4:9), to the calendar observances (4:10), and to libertinism against which the hortatory parts of Gal are directed. These features, especially the last, led W. Lütgert[2] and J. H. Ropes[3] to conclude that in Gal Paul was fighting on two fronts: against legalistic Judaizers in chs. 1–5:12 and against libertinist 'pneumatics' in chs. 5:13–6:10. This suggestion had the value of calling attention to the problem, but was not a real solution. Further, there is nothing explicit in Gal to suggest a double front.

Munck himself suggested that Paul's opponents were simply

[1] See J. Munck, *Paul and the Salvation of Mankind*, 1959, pp. 87ff. Munck points out that this is the view of M. Dibelius (1f and 69ff) and of W. L. Knox among others.

[2] *Gesetz und Geist*, 1919.

[3] *The Singular Problem of the Epistle to the Galatians* (Harvard Theol. Stud. 14), 1929.

local (Gentile) trouble makers, who had gotten hold of a number of half-baked notions, including the fact (which they misunderstood) that the original Jerusalem disciples maintained circumcision. The line of the opponents, then, was: Paul not only gets his gospel from the original Jerusalem disciples, but he also misrepresents it by omitting circumcision.

It is true that Gal nowhere states that the opponents came from outside. But it is questionable whether Munck's solution does justice to the other features in their teaching, viz., the elemental spirits, the calendar observances and the libertinism. W. Schmithals[1] has recently argued that the opponents were some kind of syncretists—and, in a way characteristic of the Bultmann school, dubs them 'gnostics'. The reference to 'knowing God' in 4:8f perhaps supports this view. In any case they were syncretists, who combined circumcision from Judaism with features from other religious movements.

There is one difficulty about Schmithals' solution: Paul argues with syncretists precisely on the same theological ground on which he had argued against the Judaizers at the Apostolic conference and against the segregationists at Antioch, viz., on the question of justification by faith rather than by the works of the law. It is notoriously difficult to be sure where Paul stops reporting the controversy at Antioch and turns to the Galatian opponents (2:14 or 3:1?). This argument was certainly applicable to the Judaizing movement but only partially relevant against syncretism. W. Marxsen[2] meets this difficulty by supposing that Paul has only a very imperfect acquaintance with these Galatian opponents and their position. He has heard, among other things, that they are advocating circumcision, and so brings out all the arguments he had used some five or six years earlier against the Judaizers at Jerusalem and against the segregationists at Antioch some months later. It was only at Corinth (2 Cor 10–13) that he really became acquainted with the precise position of his

[1] W. Schmithals, 'Die Häretiker in Galatien', ZNW 47, 1956, pp. 25–67. Repr. in Paulus und die Gnostiker, 1965, pp. 9–46.
[2] Einleitung in das Neue Testament, pp. 52ff.

syncretistic opponents, and by that time he is able to meet
them on their own terms. In support of Marxsen's position it is
noticeable how vaguely Paul refers to the opponents: '*some*
who trouble you' (1:7); '*who* has bewitched you?' (3:1); 'he
who is troubling you will bear his judgment, *whoever he is*'
(5:10).

Summary of Contents

Part I 1:1–2:21

Paul seeks to re-establish the confidence of the Galatians in
his independent apostolic authority and in the truth of his
gospel by a careful account of his conversion and subsequent
contacts with the Jerusalem authorities down to the Antioch
fracas.

Part II 3:1–5:12 (Theological)

Paul seeks to demonstrate (i) the true nature of the gospel
as justification through grace by faith, not by works; and
(ii) the place of the law in the divine economy of salvation:

- 3:1–5. A reminder that the Galatians themselves first
  received salvation through the hearing of faith, not by
  the works of the law.
- 3:6–29. Abraham, the pattern of justification by faith in
  God's promise, not by the works of the law. The law had
  only a pedagogic function, to bring home the reality of
  sin and the need of salvation.
- 4. The inferiority of the law *vis à vis* the gospel demonstrated
  by the allegory of Abraham's two sons.
- 5:1–12. Appeal to the Galatians to put this teaching into
  practice by getting rid of the false teachers and their
  teaching.

Part III 5:13–6:10 (Ethical)

The ethics of the gospel, based on the contrast between the
works of the flesh and the fruit of the Spirit, and concluding
with detailed injunctions (6:1–10).

6:11–18. Autographic conclusion, summarizing the main points of the central section (Part II), and a concluding greeting (v. 18).

The Importance of Galatians

(1) 1–2:14 provides the chief source for the biography and chronology of Paul down to the Antioch controversy. With 2 Cor, Gal is main source for Paul's understanding of his apostolic authority. With Romans, 3:1–5:12 is the chief source for the distinctively Pauline presentation of the gospel in terms of justification by faith.

(2) Gal furnishes important evidence for the earlier battle Paul had fought against the Judaizers. The significance of that earlier, successful struggle is that he emancipated the gospel from its Jewish swaddling clothes, and yet preserved its essential framework of salvation history and its continuity with the OT.

(c) THE PHILIPPIAN CORRESPONDENCE

Date and Circumstances of writing

Phil was written when Paul was in prison. See 1:7, 'you are all partakers with me of grace, both in my imprisonment and in the defence and confirmation of the gospel'; 1:13, 'it has become known throughout the whole praetorian guard and to all the rest that my imprisonment is for Christ'; 1:16, 'I am put here (sc. in prison) for the defence of the gospel'; v. 17, 'my imprisonment'. In 1:20 and 2:17 Paul is sure that when he is brought to trial this will decide for him the issue of life or death. Yet he still hopes for freedom ('I know I shall remain and continue with you all', 1:25) and hopes in fact to revisit the Philippians: 'I trust in the Lord that shortly I myself shall come also', 2:24.

Paul, then, was in prison at the writing of Phil. But where? From Acts there are two possibilities: (1) Caesarea (Acts 23:35–26:32); (2) Rome (28:16–31). The traditional view, maintained by J. B. Lightfoot and by many still today (e.g. O. Cullmann, C. H. Dodd) is that Phil belongs to the Roman imprisonment. On our chronology this would date it 56–58. If the imprisonment was at Caesarea, it would have to be placed a year or two years earlier (55).

However, there is another theory, which has been elaborated by G. S. Duncan,[1] to the effect that Phil was written at Ephesus. First, there are certain difficulties in the Roman view. The most weighty is the number of comings and goings between Philippi and place where Paul is writing from. Secondly, there is the problem of Timothy's movements. In 2:19 Paul speaks about his visiting Philippi. We know from 1 Cor 4:16, 16:10ff; cf. Acts 19:22, that Paul did send Timothy *from Ephesus* to Corinth *via* Philippi towards the end of the Ephesian residence. Again, as we have already noted, Paul hopes himself to visit the Philippians after his release from prison. But, according to Rom 15:24, after visiting Rome he hoped to go on to Spain. It is of course arguable that his plans had changed owing to his reaching Rome as a prisoner, and to his subsequent two years in custody. And if Past are accepted as authentic this is precisely what Paul did. The dating of Phil during the Roman imprisonment hangs naturally together with the acceptance of Past as Pauline, whereas the view that they are deutero-Pauline should carry with it the rejection of the Roman imprisonment as the place and time of Phil. Another general consideration is that Phil 3 fits in with the letters of the controversial period (2 Cor 10–13; Gal).

There are certain *prima facie* objections to the Ephesian hypothesis. The major difficulty is Acts' silence on an imprisonment at Ephesus (Acts 19:1ff). This, however, is not so serious as it sounds. As we have seen, Acts is full of lacunae. Indeed, the lacunae are particularly evident precisely in the Ephesian period, for there is nothing at all in Acts about the crisis at Corinth (2 Cor). And if our dating of Gal was correct, the Galatian crisis also occurred in this period. Clearly, not too

---

[1] G. S. Duncan, *St Paul's Ephesian Ministry*, 1929. For the earlier history of the theory see *ibid.* pp. 59ff.

much weight should be given to the silence of Acts on an Ephesian imprisonment. But is there any positive evidence for it in our primary sources, the Pauline letters themselves? There is no direct statement, but an accumulation of statements which make an Ephesian imprisonment possible, if not probable. In 2 Cor 11:23 (cf. 6:5) Paul speaks of imprisonment as a frequent experience ('in prisons oft'). Acts only relates one imprisonment prior to the time of writing of 1 Cor, viz., at Philippi itself (Acts 16:24ff). Obviously there were more. So it is not impossible that one or more of these imprisonments occurred during the Ephesian residence. 1 Cor 4:11; 2 Cor 1:8f (Asia!) 4:8ff, 6:9 refer to sufferings as a vivid memory at the time of writing (i.e. as we shall see, precisely during the Ephesian residence). Rom 16:3 states that Aquila and Prisca 'laid down their necks' for Paul. Paul and this married couple were together with Paul first at Corinth and then at Ephesus (1 Cor 16:19 Rom 16:3; Acts 18:2, 18, 26). In Rom 16:7 Paul greets Andronicus and Junius as his 'fellow prisoners', and, as we shall see (p. 51) the greetings in Rom 16 were probably all intended for members of the church at Ephesus rather than in Rome. Finally, and most important of all, in 1 Cor 15:32 Paul speaks of having 'fought with wild beasts at Ephesus'. Even if this is not taken literally, it strongly suggests an imprisonment at Ephesus.

There are also certain difficulties in Phil itself. In 1:13 Paul refers to the Praetorian guard and in 4:22 to Caesar's household. These references would more naturally fit the Roman imprisonment of Acts 28:16ff. But the Praetorian guards (cf. the Nazi SS) were not only the emperor's personal bodyguard, but performed police duties in the imperial provinces. So the references in 1:13 and 4:22 are equally possible for Ephesus. Indeed, there is archaeological evidence (inscriptions) that Ephesus was garrisoned by Praetorian guards.

The defenders of the traditional view that Phil was written at Rome point out that Paul is looking back as an old man on his many years of service, 1:5, 23, 4:10. Also, the imprisonment is obviously lengthy, which would correspond to the 2 years of

Acts 28:30. Timothy's presence with Paul would correspond
to Col 1:1 (though the date, place of writing and even Pauline
authorship of Col is a further problem). O. Cullmann,[1] who
favours a Roman provenance for Phil has also called attention
to the allusion to those who preach Christ out of 'jealousy'
(1:15) and has tied this with references to Paul at Rome (?) in
1 Clem 5 (date: c. 95). Paul, he contends, was denounced at
Rome by certain partisan members of the Roman church to
the emperor. But these connections are uncertain.

There is another point, not usually avowed, which enters
perhaps somewhat subconsciously into the discussion. It is
felt that Phil (like Eph and Col) implies a more advanced
theology, and had therefore better be placed as late as possible
in Paul's career. (J. B. Lightfoot vindicated the Pauline
authorship of these letters against the Tübingen critics on the
ground that they represented later developments in Paul's
thought.) The Christology of Phil 2:6–11, with its emphasis
on the pre-existence and incarnation of Christ, was an instance
of such development. But the trend today is precisely in the
opposite direction—to see in this hymn not later development
of Pauline thought, but actually a pre-Pauline composition
taken up and used (with modification) by Paul. There is much
to be said for the argument of development in the case of Col
and Eph if they are to be retained as genuine Pauline letters,
but far less for Phil. The Ephesian hypothesis is strongest for
Phil, and it will be accepted here as the best explanation of the
facts. Rejection of it seems to rest on two questionable
positions: (1) a hangover from the acceptance of Past as
Pauline; (2) Too great a deference to Acts.

Integrity

Prior to F. W. Beare's Commentary on Phil (1959), there
were few if any in the English-speaking world who seriously
considered partition theories in connection with Phil (contrast
2 Cor). And there does not seem at first sight to be such an
immediate urgency to divide it up into different letters.

[1] *Peter*, 1953[1], pp. 104f.

Quite long ago J. Weiss[1] pointed out the marked difference in tone between 3:2–4:1 and rest of the letter. In the midst of a letter remarkable for its warmth and friendliness Paul suddenly launches into a furious attack on false teachers in language reminiscent of Gal and 2 Cor 10–13. Moreover, 3:1 begins 'finally' and in 4:2 we come straight to the greetings with which a letter normally closes. This fact led Weiss to suggest that 3:2–4:1 was an interpolation from a different letter of Paul.

The question of the unity of Phil was thoroughly investigated by W. Schmithals,[2] whom Beare follows closely. In 1:17 and 28 Paul issues a warning against opponents who are undermining his preaching. These opponents are at work both where Paul is in prison and in Philippi (v. 28). In face of this opposition Paul urges the Philippians to maintain unity (2:1ff). In 2:19–30 he informs his correspondents that he will send Timothy to them shortly, and that meanwhile Epaphroditus is taking the letter. Epaphroditus is mentioned in 4:18 as the deliverer of the 'care packet' from the Philippians to Paul during his imprisonment. Epaphroditus is to report back on the situation at Philippi. 3:1 seems to draw this letter to a close, save for a concluding greeting.

Then in 3:2ff Paul launches out on his furious onslaught against the false teachers. Those who defend the integrity of Phil can only do so by maintaining (as with the similar change at 2 Cor 10:1) that fresh news had come in, or that the change is due to Paul's volatile temperament. But Schmithals points out that there is a difference between the references to the false teaching in ch. 3 compared with chs. 1–2. *There* the danger was largely hypothetical and vaguely conceived. *Here* they present an acute danger whose nature is fully known. So Schmithals (cf. Weiss) argues that 3:2–4:3 is another letter which has been interpolated into the earlier letter. This earlier letter is resumed in 4:4–7. V. 4 takes up the point left off at 3:1.

---

[1] J. Weiss, *Das Urchristentum*, 1917, p. 296; E.T. (1959[2]), p. 386f.

[2] 'Die Irrlehrer des Philipperbriefes', *ZThK* 1957, pp. 297–341. Repr. in *Paulus und die Gnostiker*, 54, pp. 47–87.

4:1–3, 8f represents the conclusion to the 'severe letter'. This explains the double 'finally' (3:1, 4:8). The first 'finally' belongs to the earlier letter, the second to the severe letter. The ends of the two letters have thus been dovetailed to form a single letter.

Then again in 4:10–23 we have Paul's 'thank you' for the care packet. It is rather surprising, Schmithals argues, that Paul should have deferred his 'thank you' to so late a point, especially as he has already mentioned Epaphroditus, the deliverer of the gift, in 2:25. So with some plausibility Schmithals argues that 4:10–23 is a separate, even earlier letter, sent after Epaphroditus had brought the parcel. This thank-you letter was not taken by Epaphroditus himself owing to his illness. To sum, according to Schmithals, Paul wrote three letters to the Philippians, and in this order:

Letter A. 4:10–23. Expression of thanks for the care parcel received *via* Epaphroditus.

Letter B. 1:1–3:1, 4:4–7. News about Paul's imprisonment, Epaphroditus' recovery, and Paul's hope of sending Timothy soon, coupled with a general exhortation to unity in face of (somewhat vaguely characterized) false teaching.

Letter C. 3:2–4:3 plus 4:8f. The severe letter condemning the false teachers, whose position is now clearly recognized.

This tripartite division of the letter will not commend itself so widely as the division of 2 Cor. For as will be seen the text of 2 Cor 1–9 actually encourages us to look for a lost severe letter, and the partition theory in that case is supported by a number of cross-references between the two parts. There is nothing of the kind in Phil. The only evidence, for what it is worth, is a statement by Polycarp in his own letter to Philippians (early second century), which speaks (ch. 3) of *'letters'* written by Paul to the Philippians. All that can be said in favour of the Schmithals-Beare division is that it clears up some of the abrupt transitions in the letter, the two 'finally's' and the perplexing order of the material. It also makes a plausible story of Paul's relationships with the Philippians:

1. Paul is in prison at Ephesus, and receives from the Philippians a gift brought by Epaphroditus (4:18).
2. Paul sends a thank-you note to the Philippians (Letter A).
3. Epaphroditus stays on in Ephesus because of his illness.
4. Epaphroditus, having recovered, is about to return to Philippi (2:25).
5. Paul hears the first rumblings of trouble in Philippi (2:15f, 21).
6. Paul sends Letter B *via* Epaphroditus. This letter should be dated close to Gal. In both letters the opposition is vaguely conceived.
7. News reaches Paul of a serious situation at Philippi due to the activities of the false teachers, and sends off Letter C. This letter should be dated close to 2 Cor 10–13. In both letters the opposition is clearly characterized.
8. Timothy goes to Philippi (2:19).
9. Paul visits Philippi on his way to Corinth (2:24).

Paul's Opponents at Philippi

The Tübingen school identified Paul's opponents at Philippi with the 'Judaizers' as in Galatia. It is clear that they boasted of their Jewishness (3:2ff; cf. 2 Cor 11:18ff). And they apparently practise and propagate circumcision ('those who mutilate the flesh', 3:2). But, save for a brief reference in 3:9, Paul does not argue out the whole question of the law as in Gal, when he was still vague about the nature of their teaching. Instead, he emphasizes (as in 2 Cor 10–11) the place of the cross and of the element of 'not yet' in the Christian life. All this suggests once more some kind of syncretism, in which circumcision (a Jewish motive) was combined with the mystery religion concept that through sacramental initiation the believer had already passed from death to life and immortality. Again, the Bultmann school (e.g. Schmithals) would call this *gnosis*, but the term is not used in Phil 3.

The Importance of Philippians

(1) 3:5ff provides biographical information about Paul, additional to and in part corroborative of Gal 1–2.

(2) 4:8 is an interesting example of Paul's use of Stoic ethical categories.

(3) The most important passage is the (probably) pre-Pauline hymn, Phil 2:6–11,[1] which provides important evidence for the development of NT christology.

(d) PHILEMON

It is clear that Philem, like Phil, was written when Paul was in prison (vv. 1, 9, 10, 23; cf. v. 22, where Paul evidently expects release).

The situation is this: Onesimus, a slave, has run away from his master, Philemon, a Christian, has somehow established contact with Paul in prison, and as a result has been converted to the Christian faith. Paul is sending Onesimus back to Philemon, and so writes to his owner this short letter. It is a private letter, though it is also addressed to Apphia, Archippus and the house church in Philemon's home. Verse 10 announces Onesimus' conversion. Verse 16 bids Philemon to receive him back, 'no longer as a slave, but as a brother beloved'. There is a hint that Onesimus had made off with some of his master's property or money, in which case Paul offers to make good the loss (v. 18).

There are three problems in connection with Philem: (1) the place of Philemon's residence; (2) the place of imprisonment where Onesimus discovered Paul and Paul wrote the letter; (3) connected with these questions—the date.

---

[1] For a traditio-historical and exegetical study of this hymn see R. H. Fuller, *The Foundations of New Testament Christology*, pp. 204ff.

(1) The traditional and still generally accepted view is that Philemon was a resident of Colossae. This however is nowhere stated in Philem but is inferred from Col 4:9, which refers to Onesimus 'the faithful and beloved brother, who is one of you'. The language here suggests that Paul is again informing the Colossians of Onesimus' conversion, as in Philem 16. Archippus also figures as a member of the Colossian church in Col 4:17, and as (apparently) a member of Philemon's house church in Philem 2. Also in both Col and Philem greetings are sent to the church from Aristarchus (Col 4:10/Philem 24), Mark (*ibid.*), Epaphras (Col. 4:12, mentioned as a member of the church at Colossae, and Philem 24, mentioned as in prison with Paul); Luke 4:14/Philem 24) and Demas (*ibid.*). All this would seem to clinch the matter: Philemon has lived at Colossae, and Onesimus had run away from there.

The matter is complicated, however, by the doubts (hardly felt in Britain, but widely entertained on the Continent, and not only within the Bultmann school) that Col is deutero-Pauline (see below). In that case all of these names have simply been lifted from Philem and inserted into Col to create the impression that both letters were written by Paul at the same time and in the same situation. It is perhaps best to content ourselves by saying that Philem does not tell us where Philemon and Onesimus lived, or where the house church was.

(2) The traditional view, again, is that Philem was written from Paul's Roman imprisonment (Acts 28:30f). Deissmann and Duncan place Philem, like Phil, during the Ephesian imprisonment. Their chief argument is that a run-away slave from Colossae would be more likely to make for Ephesus than for Rome. Secondly, it is difficult to reconcile Paul's evident hope of release and his consequent request for Philemon to provide hospitality for him with the Roman imprisonment, in view of Paul's declared intention (Rom 15:24) of going on from there to Spain. For wherever Philemon lived, it was clearly in a sphere covered by Paul's earlier missionary work, and therefore somewhere in the east. We may tentatively place Philem in the Ephesian period, but there is really no evidence in favour of

Ephesus any more than for any of the other frequent imprisonments of Paul in the east mentioned in 2 Cor 11:23.

On the other hand, if we accept Col as genuine, it can, in our
opinion, be so accepted only on condition that it was written
as late as possible in Paul's career (see below). In that case we
shall have to place both Col and Philem in the Roman
imprisonment. This is not impossible. But it is difficult to be
certain.

(3) The question of date will be determined by the place of
writing. If written during the Ephesian period, its date on our
chronology would be 52–54. If during the Roman period, its
date would be 56–58. It was clearly written towards the end of
Paul's imprisonment, for he is hoping soon to be free.

Note on Paul and Slavery

The modern reader is perhaps surprised, if not shocked, that
Paul took slavery as a social institution for granted and sent
Onesimus back to his owner without a request for his release.
But to begin a social revolution would have been utterly alien
to Paul's mission, and futile at that time anyhow. Instead,
Paul concentrates on the change of relationship between
master and slave: 'accept him no longer as a slave, but as a
brother beloved'. This does not mean (as was argued in the
American south) that slavery is scripturally justified. The
church has since come to see that the great principle of Gal
3:28 involved (for the nineteenth century though not for the
first) precisely the abolition of slavery. The NT ethic has to be
implemented in given situations. It is not a hard and fast legal
code.

(e) THE CORINTHIAN CORRESPONDENCE

1 *Corinthians*

The authenticity of 1 Cor is nowhere seriously challenged,
nor is there any question of its integrity. Some people have
tried to break it up into several letters, but apart from its
length there is no internal reason for such endeavours.

Date. 1 Cor was obviously written after Paul's foundation

visit to Corinth (49–51 on our chronology). There are a number of indications that it was written during the Ephesian residence. In 16:8 Paul says 'I will stay at Ephesus until Pentecost'. In 16:19 he sends greetings from 'the churches in Asia'. Note also 16:19, 'Aquila and Prisca salute you'. According to Acts 18:19, 26 this couple took up residence at Ephesus after they left Corinth.

1 Cor 4:17 states that Paul sent Timothy to Corinth. So far as the wording is concerned, this could mean that Timothy is carrying 1 Cor with him, since it is common in ancient languages to write letters from the standpoint of the recipient rather than of the writer, an ancient letter writer would say 'I have sent' where we would say 'I am sending'. But Timothy is apparently already on his way, and it is not quite certain whether he will get there at all: '*if* Timothy *should* come to you' (16:10). So it must not be concluded that Timothy is the bearer of the letter. He must have left earlier, and will presumably arrive later.

In 1 Cor 5:9–11 we learn that Paul had written a previous letter to the Corinthians. Here he is concerned to correct a false impression to which that previous letter had given rise: 'I wrote to you *in my letter* not to mingle with fornicators'. The previous letter had created the impression that Paul was urging his converts to avoid *all* contact with fornicators—a manifest impossibility in the streets of Corinth! He corrects this false impression by saying he had really meant that immoral *Christians*, members of the community, were to be excommunicated or disciplined.

This previous letter, or a fragment of it, has often been identified with 2 Cor 6:14–7:1 (2 Cor, as we shall see, is a collection of various letters to the Corinthians). Two circumstances have led to this identification: (1) the contents of 2 Cor 6:14ff might easily lead to the false impression Paul is at pains to correct in 1 Cor 5:9ff; (2) 2 Cor 6:14ff is clearly an interpolation. Remove it, and 6:13 runs straight into 7:2 without a break. G. Bornkamm, however, in a recent monograph[1]

[1] *Die Vorgeschichte des sogennanten Zweiten Korintherbriefes*, 1961 p.

on 2 Cor, while agreeing that 2 Cor 6:14–7:1 is an interpolation, contends on grounds of language and content that 2 Cor 6:14ff is non-Pauline. According to Bornkamm, it shows affinities with ideas from the Dead Sea Scrolls. He may be correct in this opinion, in which case, the 'previous letter' has been lost. But in any case one of the purposes in writing 1 Cor was to correct the false impression of the 'previous letter'.

There were other reasons for writing 1 Cor. First 'it was reported to me concerning you *by those of Chloe* that there are strifes and contentions among you' (1:11). Some people have come from Chloe (whoever she is, perhaps the owner of a home where a house church met) with verbal information about the goings on in the Corinthian church. There were factions in the community, three or four: centred on Paul, Apollos, Cephas and a Christ faction (a nonparty party?—or is this Paul's interjection—'I will have nothing to do with any of your factions, I belong to Christ!'?). Paul deals at length with this question from 1:13 through ch. 4. A case of incest has been reported (again by Chloe's people?) to Paul (5:1–8); the mis-understanding of the previous letter, mentioned above (5:9–13), a tendency to indulge in litigation (6:1 8), and finally an inclination to libertinist practices involving (as in Galatia) a misunderstanding of Christian freedom (6:9–20).

Ch. 7 takes a new turn. To understand this new turn we must shift to 1 Cor 16:17, where Paul writes: 'I rejoice at the arrival of Stephanas, Fortunatus and Achaicus'. In addition to 'those of Chloe', S, F, and A have turned up on the scene. We are told that S, F, and A 'made up for your absence' (*ibid.*). This probably means that these three persons brought along a letter from the Corinthians and supplemented it with further oral information. In any case, much of the material from ch. 7 on is expressly written in answer to a letter from the Corinthians inquiring about various points of doctrine and ethics, which Paul answers one by one. The references to the letter are introduced by a constantly recurring formula, 'now con-cerning', beginning with 'now concerning what you wrote about' in 7:1 and repeated at 7:25; 8:1; 12:1; 16:1 and 16:12.

In 7:1 the question is about sexual problems. Some of the
Corinthians had got hold of the idea that Christianity involved
sexual asceticism (the opposite of the group dealt with in
6:9ff, esp. 12ff—an apparent inconsistency which will be
explained later). In 7:25 we have a question about virgins;
in 8:1 the problem of meats sacrificed to idols; in 12:1 the
problems raised by spiritual gifts in Christian worship, esp.
tongue-speaking; 16:1 deals with the question of the collection
for the Jerusalem Christians, which Paul had undertaken at
the apostolic conference; finally 16:12 concerns the future
movements of Apollos.

In these chapters there are certain other matters not
covered by the formula 'now concerning', and it is reasonable
to assume that these matters were raised in the verbal com-
munications of S, F, and A. Among these problems are the
veiling of women prophets in church (11:2–16), while 11:17–34
concerns the unworthy behaviour of wealthier Christians at the
Lord's Supper, which (fortunately for us) leads Paul to quote
the earliest recorded version of the eucharistic institution
(11:23–25).

Ch. 15 also deals with the nature of the resurrection body,
which, by another stroke of luck, gives Paul the occasion to
quote the earliest available tradition of the Easter appearances
(15:3ff).

The Nature of the Troubles at Corinth

There has again been much discussion about the precise
nature of the troubles at Corinth. F. C. Baur of course detected
the presence of Judaizers versus Paulinists and understood the
groups mentioned in 1 Cor 1:12 as parties with theological
directions. J. Munck is quite right in emphasizing that they
are not parties but cliques, with no clear doctrinal significance.
Nevertheless, it was not mere bourgeois cliquishness. A
common direction or basis is discernible behind all the
questions which the Corinthians ask and behind all the accusa-
tions which Paul levels against them. There is a great deal to
suggest that it was a gnosticizing movement. Such, of course,

is the opinion of the Bultmann school,[1] and for once they appear to be right, if by 'gnostic' we mean not the full-blown gnostic systems of the second century, but religious attitudes which culminate in the boastful claim to the possession of 'gnosis' (knowledge). Note how frequently this term occurs in 1 Cor (1:5; 8:1, 7, 10, 11; 12:8; 13:2, 8; 14:6). By gnosis the Corinthians evidently mean some sort of esoteric religious experience (sacramentally mediated?) which sets them above ordinary church members who do not share it. Paul does not condemn gnosis as such. Rightly understood, it is one of the gifts of salvation, and he can thank God for its presence in the Corinthians (1:5). But it can be misused, and when misused it manifests itself in all sorts of reprehensible theological opinions and wrong behaviour. Sometimes it may (6:9ff) lead to libertinism, to uninhibited intercourse with prostitutes (temple prostitution?), sometimes to undesirable forms of asceticism, such as complete abstention from intercourse on the part of married people (7:3ff). The reason for this apparently contradictory behaviour is that gnosticism is based upon a dualistic view of the world. Gnosis puts the believer above this world into the real world. When there, he may either say that the world is a matter of indifference and that anything he does in it will not affect his soul (libertinism), or he may say, now that he is above the world he must reduce all his contacts with it to a minimum (asceticism). Paul's answer to libertinism is that the body is a temple of the Holy Spirit (6:19). His answer to asceticism is not so satisfactory. He is surprisingly sympathetic towards sexual asceticism (7:8, 17ff, 25ff, 32ff). This is due to 'the impending distress' (v. 26), the eschatological denoument, culminating in the second coming. True, he maintains a robust common sense: 'it is better to marry than to be aflame with passion' (v. 9); 'let them marry—it is no sin' (v. 36). But he lacks the balanced view of the possibility of sanctifying marriage in the Lord, such as the deutero-

---

[1] W. Schmithals, *Die Gnosis in Korinth*, 1956. R. M. Grant, *A Historical Introduction to the New Testament*, 1963, accepts this verdict for 1 Cor (pp. 204ff).

Pauline author of Ephesians was able to achieve. Another gnostic manifestation is participation in pagan meals (8:1ff, 10:23ff). This springs from a similar sense of superiority, and leads to scandal, since the weak who have not gnosis are offended. The gnostics treat the sacraments as automatic guarantees of salvation, with no ethical implications (10:1–13, 11:17–34).

In 12:3 it appears that some, under the influence of religious excitement, were saying, 'Jesus be cursed'. This surprising affirmation has been variously interpreted, but it would be in line with a gnosticizing dualism if it meant the rejection of the humanity of Jesus in favour of a docetic Christ.[1] In a similar vein they would have no truck with the doctrine of the cross. To them it was 'foolishness' (1:18, 23).

The excessive emphasis on the spectacular gifts of the Spirit (chs. 12–14) may well point in a gnostic direction. Here the same sense of superiority over the weaker members who have no such gifts manifests itself. This is the occasion of Paul's first use of the figure of the body of Christ, in which all members, even the least significant, have their necessary part to play. Note that in 13:1f he links speaking with tongues with gnosis, and that it is in this context that he places the famous hymn to charity (1 Cor 13).

The Importance of 1 Corinthians

1 Cor is invaluable for insight it gives us into the everyday problems of one of the Pauline communities. How far it is typical it is impossible to say, but certainly most of the problems which engaged Paul elsewhere crop up here, in a more acute form, and with a greater wealth of detail.

The letter is also important because it contains some of the earliest traditions of the primitive church, notably the kerygmatic formula in 1 Cor 15:3ff, as well as the eucharistic tradition in 1 Cor 11:23–25.

---

[1] W. Schmithals, *op. cit.*, pp. 45ff; J. M. Robinson, *JBR* 30, 1962, p. 203.

2 *Corinthians*

2 Corinthians poses a very nice problem for the critic. There is a striking difference of mood between chs. 1–9 and chs. 10–13. In chs. 1–9 Paul is writing jubilantly because a great crisis in his relations with the church has been satisfactorily solved, whereas in ch. 10 he launches into a furious onslaught on the Corinthians. This change calls for an explanation.

Now in 2:4 and in 7:8, 12 Paul refers to an earlier letter which he said was written 'with many tears'. and which caused much pain, both to himself and to the Corinthians. This does not at all suit the content of 1 Cor. Either we must suppose that this severe letter has been lost, or we come to the theory first put forward by A. Hausrath in 1870.[1] This theory identifies the severe letter referred to in chs. 2 and 7 with chs. 10–13 (or with part of it, so J. H. Kennedy[2]). The arguments in favour of this theory were set out with characteristic lucidity by Kirsopp Lake,[3] who points out a series of cross-references between the two parts of our present 2 Cor: 13:10/2:3; 13:2/1:23; 10:6/2:9. And 2:4 well describes chs. 10–13.

The Hausrath theory has received considerable approval from British and American scholars.[4] On the other hand, until very recently it has not enjoyed much popularity in the land of its origin or in the European continent generally.[5]

Part of the reluctance to accept the theory has been due to the presence even within chs. 1–9 of passages (e.g. 2:14–4:18, 5:11–6:10) in which Paul is seemingly just as concerned to defend his apostleship against attack as he is in chs. 10–13. Thus it is felt that the differences between the two parts have been exaggerated. The tendency among German and other

[1] A. Hausrath, *Der Vierkapitelbrief des Paulus an die Korinther*, 1870.
[2] *The Second and Third Epistles of St Paul to the Corinthians*, 1900.
[3] *The Earlier Epistles of St Paul*, 1911, pp. 154–164.
[4] The following have accepted the theory: J. H. Kennedy, K. Lake, A. Plummer, R. H. Strachan, A. D. Nock, T. W. Manson, W. L. Knox, R. P. C. Hanson.
[5] The following continental scholars have rejected it: H. Lietzmann, W. G. Kümmel, H. D. Wendland, Feine-Behm, J. Munck.

Continental scholars has been to fall back on some other explanation such as fresh news coming in after Paul had written chs. 1–9, or a sleepless night (Lietzmann).

Recently, however, G. Bornkamm has returned to the partition theory and re-examined the various possibilities.[1] His theories are not entirely new, but take up many earlier suggestions. His starting-point is that there is a great hiatus between 2:13 and 7:5. Down to 2:13 Paul is going over his relation with the Corinthians up to the post-crisis reconciliation. Then this subject is broken off, and 2:14–7:4 is a defence of Paul's apostleship, which hardly accords with the mood of reconciliation. It is this fact, as we have seen, that was the chief argument against the partition theory. It also led J. Weiss and R. Bultmann to assign 2:14–7:4 to the severe letter. But, argues Bornkamm, in these chapters Paul defends his apostleship in a rather different tone from chs. 10–13. In the severe letter he is fighting with his back against the wall. In 2:14–7:4 he defends himself as though he is quite sure his arguments will be accepted by the Corinthians, and with a sense of being on the winning side. Cf. esp. 6:8ff; 7:4 with chs. 11 and 12. Consequently Bornkamm assigns 2:14–7:4 to an earlier letter. He calls it 'the first apology'. He sees in 10:10 (in the severe letter) a reference to this 'first apology'.

Secondly, there is a problem with chs. 8 and 9. Both deal with the collection for the Jerusalem church, but at ch. 9 Paul makes a new beginning without reference to what he has said in ch. 8.

In ch. 8 Titus is commended to the Corinthians for the task of completing the collection began a year ago. Macedon is held out as an example to Corinth in this matter. 8:10 refers to the recent crisis in Paul's relation with the church. This ch., Bornkamm argues, comes very suitably at the end of the letter of reconciliation.

Ch. 9 says nothing about the Macedonian example. 9:2 speaks about the efforts of the whole of Achaea. In 9:5 it

[1] See above, p. 41, n.1.

appears that Titus and his companions are already on the job in Corinth. Paul is now looking forward to his trip to Rome and the west.

Accordingly, concludes Bornkamm, ch. 9 is best taken as a separate message written later than chs. 1–8.

The most original feature of Bornkamm's monograph is his explanation for the arrangement of our present 2 Cor. Previous explanations had attributed the juxtaposition of 2 Cor 1–9 and 10–13 to accident. Bornkamm suggests that the arrangement was quite deliberate, and that it reflects the views of the church in the second century. According to Bornkamm, 2:14ff is inserted as a triumphal hymn, because from the standpoint of the second century (though not yet from Paul's standpoint at the time!) Paul's journey from Troas to Macedon seemed like a triumphal progress. Secondly, Bornkamm suggests chs. 10–13 are placed at the end of the letter because it was convention derived from apocalyptic that warnings of false teachers should be given at the end of documents. The appearance of false teachers was a sign of the last times immediately before the parousia. The compilation of 2 Cor took place between the time of Ignatius and Polycarp (who know 1 Cor but not 2 Cor) and Marcion (who knows both).

It would be impossible either to refute or to prove Bornkamm's thesis. All we can say, is that it removes some of the residual difficulties of Hausrath's partition theory, at least as far as the insertion of 2:14–7:4 is concerned. Perhaps the division of chs. 8 and 9 is not quite so necessary. Yet Bornkamm's thesis makes a plausible story for Paul's relationships with the Corinthian church after the writing of 2 Cor. Its difficulty is that it involves postulating two further letters (1st apology and 2nd collection letter) for which there is no clear evidence.

This story may be reconstructed as follows:

After the writing of 1 Cor, when, as Paul hoped, things had quietened down, he requests Timothy to start the fund-raising campaign at Corinth. Then he hears that certain 'false apostles' (their identity will be considered later) have turned up and are attacking his apostolic authority. So he writes the first apology (2:14–7:4) (minus 6:14–7:1, which as we have seen[1] is either the 'previous letter'—or part of it—of 1 Cor 5:9, or as Bornkamm thinks, is a non-Pauline interpolation).

Hearing that this letter made no impression, he makes a lightning visit to Corinth (2:1, 12:14, 13:1). This visit was a fiasco. Paul's letters were powerful, they said, but his bodily presence weak (10:10). So Paul returns to Ephesus and pens the severe letter (10–13), sending it *via* Titus with the commission to do his best to bring the Corinthians round. Paul then leaves Ephesus for Troas, awaiting Titus' arrival from Corinth with news about his (and the severe letter's) success or otherwise. But Titus does not arrive. So in his anxiety Paul goes as far as Macedonia, to meet Titus half-way. At last Titus arrives with the news that all is well. So Paul writes 2 Cor 1–2:14, 7:5–9:15. Or, if we follow Bornkamm all the way, ch. 9 is a separate letter about the collection, written a little later.

The letter of reconciliation, then, is written for two purposes. First, Paul is thankful that the crisis is over, and that normal relations have been restored. Then gently but firmly he (chs. 8 and 9) urges upon them the resumption of the collection, which had been delayed by the crisis.

Paul's Opponents in 2 Corinthians

Most of our information about Paul's opponents in 2 Cor comes from the severe letter, chs. 10–13. They are saying that Paul has no eloquence (10:1, 10; does he not indulge sufficiently in ecstatic speech?), insufficient miraculous powers (12:12), or visionary experiences (12:1ff). They boast of their own Jewish background (11:22). They claim, falsely, to be apostles (11:5, 12f; 12:11). It is clear (11:4) that they came from outside. It would seem that the opponents are very similar to those at Galatia and Philippi, except that here is no mention of circumcision. We must[2] be careful to distinguish the situations of 1 Cor

---

[1] Above, p. 41.
[2] See D. Georgi, *Die Gegner des Paulus im 2. Korintherbrief*, 1964.

and 2 Cor 10–13. As we have seen (above pp. 43ff), the trouble in 1 Cor was of local origin. It arose from within the Corinthian community and was due to their misunderstanding of the gospel and the nature of the church. In 2 Cor the situation is quite different. Here the false teachers come from *outside* (11:4)—Hellenistic wandering preachers, Bornkamm calls them, like those at Philippi, and like the trouble makers at Galatia. Like those in Galatia they preach 'another Jesus' (11:4; cf. Gal 1:7). They found congenial soil in Corinth, for the Corinthians, given their already existing predisposition for spectacular pneumatic manifestations, for gnosis, for mystery religions, etc., were likely to succumb to the kind of syncretism which the false apostles purveyed. But there is no direct indication in 2 Cor 10–13 of any doctrinal position that we can label. Certainly it is not that of the Judaizers. Nor is there any statement which would allow us to call them gnostics.[1] But deep down there is a doctrinal position involved in the self-understanding of the false apostles. They understand themselves as Hellenistic 'divine men' ($\theta\epsilon\hat{\iota}o\iota$ $\check{\alpha}\nu\delta\rho\epsilon\varsigma$), a common type in the Hellenistic world, who display their divine nature by their spectacular gifts, ecstatic speech, miracles and visions. This suggests that they had a Christology of a similar kind, i.e. they understood Jesus as a divine man like themselves in opposition. Paul emphasizes his apostolic labours, his conformity to the cross of Christ, and therefore by implication, the 'cross side of the kerygma', as J. M. Robinson has called it (11:22ff).

Importance of 2 Corinthians

The chief importance of 2 Cor lies in its disclosure of Paul's self-understanding as an apostle. Apostleship and gospel are inseparably interwoven. This letter is the foundation for any true understanding of the ministry of the church in terms of apostolic succession (apostolorum nobis vindicamus non honores sed labores!). The apostle is in his person the embodi-

---

[1] *Contra* Schmithals, *Op. cit.*

ment of the kerygma of the cross. The church's ministry stands in this succession in so far as it reproduces the witness of the cross in word and life.

(ƒ) ROMANS

In connection with Romans there are three main problems. First, its integrity; second, the foundation and character of the Roman church; third, its occasion and relation to the situation of the church in Rome.

1. *Integrity*

The problem of the integrity of Romans is not like that which confronts us in 2 Cor or even in Phil. Rom 1–14 clearly forms a unity. With Rom 15–16 the difficulties are partly integral (ch. 16) arising from its content, and, with both 15 and 16, they are external, arising from the textual transmission.

Ch. 16 includes 26 greetings to the church addressed. Among the 26 are Prisca and Aquila. We know from 1 Cor and Acts that this couple left Rome, *c.* A.D. 49 for Corinth, then moved from Corinth to Ephesus. Now it is possible that they had returned to Rome between the writing of 1 Cor and Rom, especially since Claudius died in A.D. 54 and was succeeded by Nero, whose wife Poppea was sympathetic towards Judaism. But 26 is a surprising number of greetings for a church Paul had never visited. On the other hand, Paul had been at Ephesus for about two years, and would have had many friends there.

The sudden attack in 16:17 on 'those who create dissensions and difficulties' is equally surprising for a church which Paul had not founded, and which was not his direct responsibility. Finally, in 16:7 Paul greets two 'fellow prisoners' of his, Andronicus and Junias.

For these reasons it was long suggested that ch. 16 is a letter, or part of a letter to the church in Ephesus.

The situation is further complicated by the MS evidence. Marcion, we are informed by Origen, used a text comprising chs. 1–14. Marcion of course was capable of expunging ch. 15, particularly in view of its laudatory reference to the OT (15:4) and the ensuing OT quotations. However, there is the further fact that some MSS of the Latin vulgate place the concluding doxology (Rom 16:25–27) after 14:23. This may indicate that the omission of ch. 15 was not the work of Marcion, but represents the form in which the text reached him. So there is evidence for a version of Romans which included only chs. 1–14.

But what of a version including chs. 1–15? Until 1935 such a possibility rested only on scholarly speculation based on the contents of ch. 16.[1] In 1935 this scholarly speculation was triumphantly vindicated by the publication of the papyrus MS, p 46 (third century). This places the concluding doxology (Rom 16:25–27) *at the end of chapter* 15. This was just what the critics had been suggesting!

The MS evidence thus suggests that in early times there were *three* current versions of Romans: (1) Rom 1–14; (2) Rom 1–15; (3) Rom 1–16, each concluding with the doxology now at Rom 16:25–27. How are these facts to be explained?

In 1948 T. W. Manson,[2] writing after the publication of p 46, propounded the theory that the three different versions of Romans go back to Paul himself. 1–15 is the version which Paul intended for Rome itself, containing the information about Paul's plans to visit that church on the way to Spain. 1–16 is a version sent to Ephesus, i.e. the Roman letter with greetings and warnings to the Ephesian church appended. Finally, Manson suggests the version 1–14 was sent to other Pauline churches (Syria, etc.).

Manson then draws certain conclusions as to the nature of Rom. It is in fact a circular letter,[3] not addressed specifically to Rome, but summing up the theological position which Paul

[1] The last and most lucid statement of this theory, while it was still only a matter of speculation, is in the first (1932) edition of C. H. Dodd's commentary on Romans (Moffatt series), pp. xvii–xxiv.

[2] 'St Paul's letter to the Romans—and Others'. *BJRL* 31, 1948, pp. 224–240. Repr. *Studies in the Gospels and Epistles* (Ed. M. Blake), 1962, pp 225–241.

[3] This had already been mooted before, on the ground of the omission of ἐν ʽρώμη (1:7, 15) in some MSS.

had worked out during the controversies of Gal and 1 and 2
Cor (and, we would add, Phil). This would mean that Romans
is not simply occasional, though there was a specific occasion
for sending it to Rome, viz., his impending visit. It is much
more systematic than Paul's previous letters. Looked at in
this way, Rom ceases to be just a letter introducing Paul and
his teaching to Rom, and becomes a manifesto, setting forth
his deepest convictions on certain issues. Here introduction
becomes determinative for exegesis.

The flaw in this brilliant reconstruction is that in Rom
Paul's central concern is the Jewish law. If Rom is a summary
of the theology worked out in Gal, Phil, and 1 and 2 Cor, one
would expect it to be directed towards the questions raised by
syncretism and gnosis. Instead, it harks back to the earlier
problems of the Jerusalem conference and the Antioch fracas
(Jew and Gentile, segregation). Paul had touched on these
problems when first confronted with the trouble in Galatia, but
by Phil and 2 Cor had come to see that they were not directly
relevant (save on the one point of circumcision) to the questions
posed by syncretism and gnosis. While Manson has given a
plausible account of the origin of the three versions, his con-
tention that Rom has no direct bearing on the situation in
Rome needs reconsideration.

2. *Foundation and Character of the Roman Church*

We do not know when the gospel was first brought to Rome,
or when a Christian community was established there, but the
Suetonius reference and the banishment of Aquila and Prisca
(see above, p. 12) indicate that a Jewish Christian church
existed there by *c.* 49, when it came to an abrupt end. Rom,
preoccupied as it is with the question of Jew and Gentile,
suggests that by 55 there was again a Christian church in
Rome, but that it now consisted *both of Jews and Gentiles*. The
Jewish Christians probably returned to Rome on the death of
Claudius in 54 (see above, p. 51). It is quite possible that they
found that between 49 and 55 there had grown up a Gentile
(Pauline) Christian community. It is with the consequent

tension between these two groups that Rom is primarily concerned. Paul feels a particular responsibility for the Roman church because of his own Gentile Christians there, uncircumcised Gentiles who found difficulty living side by side with Jewish Christians in a single community. Hence all the arguments about the law and justification (chs. 1–8), about the place of Israel in salvation history (chs. 9–11) and about the relation of the 'strong' (Pauline Christians) and the 'weak' (Jewish Christians) in the Christian community (14:1ff).

3. *Occasion and Date of Writing*

Paul is hoping to visit Rome on his way to Spain after his journey to Jerusalem with the collection (1:11; 15:24, 28f). He has completed his mission in the eastern Mediterranean and is now ready for work in the west.

Meanwhile, he has heard (how we do not know) about the tensions in Rome, so he writes Rom 1–15 sending further copies to Ephesus (1–16) and (if Manson's speculation is correct), to Syria (1–14).

The situation indicates that Rom was written at Corinth (or Cenchreae, the port of Corinth, 16:1) just before Paul's last journey to Jerusalem with the collection. The date, on our chronology, would be 55.

Summary of Contents

Following Nygren,[1] we find the organizing principle of Rom in the apocalyptic scheme of the two aeons (ages).

I. *Introduction*

    1:1–7. Opening address and greeting.
    1:8–17. Paul's self-introduction.

In these two sections Paul skilfully enunciates the gospel, first in traditional terms (1:2–4) and then in his own understanding of it (v. 17). To Paul both formulae mean the same thing, whether stated in terms of the 'facts of salvation' (*extra*

---

[1] A. Nygren, *Commentary on Romans*, 1949.

nos) or in terms of our appropriation of it (*pro nobis*). Verse 17
serves as the title—the gospel of the new aeon.

A. *Negative: man in the old aeon*

    1:18–32. Gentiles have sinned by idolatry and immoral-
    ity.

    2:1–3:20. Jews have sinned: the law creates false sense
    of security and pride.

B. *Positive: the gospel of the new aeon*

    3:21–31. The righteousness of God (= his saving act) in
    Jesus Christ.

    4:1–25. Scriptural proof (Abraham).

    The four freedoms of the new aeon

    5:1–11. Freedom from wrath.

    (5:12–21. The two aeons = Adam/Christ.)

    6:1–23. Freedom from sin.

    7:1–25. Freedom from the law.

    8:1–39. Freedom from death.

C. 9–11. *The place of Israel in the salvation history of the new
    aeon.*

    9:1–5. Israel has rejected the gospel of the aeon through
    unbelief.

    9:6–13. God's promise still stands, to erect an Israel
    according to the Spirit.

    9:14–21. God's freedom, like that of a potter with his
    clay, to call a new Israel after the Spirit.

    9:30–10:21. Old Israel has been rejected because of its
    rejection of the Gospel.

    Ch. 11. The course of salvation history in the new aeon.

    11:1–10. A remnant of Israel has been saved.

    11:11–30. The Gentiles are now being brought in. This
    will provoke Israel to jealousy, so that Israel will
    come in and all will be saved.

C

D. *The ethics of the new aeon*

> 12:1–2. The true Christian liturgy as a response to God's saving act is self-oblation.
>
> 12:3–13:7. The self-oblation defined: Christian behaviour:
>
>> in the church, 12:3–16;
>> in the world, 12:17–21;
>> in the state, 13:1–7.
>
> 13:8–10. The ethic of the new aeon summarized as the love of neighbour.
>
> 13:11–14. Eschatological motivation of the ethic.
>
> 14:1–15:13. Specific application of the ethic to the Roman situation: the weak and the strong.

E. *Conclusion* 15:14–33

> Paul's future plans.
>
> 15:33 forms the concluding blessing.

The 'wandering doxology' (Rom 16:25–27) is widely regarded as a post-Pauline addition. See Dodd *ad loc.*

The Importance of Romans

Even if we do not accept fully Manson's view that Rom is a circular letter treating Paul's gospel systematically, it remains the most comprehensive statement of the specifically Pauline theology. All treatments of that theology are inevitably based principally on Rom (e.g. R. Bultmann's *Theology of the New Testament*). It shows that Paul's distinctive contribution to NT theology is its emphasis on the subjective, existential side (justification by faith), but at the same time this subjective aspect is set in the framework of a salvation history conceived in terms of the two aeons, and (cf. 1:2–4 with 1:17) is correlated to the objective side, the saving acts of God in Christ.

The part played by Rom in the history of the church can hardly be overestimated. It was Rom which led to the conversion of Augustine of Hippo, to Luther's discovery of a gracious God, of *sola fide*, and *sola gratia*, to that occasion when John Wesley's heart was 'strangely warmed', and to the bell that K. Barth accidentally rang and startled the sleeping tents of liberal theology in 1918.

4. *The Disputed Pauline Letters*

We come now to a group of letters whose Pauline authorship has been questioned for a number of reasons, but which are still widely defended as Pauline. The arguments in favour and against are about equal in weight, and a verdict of *non liquet* is the position maintained here. The letters in question are 2 Thess, Col, and Eph.

(*a*) 2 THESSALONIANS

2 Thess is at once so similar to 1 Thess and so different from it, that the traditional authorship raises serious difficulties.

First the similarities.[1] There is a whole series of literary parallels between 1 and 2 Thess. The opening address is identical (1 Thess 1:1/2 Thess 1:1). 2 Thess 1:3–12 exhibits a number of verbal parallels with 1 Thess 2:10; 3:12f; 4:16; 2:14ff, 19; 2:12; 4:5f. 2 Thess 2:1–12 with 1 Thess 4:14–17; 5:12; 3:4; 2:12f; 1:2–4; 4:7; 5:9. 2 Thess 2:15–3:5 with 1 Thess 3:2; 3:8–4:2.

On the other hand, Wrede noted marked differences of a theological kind between 1 and 2 Thess. Most striking is the different eschatological perspective. In 1 Thess the parousia is near—so near, that the deaths of certain Christians before the parousia has created a problem (see above, p. 22). In 2 Thess 2:3–12 there is a remarkable passage, unlike anything elsewhere in Paul, which sets out an apocalyptic programme, one involving a considerable delay in the parousia. First, there is the present period during which the 'restraining force' is holding back the 'lawless one' (Antichrist). Then the Anti-

---

[1] See W. Wrede, *Die Echtheit des 2. Thessalonicherbriefs*, TU NF 9, 2, 1903, pp. 4-12, where the passages are set out in parallel columns and identical words and phrases underlined.

christ will appear and reign temporarily until the parousia of
the Lord Jesus. Much more recently, H. Braun[1] has noted a
number of other features suggesting a sub-apostolic theological perspective. There is a different view of the last judgment. In Paul every man, pagan and Christian alike, will be
judged according to his works (pagans: Rom 2:6–11; Christians: Rom 14:10–12; 1 Cor 4:4f; 2 Cor 5:10). In Paul only false
teachers will be judged as such (Gal 5:10; 2 Cor 11:15). In 2
Thess, on the other hand, the last judgment relates to two
general classes, the persecuted church and its persecutors. At
the last judgment there will be a reversal of fates: the persecutors will have tribulation and the persecuted relief (2 Thess
1:5ff; cf. Rev 16:6f, 19:2). Finally, Braun notes a tendency,
characteristic of the post-Pauline generation, to transfer
attributes, functions, etc., from God to Christ, e.g. 2 Thess
2:16, 3:5 compared with 1 Thess 3:11f.

It is possible to explain away these difficulties and to retain
2 Thess as genuinely Pauline. The close similarities of vocabulary and style between 1 and 2 Thess are usually explained
by dating the two letters within a few months of each other.
The major theological differences may be due to the use in
2 Thess 2:3–12 of an early Christian apocalypse, adopted for
the special purpose of damping down the eschatological
excitement at Thessalonica by announcing a delay in the
parousia. But it is difficult to account for the other differences
of theological perspective (Braun) on the assumption that the
letter is genuine to Paul.

The Occasion of the Letter

2 Thess deals with two major problems. First, there are false
teachers in the church announcing that (2:2) 'the day of the
Lord has come' (ἐνέστηκεν)[2]. This suggests the kind of gnostic-

---

[1] *ZNW* 44, 1952–3, pp. 152–6. Repr. *Ges. Stud.*, 1962, pp. 205–209.

[2] 'At hand' is a possible translation, and more likely if the letter is
by Paul himself. For in that case the situation, as in 1 Thess, is one of
apocalyptic excitement. Here introductory questions tend to determine
exegesis.

ism found in 2 Tim 2:18. Such a view is possible in Paul's time (cf. 1 Cor 15), but a little difficult to assume for Thessalonica in view of 1 Thess, where the trouble was apocalyptic fanaticism. This gnostic over-realized eschatology is countered with the apocalypse (2:3–12).

The second problem is the libertinist ethic attacked in 3:6–15. This again is possible for Thessalonica in Paul's life time. Indeed, 1 Thess 4:10b–12 already suggests that apocalyptic excitement was leading to idleness. But once more, it is perhaps a little more intelligible in a gnostic context.

Date. If Pauline, 50: if post-Pauline, somewhere between 65 and *c.* 115 (Polycarp). Marxsen[1] conjectures soon after 70.

Summary of Contents

1:1–2. Opening address = 1 Thess 1:1.

1:3–12. Opening thanksgiving for the church's growth in faith.

2:1–12. The over-realized eschatology of the false gnostic teachers, countered with a 'little apocalypse'.

2:13–3:5. Further thanksgiving and prayer that the church may hold fast to the Pauline traditions.

3:6–16. Exhortation to deal with the idle brethren who walk disorderly.

3:17f. Autographic conclusion. If the letter is not Pauline this will be a strong, but suspect, claim to authenticity. If genuinely Pauline, it is Paul's reaction to the false letters circulating at Thessalonica (2:2).

(*b*) COLOSSIANS

The authenticity of Col was first questioned by the Tübingen school, who assigned it to the 'synthesis' period of early church history. The more moderate successors of the Tübingen school continued to have doubts about it after they had withdrawn from some of the more extreme positions of

[1] *Einleitung*, p. 44.

F. C. Baur. Thus H. J. Holtzmann retained the bulk of Col as
Pauline but held that the christological hymn (1:15ff) was a
post-Pauline interpolation. In this hymn Christ is accorded
not only inactive pre-existence as in Phil 2:6ff but an active
role as agent of creation.

Again, Col is clearly attacking some kind of gnosticism.
The Christology of the hymn is slanted against gnostic ideas.
Christ is the 'head' over the invisible powers (1:16). This
suggests a gnostic system of celestial hierarchies. In 2:8 we
read: 'beware lest anyone carry you off captive through
philosophy and vain deceit'. By 'philosophy' the writer means
not the serious philosophies of Plato, etc., but the syncretistic
mythologies of gnosticism. In 2:9 it is asserted that Christ is
the 'fullness' (πλήρωμα, a gnostic word!)—i.e. the cosmic
headship belongs to Christ, not to any gnostic *pleroma*. In
2:16 there is an allusion to various cultic observances:
'questions of food and drink', 'a new moon or a sabbath'. Col
2:18 condemns the worship of angelic (demonic) powers, i.e.
gnostic mythological hierarchies. The same verse also protests
against those who speculate about visions they have received.
2:21 refers to certain ascetic practices: 'do not touch, do not
taste'. Ascetic abstention from certain foods and drinks is
likely to arise from a dualistic gnostic world view.

At a time when gnosticism was thought to be merely a
second-century Christian deviation,[1] all this was enough to
relegate Col to a later date. Since the history of religions
school, however, gnosticism has come to be regarded as a
first-century syncretistic movement both in and outside the
church. So the gnosticism in Col is no longer an argument
against Pauline authorship. Many of the features combated in
Col are already found, e.g., in Gal. But there are other
problems.

Style and Vocabulary. Compared with the other Pauline
letters, Col contains a remarkable number of *hapax legomena*
both NT and Pauline. Morton's computer, not surprisingly,

---

[1] Following the patristic evidence of the full-blown gnostic systems,
which are second-century Christian heresies.

rejects Col: Marxsen[1] reports 34 words in Col not found elsewhere in the NT and 25 words not found in other Pauline writings.

Theology. We have already mentioned the high Christology of Col. In addition there is the different way in which the term 'body of Christ' is used here compared with 1 Cor and Rom. In the latter it is a figurative comparison, the point of which is mutual interdependence in the church. In Col (followed by Eph) the body of Christ is a cosmic reality, of which Christ is the head (Col 1:18, 24; 2:19; 3:15).

Circumcision is treated in Col in a different way from Rom. In Rom (2:25ff; 3:1, 30; 4:9ff) circumcision was a Jewish rite, now abolished. In Col there is a Christian circumcision, which is baptism (Col 2:11).

Baptism is also presented differently. In Rom 6 the believers die with Christ in baptism but their rising with him is always future and potential, to be constantly striven after by moral effort, but never completely realized until the parousia. In Col this eschatological reserve has disappeared. In baptism we are already risen with Christ (Col 3:1).

Marxsen (*ibid.*) makes the further point that the position of Epaphras (4:12) is that of a successor to Paul, and that his position is therefore like that of the presbyters, etc., in the Past. Here is the doctrine of apostolic succession, characteristic of the 'early Catholicism' of the sub-apostolic age.

What are we to make of these arguments? The developed concept of the body of Christ is not beyond the bounds of possibility for Paul, especially if the concept has been further developed polemically in response to the gnostic threat. Granted that its roots lie in the concept of Christ as the second Adam (1 Cor 15; Rom 5),[2] it is quite within the orbit of Pauline thought.

With regard to baptism, there is a difference of accent, it is true. And yet Col still maintains the moral imperative: 'If you

[1] *Einleitung,* p. 160.
[2] For this derivation of the doctrine of the body of Christ see R. H. Fuller, *The Foundations of New Testament Christology,* pp. 211ff.

then have been raised with Christ . . . *seek* the things that are above. . . . *Set* your mind on things that are above' (Col 3:1f). Then follows a whole series of concrete imperatives (5ff).

As to circumcision, here again Paul may well have gone beyond his position in Gal 3–4 and Rom 4. But these passages already *imply* the replacement of circumcision by baptism.[1] In short, all of the doctrinal differences can be adequately accounted for on the supposition that Col represents a later development of Paul's thinking in response to a more developed situation.

The Christology of Col is certainly more advanced than that of the earlier epistles. But it is not without precedent. The pre-existence of the Son is already found in Phil 2:6ff, and is in fact a pre-Pauline doctrine (see above, p. 38). Nor is the idea of the active pre-existence and agency of creation completely new to Paul as 1 Cor 8:6 shows. In fact, the whole concept of active pre-existence seems to have been worked out in connection with the identification of the Son with the wisdom of God[2] *before* Paul, and is presumed in all the passages which speak of pre-existence, even where it is not expressed (e.g. Phil 2:6ff). Paul himself identifies Christ quite casually with the wisdom of God in 1 Cor 1:24. If Paul accepted it all along, it was easy for him to bring it forth in the Colossian context, where he has opposing the gnostic ideas of other mediatorial principles.

The differences of vocabulary can probably be adequately accounted for (1) by the vocabulary of the syncretistic opponents; (2) the development of Paul's thought; (3) the use of hymnic sources (e.g. Col 1:15ff); (4) an argument which would also explain the stylistic differences of which the computer is aware—a 'secretary hypothesis'. According to the latter, Paul in prison would have used a secretary to whom he gave the headings of what he wanted said, the secretary would then take home his notes, write up the letter, and bring it to Paul for approval and signature.

[1] See O. Cullmann, *Heil als Heilsgeschichte*, 1965, p. 239.
[2] See *The Foundations of New Testament Christology*, pp. 72–5; 208ff.

The only argument unaccounted for is the position of Epaphras. In 4:12 Epaphras is really no more than a trusted assistant of Paul. He is a fellow-labourer rather than a successor to the apostle.

There is, however, one remaining difficulty. We can maintain the traditional authorship of Col provided we allow for a development in Paul's thought, i.e. if we place it at a later date than Rom. Yet, it is clear (see above, pp. 39f) that Col is written, or purports to be written, in precisely the same situation as Philem. Now we saw that there were good reasons for placing Philem during the Ephesian captivity, rather than during the imprisonment at Rome. But we now want to place Col at Rome. This is a baffling problem, and the only solution seems to be to place Philem after all in the Roman period. If Philem is dated in the Ephesian period, then Col must be included among the deutero-Paulines.

Let us then, recognizing the difficulties, proceed on the assumption that the letter is written during the Roman imprisonment (1:24, 4:10). According to Col 2:1, Paul had never visited the church, and it is possible that its actual founder was Epaphras, who in that case would have founded it as Paul's agent during the Ephesian ministry. Epaphras accordingly has arrived at Rome with news of the situation in Colossae. Onesimus is also there. Tychicus is returning to Colossae with Onesimus (Col 4:7–9). So Paul takes the opportunity to write a letter to the Colossians, exhorting them to faithfulness in view of the syncretistic threat.

Col 4:16 speaks of a simultaneous letter to the Laodiceans. This has been variously identified with Ephesians, with Philem, and with a letter now lost. If Col is genuine, the last is the most likely possibility. That letters should have been read in the church service during Paul's lifetime (a further objection raised by Marxsen) is not at all surprising, for this is precisely the context in which e.g. 1 Cor was read (see above, p. 17).

While the traditional view of the authorship and date is not without its difficulties, Col points to a situation fully intelligible in Paul's lifetime, and (unlike 2 Thess and Eph) nothing is gained exegetically by transferring it to the deutero-Paulines.

Summary of Contents

Part I (Doctrinal)

1:1f. Opening salutation.

1:3–14. Thanksgiving and prayer for the Colossian community.

1:15–20. Christological hymn. Finality of the revelation in Christ and his superiority over all other mediatorial principles. Christ is pre-existent the Head of the creation and the Head of the new creation.

1:21–23. The participation of the Colossians in this cosmic redemption.

1:24–2:5. Paul's present situation: his imprisonment carries forward God's purpose of salvation.

2:6–23. Attack on the false teaching of the syncretists. Through baptism the Colossians have passed over into the new aeon, but by succumbing to syncretism they are reverting to the old aeon (cf. Gal). The refutation in Col 2:6ff cannot be dismissed as inadequate and un-Pauline. Paul does not merely blast his opponents, but undermines their position by recalling the Colossians to the realities of their Christian existence.

3:1–17. Ethical exhortation. As in Gal this may be directed against the libertinism of the syncretists.

Part III (Ethical)

3:10–4:1. Household code. This is the first example of this form of ethical teaching in Paul. Since household codes become regular features of the post-apostolic letters (Eph 1, Pet, Past) this is a possible argument for deutero-Pauline authorship. But as such the household codes were older than Paul, and derived ultimately from Stoicism *via* the teaching of the Hellenistic Christianity.

It is not impossible that Paul should have used a house-hold code.

4:2-6. General exhortation to prayer.

4:7-17. Concluding greetings.

4:18. Autographic signature and blessing.

(c) EPHESIANS

The Pauline authorship of Eph is more widely disputed than that of Col.[1] The reasons are as follows:

1. *The style.* This is remarkably different from that of the unquestioned Paulines. (1) The inordinate length of the sentences impresses anyone who reads it in AV(KJV). Look at 1:15-23 and 3:1-7. By splitting up these sentences, RSV has concealed their length in the original Gk; (ii) *The piling up of synonyms*, e.g. 1:19, where four words for 'power' occur, three in the same phrase ('the energy of the power of his might'). (2) The repetition of a number of favourite phrases not found elsewhere in Paul, such as 'in the heavenlies'.

2. *The vocabulary.* Forty words occur in Eph not found in other Pauline letters; e.g. 'devil' (διάβολος), whereas Paul uses 'Satan'. A number of key words from Col are used in a different sense in Eph, e.g. 'mystery', 'body'. (The force of this argument is nullified for those who regard Col as also deutero-Pauline.)

3. *The literary relationship* between Col and Eph. A glance at the cross-references in the margin of Eph in RSV or the Gk Text (Kilpatrick or Nestle) will show how frequent the parallels are. Note esp. Eph 6:21f/Col 4:7, where the situation envisaged (Tychicus as the deliverer of the letter) is the same.

4. *Theology.* The Pauline doctrine of justification comes out clearly (2:5, 8). Yet, as already hinted, there are striking

---

[1] The doubts about Col are confined mainly to German-speaking scholars. The doubts about Eph are shared by the Anglo-Saxon world. See D. E. Nineham in *Studies in Ephesians*, ed. F. L. Cross, 1956, pp. 21–35.

differences between Col and Eph. Note how Eph stresses the
cosmic functions of the church (3:10, the church makes known
its redemption to the cosmic powers). Note too the presentation of marriage as a 'mystery' representing the unity between
Christ and his church (Eph 5:21ff).

5. *The literary character*. Eph refers to no specific conflict or
problems. It is really a tract dressed up in epistolary form,
(1:1f; 6:21–24 and the references to Paul as a prisoner, 3:1;
4:1), i.e. precisely an 'epistle' in Deissmann's sense.

6. Finally, there are a number of features suggesting a sub-
apostolic and 'early catholic' standpoint. Eph looks back upon
the apostles as a closed group (2:20, 3:5). In 4:11 the ministries
are listed: apostles, prophets and evangelists belong to the
past: now there are pastors and teachers who hand on the
tradition of the apostolic age. The author, by speaking in
Paul's name, endeavouring as a pastor and teacher to hand on
the apostolic tradition. The ministerial organization is developing towards the point reached by Past, though the terminology
is not yet fixed (elders, bishops).

Eph is directed to quite a different subject from Col. Col is
concerned with syncretistic heresy, Eph with the unity of
Jews and Gentiles in one ecclesia. All through, the thoughts of
Col are given a wholly different application.

Some of these difficulties can be explained away.

1. The style, vocabulary, etc., may be explained on the
'secretary hypothesis' (cf. Col).

2. The general character and impersonal approach may be
explained from the indication that Eph was intended as a
circular letter.

There is some MS evidence for this. ἐν Ἐφέσῳ (1:1) is
omitted in the earliest MS, p 46, inserted in the margin by
א and B, and finally assumed into the text.[1]

[1] Some following Marcion have identified Eph with the letter to
Laodicea of Col 4:16. This could explain the impersonal attitude (Paul
had not founded or visited the Colossian church), but not its general
character.

3. The literary affinities with Col coupled with the remarkable developments of thought may be explained from Paul's prolonged meditation on the themes of Col. The re-application of the thoughts to the unity of the church is suggested by Paul's reflections at the end of his long career.

Argument 1 may stand—we have already used it for Col. But it would require a different secretary from Col. Argument 2 is tenable (indeed it is the only viable explanation of the original reading of Eph 1:1). But a circular letter without concrete occasion is unprecedented among the Paulines. Even Rom, as we have seen, has a concrete occasion. Argument 3 is a valiant attempt, but how then can we explain the fact that Tychicus must have taken both letters together (Col 4:7/ Eph 6:21)? Prolonged meditation would surely require a greater distance between the writing of Col and Eph.

Undefended is the objection that Eph is sub-apostolic and 'early catholic'. This remains the decisive objection against Pauline authorship.

Ephesians as a sub-Apostolic Writing

The author, standing in 'apostolic succession' to Paul and speaking with his authority, announces the revelation of a 'mystery', i.e. a deeper knowledge into the economy of the divine salvation in history (3:1ff), viz., 'that the Gentiles are fellow heirs, member of the same body' (3:6). This of course, is not entirely new: Paul had implied the same thing in his treatment of the problem of Israel's unbelief in Rom 9–11. But now Paul's insight is carried further. Instead of a brief period in which the Gentiles are being admitted and Israel is being provoked to jealousy, there is an extended period of salvation history in which Jews and Gentiles live together in the one ecclesia, with the task of growing up in love to maturity. Compared with Paul, Eph places the parousia in the more distant future—when the church will be finally presented to Christ 'without spot or wrinkle or any such thing' (5:27). As O. Cullmann has shown,[1] the basic scheme of salvation history

[1] *Heil als Heilsgeschichte*, esp. pp. 104–8.

undergoes constant re-interpretation and adjustment in the light of fresh historical situations. Eph is an example of such a re-interpretation as the result of the Pauline mission, the death of the apostles, and the extension of salvation history consequent upon the delay in the parousia.

Date. The *terminus a quo* is the death of Paul, the exact date of which is unknown, but in any case Eph is later than 64 (on our chronology it would be 58). Yet Eph presumes the continued presence of Jews in the ecclesia. Therefore in any case it cannot be much later than 70. Marxsen[1] places it 'early in the post-apostolic age'.

Summary of Contents

Part I (Doctrinal)

Ch. 1. Thanksgiving for the revelation and redemption in Christ.

Ch. 2. The call of the Gentiles into the ecclesia.

Ch. 3. The unity of Jew and Gentile in the one ecclesia, with concluding prayer for growth (3:14–19), and doxology (20f).

Part II (Ethical)

4:1–16. Unity as a constant task as well as a gift.

4:17–5:20. Detailed ethical injunctions.

5:21–6:9. Household code.

6:10–20. Final exhortation to Christian conflict in the world.

6:21–24. Epistolary conclusion and blessing.

[1] *Einleitung*, p. 171.

III.—THE SYNOPTIC GOSPELS AND ACTS

(a) THE HISTORY OF THE SYNOPTIC TRADITION

The synoptic gospels and Acts are placed here, after the Pauline letters, because as literary products they are later. The Pauline letters, with the possible exceptions of Philem and Col, were all written by 60. Our earliest written gospel, Mark, is dated 65–70 (see below).

The modern critical study of the synoptic[1] gospels has passed through two overlapping phases. The first, from the last half of the eighteenth century to *c.* 1924 (the date of Streeter's *The Four Gospels*), concentrated upon the literary relationship between the first three gospels, the second, from 1918 onwards, upon the preliterary history of the gospel material.

The Synoptic Problem

In order to appreciate the obvious literary relationship between the first three gospels the student should write out in parallel columns from his Gk NT (if possible), or failing that, from the English, preferably RV (the most literal translation available), Mt 4:1–11, Mk 1:12f and Lk 4:1–13. The verbal similarities will show that some literary relationship is demanded. The following literary relationships are possible: (1) Mt is the earliest: Mk has abbreviated Mt while Lk has copied Mt with some re-arrangement; (2) Mk is the earliest: Mt and Lk have used Mk plus a common source now lost; Mt alternatively has used Mk plus Lk, or Lk has used Mk plus Mt; (3) Lk is the earliest: Mt has followed Lk with re-arrangements,

---

[1] The term 'synoptic' is itself the result of the first phase of this study. The literary relationship between Mt, Mk, and Lk made it possible to draw up the first three gospels in parallel columns, i.e. in the form of a 'synopsis' συνόψεσθαι=to 'see together'). The term came into use at the end of the eighteenth century (so Marxsen).

and Mk has abbreviated k. The choice between these possibilities can only be determined from an overall synoptic analysis.

The Priority of Mark

Although from time to time the theory of the priority of Mt is revived,[1] it is now generally accepted that Mk is our earliest gospel, and that both Mt and Lk have used Mk.[2] There is no single argument for this: the force of arguments is cumulative.

(1) Common subject-matter: Mk contains 661 verses. Of these, Mt reproduces some 600 and Lk some 300.

(2) Verbal agreement. These verses exhibit not only common subject-matter, but extensive verbal agreement. Most important, *Mt and Lk never agree in diverging from Mk wording.*[3]

When Mt or Lk diverge in wording from Mk these divergences are clearly deliberate. Sometimes they alter Mk for stylistic reasons, i.e. from a desire to improve Mk's Gk (e.g. Mk 2:4 uses for the paralytic's litter the coarse word κράβατον Mt alters this to κλίνη and Lk to κλινίδιον. Sometimes Mt and Lk alter Mk for dogmatic reasons. E.g. Mk 6:5 says 'Jesus *could do* mighty works'. Mt 13:58 alters 'could do' to 'did'. Cf. also the alteration of Mk 10:17f in Mt 19:17. The young man addressed Jesus as 'Good Master'. In Mk Jesus replies, 'Why do you call me good'? and in Mt, 'Why do you ask me about what is good?' It is easier to suppose that Mt altered Mk than *vice versa*.

(3) Mk is full of picturesque details, suggesting that Mk is closer to oral tradition. In Mk 4:38 Jesus is said to be

---

[1] This possibility was first propounded in modern times by Griesbach in 1789, but generally abandoned after the work of Lachmann (1835). Recent examples of the revival: B. C. Butler (R.C.), *The Originality of St. Matthew*, 1951; N. B. Stonehouse (conservative evangelical), *Origins of the Synoptic Gospels*, 1963; W. R. Farmer (critical), *The Synoptic Problem*, 1964.

[2] The number of treatments of the Marcan hypothesis in English is legion. B. H. Streeter's work *The Four Gospels*, 1924, is still definitive.

[3] But see below, p. 71.

sleeping on a 'pillow' during the storm at sea. Mt and Lk omit this detail.

(4) Common order. By and large, Mt and Lk follow Mk in the order in which they present the units of material. When they diverge from Mk's order they do so independently of each other. This fact is as important as the non-agreement of their divergences in wording.

The Priority of Mark

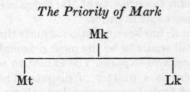

Ur-Markus

There is the residual problem of the few passages where Mt and Lk do agree in wording against Mk (see Streeter, pp. 295ff). This has led German scholars to postulate an 'Ur-Markus', an earlier form of Mk used by both Mt and Lk, now lost. Our present Mk is on this theory a later revision of the Ur-Markus. B. H. Streeter (*ibid.*) has examined these residual agreements of Mt/Lk against Mk and demonstrated that in every case they are the result of assimilation of Lk to Mt in the course of textual transmission.

When these minor agreements of Mt/Lk against Mk have been thus removed, there are still two major agreements in omission, viz., the two miracle stories, Mk 7:32ff (deaf mute) and 8:22ff (the blind man of Bethsaida). The proponents of the Ur-Markus theory hold that the original Mk, as used by Mt/Lk, did not yet contain these stories. This is doubtful because the stories in question play an integral part in the Marcan theology, esp. the blind man of Bethesda.[1] The agreement of Mt/Lk in omitting them is probably due to coincidence in intention.

[1] See R. H. Fuller, *Interpreting the Miracles*, 1963, p. 74.

Non-Marcan Material common to Mat/Luke

There remain some 200–250 vv. not in Mk but common to Mt/Lk. This material could have arisen through Mt's using Lk as a second source or *vice versa*. But since Holtzmann (1863) the commonest explanation has been that this is due to their use of common source now lost, generally referred to as Q (Ger.: *Quelle*). The arguments for the Q hypothesis are similar to those for the priority of Mk: agreement of Mt/Lk in wording and agreement in order.

The Q hypothesis has been questioned more than the priority of Mk,[1] but it still seems to be the most reasonable account of phenomena it seeks to explain. The extent to which Q was a written document is a matter of dispute. There are many passages of exact verbal agreement, but other passages where the verbal agreement is considerable but far from total, and still others where the verbal agreement is minimal, e.g. the parable of the talents/pounds (Mt 25:14–30; Lk 19:12–27).

In the third case, it is best to assume that the material in question is not from Q but from distinct traditions peculiar to Mt and Lk respectively. The second case is probably due to alternative translations from Aramaic. Only the first class can be confidently assigned to a common written Gk source. For these reasons it is difficult to define with any certainty the exact limits of Q. It is thus best to speak of the 'Q material', including both exact and partial verbal agreements. If we do use the symbol Q, it is shorthand for a common layer of tradition, partly written and perhaps partly oral.

The Contents, Character and Purpose of Q

It will have been noticed that Q consists almost entirely of sayings. There is some evidence that collections of dominical sayings did exist. Paul, e.g., seems to quote from a recognized body of sayings of the Lord (see above, p. 19). The recently

[1] Most notably, in the English-speaking world, by A. M. Farrer, 'On Dispensing with Q' in D. E. Nineham (ed.), *Studies in the Gospels*, 1955, pp. 55–88.

discovered Coptic Gospel of Thomas[1] indicates the survival of such collections into the second century.

Reconstructions of Q have frequently been attempted and none agree exactly. T. W. Manson[2] gives a useful list of those passages upon which v. Harnack, Streeter and Bussmann agree. They are: Lk 3:7–9; 4:1–13; 6:20–23, 27–33, 35–44, 46–49; 7:1–10, 18–20, 22–35; 9:57–60; 10:2–16, 21–24; 11:9–13, 29–35, 39, 41, 42, 44, 46–52; 12:2–10, 22–31, 33, 34, 39, 40, 42–46, 51, 53, 58, 59; 13:18–21, 24, 28, 29, 34, 35; 14:26, 27, 34, 35; 16:13, 16–18; 17:1, 3, 4, 6, 23, 24, 26, 27, 33–35, 37.

Q began with the eschatological proclamation of the Baptist. It included the temptations of Jesus, the Great Sermon, the healing of the centurion's boy, the missionary charge to the disciples, sayings about the Baptist, and anti-Pharisaic sayings. It concluded with eschatological sayings about the parousia.

The prevailing view of Q until recently was that it consisted of didache (ethical teaching) rather than kerygma (i.e. the proclamation of the passion and resurrection.[3] This circumstance led to much discussion about the reason for the omission of the kerygma, and of the relation to the Q material to the kerygma. Manson's view is that Q presumes a knowledge of the kerygma, and is intended to inculcate the kind of life which acceptance of the kerygma demands.

More recently H. E. Tödt, in the most important study of the Q material since Manson[4], has seriously questioned this view of Q following earlier suggestions of Dibelius[5] and Bultmann[6]

---

[1] A. Guillaumont et al., The Gospel According to Thomas, 1959.

[2] The Sayings of Jesus (1937), 1948, p. 16.

[3] So above all Manson, ibid.

[4] The Son of Man in the Synoptic Tradition, 1965, pp. 235–269.

[5] M. Dibelius, The Sermon on the Mount, 1940. Dibelius points out that the Q material relates the ethical teaching to Jesus' own eschatological message.

[6] R. Bultmann, Jesus and the Word, 1934, pp. 27ff, Primitive Christianity, 1956, pp. 71ff. Here Bultmann treats the Q material as containing primarily not ethical teaching, but the eschatological proclamation of Jesus. Also Theology of the New Testament I, 1952, p. 33. Here Bultmann asserts that the earliest church, side by side with its own kergygma, continued Jesus' own eschatological proclamation.

shows that the Q material contains much that cannot be
included under didache, but that is in fact primarily concerned
with Jesus' own proclamation of the near approach of the
eschatological kingdom of God. Thus Q shows that the early
church continued Jesus' own proclamation.

This still does not solve the problem of the relation between
this continuation of Jesus' own proclamation and the church's
own kerygma of the passion and resurrection. In answer, Tödt
points out that Q presupposes the death and resurrection of
Jesus. Jesus had staked all on his eschatological proclamation.
This proclamation had been radically called in question by the
cross. But God had vindicated Jesus' proclamation by reveal-
ing him in the resurrection appearances as raised from the
dead. Only because of this could the church continue Jesus'
own eschatological proclamation. Therefore the cross and
resurrection are the indispensable presuppositions of Q. Jesus'
word still has authority because its authority has been
vindicated by God in the resurrection. Thus side by side with
the continuation of Jesus' eschatological proclamation Q also
contains a christological kerygma—not the kerygma of the
saving significance passion, to which the circles from which Q
emanates had not yet arrived, but the kerygma of Jesus who
in his earthly ministry spoke with the authority of the Son of
man vindicated in face of the rejection of men (Lk 7:34; 9:58),
and who will come again in order finally to vindicate the
authority of his word (Lk 11:30; 12:8f, 40; 17:24–30).

The Date and Provenance of Q. From the foregoing discussion
it is clear that the basic nucleus of the Q material, reflecting
as it does the Christology of the earliest Aramaic-speaking
church[1] goes back, in its original Aramaic form, to Palestine in
the thirties. The church in Q is faced with three main preoccupations: Israel's rejection of Jesus proclamation and the
continued rejection of its own kerygma, the hostility of the
Pharisees, and relations with the continuing Baptist disciples.
But Q was translated into Gk, and therefore passed into the

[1] See R. H. Fuller, *The Foundations of New Testament Christology*,
pp. 142ff.

Hellenistic church. As a consequence it received some Hellenistic colouring. This is apparent in the present form of the temptation narrative (Jesus as the Son of God), in the story of the centurion's boy, which justifies the Gentile mission and perhaps also the revelation hymn (Lk 10:21f). Manson dates Q *c.* 50 or earlier, and sees Antioch as its place of origin. If we are right in putting Mk at Antioch (see below, p. 107) Q must have taken on its Gk dress somewhere else in close touch with Palestine, perhaps at Caesarea, where it was later expanded by the addition of special Lucan material—see below, p. 78.

The Q Hypothesis

The Special Matthean Material

Aside from the editorial work of Matthew himself (on which see below, pp. 113–18), the Special Matthean material consists of: (1) the infancy (chs. 1–2) and resurrection narratives (ch. 28); (2) narrative additions (e.g. the dialogue between Jesus and the Baptist, Mt 3:14f, the stater in the fish's mouth, 17:24–27; the suicide of Judas, 27:3–10; Pilate's wife's dream, 27:19; Pilate's washing of his hands, 27:24; and the resurrection of the saints 27:52f; (3) the testimonia (OT quotations); (4) teaching material.

Of these, the infancy and resurrection narratives probably have some previous history in the oral tradition, but in their present form appear to be compositions of Mt for apologetic (anti-Jewish) motives. The narrative additions are highly legendary in character, and appear to be quite late. The testimonia will be discussed later under Mt's own theological presentation. They draw largely upon a traditional stock of such quotations. Some of them are from the LXX, others apparently from the Heb. This points to diverse origins. It is the teaching material which is important and most characteristic.

The teaching material occurs in conjunction with matter partly from Mk and partly from Q, and most of it is in the five great discourses (see below). It consists (roughly) of: 5:4, 5, 7-10, 14, 16, 17, 19f, 21-23, 33-37, 38f, 41, 43, 47; 6:1-18, 34; 7:6, 15; 10:5b-6, 16b, 23, 41; 11:29 (?); 13:14-30, 36-43, 44-52; 18:15-20, 23-35; 19:10-12; 20:1-16; 21:28-32; 22:11-13; 23:2f, 5f, 7b-10, 15-22, 32f; 25:1-13, 14-30 (?), 31-46. It is not always easy to decide when material is from Q but not used by Lk, or when material is an editorial addition of Mt. But it is clear that we have here a body of material comparable in its forms to that of Q, viz., sayings and parables. T. W. Manson believed that it came from a single document arranged in a topical order and corresponding closely to the arrangement of the Q as given by Lk.[1] Unfortunately, owing to Mt's habit of conflation we cannot be sure of this. For its order in Mt may be due entirely to Mt's having taken the Q material as his basis and combining it with Special Matthean material wherever the latter appeared suitable. But at least we can say that the Special Matthean material is in content remarkably like that of Q. Its contents are: Jesus' preaching; missionary charge; missionary parables; community rules; denunciation of the Pharisees; parousia parables.

This material evidently has a long history behind it. Some of it (e.g. the Matthean beatitudes and antitheses in the Sermon on the Mount) has a high claim to belong to the authentic Jesus tradition, and has figured in much recent reconstruction of the original message of Jesus.[2] Some of it is highly legalistic, and represents the narrowly Judaistic outlook of some Palestinian community. It appears to be opposed to the admission of Gentiles without submission to the Law (5:19), and may even be specifically anti-Pauline (cf. 10:5b)

---

[1] *Op. cit.*, p. 22. He points out that the same topical arrangement of material is reproduced in the *Didache*.

[2] E.g. G. Bornkamm, *Jesus of Nazareth*, 1960, pp. 97ff. For a discussion of the implied criteria of authenticity see below, pp. 94-98.

polemic, reflecting the tensions of Gal 2, Acts 15 and 21. Some
of it again has a highly apocalyptic colouring (see esp. 10:23).[1]
Clearly it is material with a long history behind it. Since Mt has
incorporated his special tradition into the post-Pauline
Hellenistic Mk we may conjecture that the confluence of the
two traditions occurred after the fall of Jerusalem (70).
Manson, who thinks Special Matthew is a single document,
puts the date of its compilation at 65 (*op. cit.* p. 24). We can
argue that the special material reflects the history of the
Jerusalem Church down to that time.

The Special Lucan Material

The material peculiar to Lk consists of: (1) Baptist and Jesus
infancy cycles (chs. 1–2), genealogy (3:23–38), and passion-
resurrection tradition (chs. 22–24).[2] (2) A considerable
expansion of the Q[3] material with the addition of the Baptist's
preaching, parables, sayings and a few healing narratives. This
material includes the following: Lk 3:10–14; 4:16–32; 5:1–11;
6:24–26 (?); 7:11–17, 36; 8:3; 9:51–56, 61f (?)[4]; 10:17–20,
29–42; 11:5–8, 27f (?); 12:13–21, 32 (?), 47–49 (?); 13:1–17,
31–33; 14:1–24, 28–33; 15:8–16:12, 14f, 19–31; 17:7–22, 32 (?);
18:1–14a (b?); 19:1–27, 39–44. Again, it is not always easy to
decide whether any given verse is from the special material
or is an editorial composition of Lk.

As Manson (*op. cit.*, p. 27) rightly points out, there is no hint
of topical arrangement in the special Lucan material. From
this he concludes that it was not a written document, but oral
tradition.[5] Also, there can be no doubt that Luke himself has

[1] This apocalyptic material again has received much attention
recently as evidence for the preaching of the earliest post-Easter
community. E. Käsemann, 'Die Anfänge christlicher Theologie',
ZThK 57 (1960), pp. 162–85.
[2] For the view that Lk's passion narrative is basically independent of
Mk's though supplemented from Mk, see below, pp. 89–91.
[3] For this way of stating the case, see the discussion of the proto-
Luke theory below.
[4] More likely this is from Q, not used by Mt (so Taylor and Bornkamm).
[5] In our view much of it had been combined with the Q material
prior to its use by Lk. See below, p. 80.

coloured the style. This is generally recognized in the case of
the long narrative parables (Good Samaritan, Prodigal Son,
Unjust Steward, Dives and Lazarus). In the long travel
narrative, 9:51–18:14, the framework giving the impression
of a journey is doubtless the editorial work of Lk rather than
derived from the special material.

The good Palestinian character of the Special Lucan
material has frequently been recognized. At the same time, it
is not, like the Special Matthean material, narrowly Judaistic
in its attitude to the Law and to the Gentile mission. There are
apocalyptic sayings, but not so strongly coloured as the
Special Matthean material. Special Luke is interested in the
graciousness of Jesus towards the outcast, the poor, women,
non-Jews (particularly Samaritans). The history of this
material is difficult to trace. Conjecturally, we might say that
it came from Galilee into Samaria *via* the Samaritan mission
(Acts 8), and thence to Caesarea, where it was combined with
the Q material. We incline to agree with Manson that this
could have happened *c*. 60.

The Four Source Theory

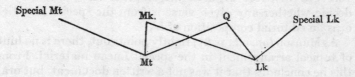

The Proto-Luke Theory

Streeter, *op. cit.*, pp. 201ff,[1] made a very acute observation
about Lk. Lk, it is well known, tends to follow one source at a
time, whereas Mt tends to conflate his sources. Now the Special
Lucan material, prior to the passion narrative, always occurs
in blocks of Q material, never in blocks of Mk (i.e. the order is
always Q-Special Lk-Q, never Mk-Special Lk-Mk). This

---

[1] He had first called adumbrated his theory in *Hibbert Journal* 20
(1921), pp. 103–12.

phenomenon led Streeter to propound his proto-Luke theory. Proto-Lk consisted of L + Q, with a special Lucan introduction and a passion narrative. Later, according to Streeter, Lk secured a copy of Mk, and used it to supplement proto-Lk. This theory explains certain perplexing phenomena, e.g. what has been called Lk's great omission (Lk's omission of Mk 6:45– 8:26). It is rather a great 'non-insertion'. Lk did not insert it because its contents are adequately covered elsewhere in Lk.

Lk has generally been regarded, like Mt, as a new edition of Mk, with lesser and greater insertions, Lk 6:20–8:3 and 9:51– 18:14 plus infancy and resurrection narratives and supplements to the passion narrative. For Streeter, Lk is basically an independent gospel with Marcan insertions.

The Proto-Luke Theory

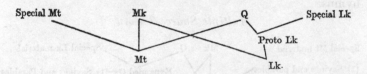

The proto-Luke theory has not met with general acceptance. Some British scholars have adopted it, notably V. Taylor[1] and T. W. Manson. In the U.S.A. it was accepted by B. S. Easton and A. M. Perry, and quite recently J. M. Robinson regards it with favour. In Germany, so far as we are aware, only J. Jeremias has accepted it (*N.T.S.* 4, 1957–8, pp. 116f).

J. M. Creed in his commentary on Lk (1931) rejects it in a footnote (!). It has never received a full length refutation. The common argument against it is that proto-Lk is too fragmentary to be a gospel.

Nevertheless, Streeter called attention to two phenomena that required explanation; (1) The invariable combination, Q + Lk, and the absence of Mk + L; (2) Lk's unusually

[1] Taylor made it the basis of further research in his *Behind the Third Gospel*, 1926.

extensive departures from Mk in the passion narrative. These phenomena are best accounted for if: (1) Q as Lk found it had already been expanded to include further material (mainly sayings and parables) peculiar to Lk; (2) Lk used an independent passion narrative and supplemented it from Mk. This is the more feasible since form criticism has made the existence of the continuous passion narrative in oral tradition exceedingly probable.

The Infancy Narratives

Finally, there are the Infancy stories in Mt 1–2 and Lk 1–2. Whatever their sources in tradition, in their written form they appear to be the work of the respective evangelists. The Lucan infancy narrative contains a cycle of Baptist traditions, probably emanating from Baptist sources and liturgical hymns.

Multiple Source Theory

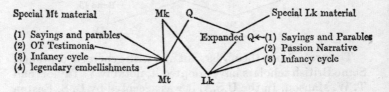

Special Mt material   Mk   Q   Special Lk material

(1) Sayings and parables   Expanded Q←(1) Sayings and Parables
(2) OT Testimonia   (2) Passion Narrative
(3) Infancy cycle   (3) Infancy cycle
(4) legendary embellishments
                    Mt   Lk

The Importance of Source Criticism

As a working solution of the synoptic problem, the source theory of which the two source theory (Mk and Q) is the basis has important consequences, both historical and theological.

1. *Historical.* When a unit of tradition has threefold attestation (Mk = Mt = Lk), Mk is to be followed as the earliest accessible form of that tradition. Where Mk and Q overlap (see below, p. 95), we can take the doubly attested tradition back even further.

2. *Theological.* Mt's and Lk's editorial alterations of Mk provide invaluable clues into the theological stance of Mt and

Lk, and have borne great fruit recently in the method known as *Redaktionsgeschichte* (see below, pp. 81f).

Despite the continuing attacks upon it, the two source theory may be regarded as one of the assured results of the modern criticism, which has proved very fruitful both for historical reconstruction and for exegesis.

Redaktions-, Form-, and Traditionsgeschichte

The demonstration of the priority of Mk inaugurated an era of what might be called 'Marcan fundamentalism'. In the old 'quest of the historical Jesus'.[1] it was long assumed that Mk was a straightforward historical account of the life of Jesus from His baptism to the crucifixion, with a few miracles to be substracted or rationalistically explained away. At the turn of the present century, however, it began to become clear that Mk was in fact a highly theological document.

W. Wrede began the process with his study of the 'Messianic secret' in Mk.[2] Mark was far from being a straightforward historical report. It was in fact a highly theological interpretation of Jesus.

Next J. Wellhausen[3] extended the same observation to the other gospels, and showed the presence in them of older and more recent materials. In other words, the synoptic tradition had a history behind it.

While his fellow form critics were examining the separate units of material of which the gospels are composed (see below), K. L. Schmidt[4] examined the framework in which these units of (Mk's) material were set. He first distinguished between the 'tradition' (the units of material) and the 'redaction' (the connecting-links between the units). Next he discovered a certain disparity between the units and their connecting-links, indicating that the connecting-links were the

[1] The English title of A. Schweitzer's classic history of the life of Jesus research in the late eighteenth and nineteenth centuries. ET 1910.
[2] See R. H. Fuller, *The New Testament in Current Study*, pp. 93–5, (U.S. Ed., pp. 80–82).
[3] *Einleitung in die drei ersten Evangelien*, 1905.
[4] *Der Rahmen der Geschichte Jesu*, 1919.

creation of the evangelist. Further, these units are frequently combined into collections according to topic (e.g. conflict stories in Mk 2:1–3:6). As a consequence, it became clear that Mk cannot be used to construct a continuous life of Jesus from His baptism to the crucifixion. The order of the material is partly the work of the pre-Marcan collectors, partly the redaction of the evangelist. The geographical and chronological data in the framework are Mk's creation. The earliest recoverable form of the gospel material is the separate unit.[1]

Consequences for History and Exegesis

Historically, this means that we can place little reliance on the Marcan order of events. Only the broadest outline is secured: the baptism, Galilean ministry, Jerusalem ministry, crucifixion and Easter. We cannot, e.g., say that immediately after healing the paralytic Jesus called Levi (Mk 2:1–12 followed by vv. 13f). Nor can we infer from Jesus' change of activity any development in his sense of mission, purpose or self-consciousness.[2] We cannot write a continuous story of Jesus' ministry. All we can do is to classify his words and deeds.

Exegetically, it means that the order in which the units of material are placed the connecting-links between them and the generalizing summaries provide important clues to the theology of the evangelist himself. E.g. the blind man of Bethsaida is followed immediately by the Petrine confession (Mk 8:22–26 followed by vv. 27–30) and interprets the latter as the gradual removal of the blindness of the disciples to Jesus' identity.

[1] Dr C. H. Dodd has attempted to establish against Schmidt a pre-Marcan framework. See 'The Framework of the Gospel Narrative' (1932), repr. in New Testament Studies, 1953, pp. 1–11.

[2] The present writer would make one exception to this. There is a central crisis in Jesus' ministry which is attested in three strands of tradition: the Galilean feeding, followed by the desertion of the crowds (after they tried to make Jesus king?), Peter's declaration of Jesus' Messiahship, and the departure from Galilee for Jerusalem. This succession of events is in part doubly attested in Mk (Mk 6:30–7:37/ Mk 8:1–26) and independently of Mk (see below, p. 169) by Jn 6.

The Separate Units of Material

If, as K. L. Schmidt established, the tradition behind the gospels consisted of isolated units of material, the next stage will be to discover what we can about the previous history of these units of material. This was the task which *Formgeschichte* proper, i.e. 'form history', generally rendered 'form criticism',[1] set itself.

This method of study was first applied by German philologists to secular traditions, specifically to folk lore, fairy tales, etc. It sought to identify the forms in which traditions are enshrined and transmitted and the laws which govern their growth.

In Biblical studies the method was first applied to the OT by H. Gunkel[2] in a study of the creation stories, and was extended to other OT traditions prior to World War I. Later, R. Bultmann and M. Dibelius applied the method to the study of the gospels. In 1919 Dibelius published his *Formgeschichte des Evangeliums*,[3] and in 1921 Bultmann his *Die Geschichte der synoptischen Tradition*.[4] The form critical process comprises three operations: (1) classification on the units of material according to form; (2) assignment of these forms to a *Sitz im Leben* ('life situation'), the creative milieu, the activity or interest of the community which created the particular form;

---

[1] Experience shows that the student needs to be warned about this word. It does *not* mean *any* kind of Biblical criticism, but that limited aspect of Biblical criticism which deals with the history of the 'forms' or units of material our written gospels and, to some extent, of the traditional material in the epistles.

[2] *Schöpfung und Chaos*, 1895. See Anderson, pp. 4–7.

[3] The ET *From Tradition to Gospel*, 1934, is from the 2nd (expanded) Ger. edition of 1933. The third Ger. edition of 1959 contains an essay on Form Criticism since Dibelius by G. Iber.

[4] The ET *The History of the Synoptic Tradition*, 1964, is from the 3rd Ger. edition of 1958, itself a reproduction (with supplementary notes) of the enlarged 2nd ed. of 1931. Prior to the publication of the two basic works in ET a number of reports (with critique) were published in English: V. Taylor, *The Formation of the Gospel Tradition*, 1933; E. B. Redlich *Form Criticism*, 1939; F. C. Grant, *The Growth of the Gospels*, 1933 (which also contains a tr. of a short essay by Bultmann).

(3) assessment of the historical value of the particular unit of tradition.

The Forms

The first type of unit is the 'paradigm' (Dibelius) or 'apophthegm' (Bultmann), 'pronouncement story' (Taylor). Such stories have a threefold structure: (1) setting; (2) action; (3) significant saying of Jesus. (For list of such units see below.) The setting and action are brief, the whole interest and purpose of the unit being concentrated on the significant saying, or 'punchline'.

The form critics differ as to the creative milieu of this form. Dibelius assigns it to preaching, hence his term 'paradigm', meaning sermon illustration. Bultmann subdivides the apophthegms into three categories; controversial dialogues, conflict stories (*Streitgespräche*), didactic sayings (*Jüngergespräche*) and biographical apo hthegms. In the first case the creative milieu is the church's catechetical instruction, in the second its controversies with outside opponents, in the third case Bultmann agrees with Dibelius that this type has its origin in preaching.

The historical value of the forms is assessed from the creative milieu. Dibelius thinks that since the paradigms originate in preaching, and since preaching was a central activity of the community and therefore under the control of the original eyewitnesses, the relative antiquity and reliability of the paradigms is assured. Bultmann is of the opinion that the bulk of the apophthegms are early Palestinian tradition, since the apophthegm is found also in rabbinic literature. However, the scene (particularly in the biographical apophthegms) is often artificially constructed in order to carry the saying, and is therefore an 'ideal scene'.

The form critics' classification of this type of material has met with widespread recognition, and has proven a valuable insight for exegesis and preaching.[1] Dibelius' and Bultmann's

---

[1] See R. H. Fuller, *What is Liturgical Preaching?* 1957, pp. 34ff.

names for them (apophthegms, paradigms) are less satisfactory, since they are determined by their second and third questions respectively, rather than by the form. Taylor's term, 'pronouncement stories', is to be preferred, for it gives equal weight to the scene and the setting.

The disagreement between Bultmann and Dibelius over the creative milieu warns us of the uncertainty of their conclusions here. Many of the punchlines seem more suitable to instruction than to preaching (e.g. 'Render unto Caesar'), Bultmann's threefold division with the consequent distinction in their respective creative milieux is therefore to be preferred.

The historical verdict of Dibelius as to the relative reliability of these stories has been generally welcomed, and Bultmann's scepticism about the settings has frequently been repudiated. It is indeed questionable whether the creative milieu can give any real clue about historicity. It is more promising to ask the question, whether the setting is compatible with Jesus' ministry, or whether it reflects the situation of the post-Easter church. In the latter case can the setting be explained as having been constructed out of the significant saying? In such cases we may suspect that the scene is certainly a construction of the church intended as a carrier for the saying, but that it is a 'typical scene' rather than, as Bultmann maintains an 'ideal' one. That is to say, it is constructed not out of the church's own imagination, but out of its generalized memory of the sort of situation which was typical of Jesus' ministry: e.g. Jesus teaching in the synogogue, sitting at a meal with a Pharisee, eating with the outcast, surrounded by his disciples, etc. In such cases we may trust the setting as truly reflecting the conditions of Jesus' ministry, but cannot say that it refers to some specific occasion, still less that the significant saying was uttered on this occasion.

List of Pronouncement Stories

A. The following list includes those recognized as such by Dibelius, Bultmann and Albertz:

The paralytic, Mk 2:3–12 parr.

Eating with the outcast, Mk 2:15–17.

The question about fasting, Mk 2:18–22 parr.

Plucking grain on the sabbath, Mk 2:23–28 parr.

The man with the withered hand, Mk 3:1–5 parr.

The Beelzebul controversy, Mk 3:23–30 (par. Q, Lk 11:14–23 par.).

On Purity, Mk 7:5–23 par.

Marriage and Divorce, Mk 10:2–12 par.

The rich man, Mk 10:17–22 parr.

The sons of Zebedee, Mk 10:35–40 (41–45) par.

The question about authority, Mk 11:28–33 parr.

The tribute money, Mk 12:14–17 parr.

The question about resurrection, Mk 12:18–27 parr.

The great commandment, Mk 12:28–34 par. (par. Q, Lk 10:25–28).

The baptist's question, Lk 7:18–23 par. (Q).

The man with the dropsy, Lk 14:1–6.

B. The following additional pronouncement stories are recognized by Taylor from Bultmann's list of 'biographical apophthegms':

Jesus' real brethren, Mk 3:31–35 parr.

The blessedness of Jesus' mother, Lk 11:27f.

Claimants to discipleship, Lk 9:57–62 par. (Q).

Blessing of the children, Mk 10:13–16 par.

The widow's mites, Mk 12:41–44.

The anointing at Bethany, Mk 14:3–9.

C. Further examples of biographical apophthegms (Bultmann), designated by Taylor (pp. 75f.) as 'stories about Jesus', in which 'the interest appears to lie in the incidents themselves rather than in the words of Jesus':

Call of the first disciples, Mk 1:16–20 par.

Call of Levi, Mk 2:14 parr.

Rejection at Nazareth, Mk 6:2–6 par.

Syro-Phoenician woman, Mk 7:25–30 par.

Cleansing of the Temple, Mk 11:15–17.

Centurion's servant, Lk 7:1–10 (Q).

Martha and Mary, Lk 10:38–42.

Departure for Galilee, Lk 13:31–33.
Zacchaeus Lk, 19:1–10.
Rejoicing of the disciples, Lk 17:39f.
Weeping over Jerusalem, Lk 19:41–44.

D. Pronouncement Stories identified by Albertz and accepted by Taylor:

David's son, Mk 12:35–37 parr.
Demand for a sign, Mk 8:11f par.

The second narrative form consists of 'miracle stories' (Bultmann, Taylor) or 'tales' (*Novellen,* Dibelius). Again, the structure is threefold, consisting of setting, cure and demonstration, the latter being indicated by an action on the part of the patient (e.g. the paralytic takes up his bed and walks) or by a choric ending (the by-standers say: 'we never saw such things').

As for the creative milieu, Dibelius holds that these stories were not used in preaching or any of the central activities of the church. He postulates a class of story tellers, on the ground that these stories have a popular, 'secular' character. Bultmann concludes from the fact that the interest is concentrated on the cure that they are concerned to display Jesus as a (Hellenistic) wonder worker.

From these considerations it follows that neither Dibelius nor Bultmann have a high opinion of the historicity of the miracle stories. For Dibelius they lack the control of the original eyewitnesses, since they were not shaped in a central activity of the church. For Bultmann they are Hellenistic rather than Palestinian, and therefore lack the mark of antiquity.

The present writer has discussed these form-critical conclusions in *Interpreting the Miracles,* pp. 18ff, to which the reader is referred. It should be added that the Palestinian provenance of the miracle stories is becoming increasingly clear. The miracle stories present Jesus most frequently as the eschatological prophet, which is a christological concept of the

D

earliest Palestinian church (see *The Foundations of Christology*, pp. 167ff).[1]

List of miracle stories (excluding those which are classified as pronouncement stories, and included in the lists, pp. 85–87):

The Capernaum demoniac, Mk 1:23–27 parr.
Peter's mother-in-law, Mk 1:30f parr.
The leper, Mk 1:40–45.
The stilling of the storm, Mk 4:37–41 parr.
The Gerasene demoniac, Mk 5:1–20 parr.
The ruler of the synagogue's daughter, Mk 5:22–24, 35–45 parr.
The woman with the haemorrhage, Mk 5:25–34.
The feeding of the multitude, Mk 6:34–44 parr., Mk 8:1–9 par.
The walking on the water, Mk 6:47–51 par.
The deaf mute, Mk 7:32–37.
The blind man of Bethsaida, Mk 8:22–26.
The epileptic boy, Mk 9:17–29 parr.
Blind Bartimaeus, Mk 10:46–52.
The cursing of the fig-tree, Mk 11:12–14, 20f par.
The miraculous draft of fishes, Lk 5:1–11.
The widow's son of Nain, Lk 7:12–16.
The ten lepers, Lk 17:12–16.
The bent woman, Lk 13:11–17.

The third class of narrative units are what both Dibelius and Bultmann designate 'legends'—an unfortunate term which in English at any rate appears to pre-judge the question of historicity, though it is intended to be based purely on form. A legend, technically, means a story of the doings of some religious hero. Taylor prefers to call them 'stories about Jesus', while Bornkamm classifies them as 'stories about Christ' (*Christusgeschichten*). This last term is better, for they

---

[1] For a recent recognition of the Palestinian origin of the miracle stories see U. Wilckens in *Offenbarung als Geschichte*, ed. W. Pannenberg, 1963, p. 59: 'The miracles of Jesus, of which a considerable number is most probably to be adjudged historical'—this from a group of writers who follow the radical methods of the Bultmann school, as far as historical criticism is concerned!

all have a definitely christological thrust. However, it should be noted that all of these designations are based on content, and it seems to be impossible to discern any fixed form in this type of story. That is why Redlich calls them 'formless stories'.

It is not easy to assign all of these stories to a single creative milieu, although Bultmann assigns them all to cultic activities. This is entirely plausible for some of them, such as the baptism of Jesus and the institution of the Lord's Supper. Others, with their strong christological concern, would appear rather to be suitable for preaching purposes.

Bultmann's judgment on the historicity of the legends is almost as negative as his designation suggests. The baptism and institution narratives certainly have a basis in fact, but their christological and soteriological colouring are entirely due to the post-Easter church. Others he regards as transposed resurrection appearances (the confession of Peter and the transfiguration). Dibelius recognizes that these stories may have some historical basis.

It must be confessed that considerations of form are of no help whatever in determining the historicity of this type of material. Historical verdicts must depend entirely on the application of another method, namely that of tradition-history (see below, pp. 96f).

List of Stories about Christ

The baptism, Mk 1:9–11.
The temptation, Mk 1:12f parr.
Peter's confession, Mk 8:27b–33 parr.
Entry into Jerusalem, Mk 11:1–10 parr.
Institution of the Lord's Supper, Mk 14:22–25.
Infancy narratives, Mt. 1–2; Lk 1–2.
Resurrection narratives, Mk 16:1–8; Mt 28; Lk 24.

Passion Narratives

The last type of narrative material is the passion story. This is the only type of narrative material which, according to the

form critics, existed from the earliest days in continuous
narrative form—an observation confirmed by the treatment
of the passion in the liturgical gospels of Holy Week. True,
there are also separable, if not separate, pericopes which have
been worked into the passion narrative, e.g. the institution of
the Lord's Supper, whose separate existence is demonstrated
by 1 Cor 11:23–25, and perhaps also by its absence from the
Johannine passion narrative. By and large, however, the
passion narrative is constructed in the form of day to day, and
even hour to hour narration.

Despite its earlier origin, however, the passion narrative,
according to the form critics, is not a mere historical trans-
script of the actual events. Like the rest of the gospel material,
it is 'kerygmatic'—i.e. concerned to proclaim the redemptive
significance of the events related. Three motives in particular
have coloured to telling of the story (cf. 1 Cor 15:3f): (1) Jesus
died as Messiah (the trial scenes and the inscription from the
cross); (2) Jesus' death was a vicarious atonement for sin
(Mk 14:24); (3) Jesus' passion and death as the fulfilment of OT
prophecies (Mk 14:18 = Ps 41:9; Mk 14:27 = Zech 13:7; Mk
14:34 = Ps 42:6, 12; Mk 15:5, cf. Isa 53:7; Mk 15:23, cf. Ps
69:22; Mk 15:24 = Ps 22:19; Mk 15:34 = Ps 22:1; Lk 22:37 =
Isa 53:12; Lk 23:30 = Hos 10:8; Lk 23:35 = Ps 22:8; Lk 23:46
= Ps 31:6; Lk 23:49 = Ps 88:9; Jn 19:28 = Ps 69:22; Jn 19:36
= Exod 12:46, etc.; Jn 19:37 = Zech 12:10).

The creative milieu of the passion story has been variously
designated as preaching, apologetic and the cultus. Of these
three suggestions, the cultus seems the most probable. I have
suggested elsewhere[1] that the passion narrative is the Christian
passover haggada, formulated for use at the Christian passover
festival.

Source criticism can enable us to carry the study of the
passion tradition back further than the form critics have done.
If, as we have contended (see above, p. 80), the Lucan passion
narrative is basically independent of Mk, and if also the

[1] 'The Double Origin of the Eucharist' in *BR* 8 (1963), pp. 60–72.

Johannine narrative is an independent tradition, we have in the NT three different versions of the passion narrative, all of which agree in the same basic outline of events. This common agreement enables us to infer a primitive passion narrative underlying all three traditions:

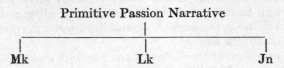

Primitive Passion Narrative

Mk   Lk   Jn

The proper procedure to arrive at the earliest available tradition is to extract this primitive passion narrative, and then submit its contents to the tests of theological motivation, in order to distinguish between authentic memory and theologically motivated creativity on the part of the church. Even so, caution is advisable in applying these tests. In certain important instances it would appear that it was the scandalous nature of the historical facts that lead the church to seek relief from the scandal by finding those events foretold in scripture, rather than that the church created scandalous facts merely to square with prophecy. Instances of the latter are the Judas's betrayal and the disciples' forsaking of Jesus.

The Words of Jesus

The words of Jesus in the synoptic gospels are of two main types: parables and sayings (aphorisms). The extended discourses in the synoptic gospels (e.g. the Little Apocalypse of Mk 13 parr. and Mt's Sermon on the Mount) are (unlike the discourses of the fourth gospel) sayings and parables strung together either in the tradition or by the evangelists.

The basic modern study of the parables was done by A. Jülicher.[1] Bultmann, the one form critic who has studied the parables in detail, takes over Jülicher's classifications.[2] Jülicher divided the parables into five classes; (i) metaphors

---

[1] *Die Gleichnisreden Jesu*, 1899.
[2] *The History of the Synoptic Tradition*, pp. 166–205.

(e.g. Mk 2:21, 22); (ii) similitudes (e.g. Lk 17:7ff); (iii) the parable proper, narrating a typical incident from life (e.g. Lk 15:1–10); (iv) the illustrative story, narrating a concrete incident from life (e.g. Lk 15:11ff); (v) allegory. According to some, Mk 12:1–9 is pure allegory; according to others it contains only allegorical traits. Other parables have received allegorical traits but were not originally allegories, e.g. Mt 22:1ff, the great supper, or an allegorical interpretation (Mk 4:13–20, the sower).

The exposure of the forms of the parables makes possible the detection of modifications to them in the course of tradition. The detection of these modifications has been performed notably by C. H. Dodd[1] and J. Jeremias.[2] When the later additions have been removed, the resulting material is recognized almost universally to have a high claim to belong to the authentic Jesus tradition.

The main form-critical study on the sayings of Jesus was done by R. Bultmann.[3] He distinguishes four classes of sayings: (i) gnomic sayings (e.g. Mt 6:34b); (ii) apocalyptic words, i.e. warnings of impending crisis, summonses to repentance and promises of future reward (e.g. Mt 5:3–11); (iii) law words and community rules (e.g. Mt 5:32); (iv) christological sayings, including 'I-words' (e.g. Mt 5:17b) and those sayings where Jesus is explicitly identified with the Son of man sayings in his present ministry or impending passion. Of these classes, (i) are paralleled in Judaism and in the Hellenistic world, and are generally the result of erroneous transferences to Jesus; (ii) are often authentic, but sometimes the creation of Christian prophets—or better, words of the risen Lord received by prophets (cf. Rev 1:17f) which have coalesced with the authentic Jesus tradition; (iii) are sometimes genuine, but often the creation of the post-Easter community legislating for its own life. Sometimes an earlier form, e.g. a parable, has been turned into a community rule (e.g. Mt 5:25; cf. Lk 12:58f);

[1] The Parables of the Kingdom, 1935[1].
[2] The Parables of Jesus, 1963[2].
[3] Op. cit., pp. 69–166.

(iv) for Bultmann, these all reflect the post Easter Christology and are therefore church formations.

The Assured Results of Form Criticism

1. The gospels are kerygmatic in intention, not biographies of Jesus.

2. The gospel tradition, prior to our written documents or their written sources now lost (Q), was transmitted orally. The gospels were not written direct from personal reminiscence.

3. At every stage in the transmission, the selection and shaping of the material was governed by the practical needs of the community, preaching, teaching, liturgical, apologetic, controversial, etc.

4. Almost certainly, collections of like material were made prior to our written documents (e.g. parables, Mk 4).

5. The order of our written gospels is determined by topical and theological considerations rather than (except in the broadest outline) by the actual course of events.

The Limitations of Form Criticism

1. While the principle of the *Sitz im Leben* is legitimate, the assignment of specific forms to particular life situations is not always successful. Here the form critics differ among themselves (e.g. Bultmann and Dibelius on the pronouncement stories). But it is sometimes well grounded: e.g. cultic interests as the creative milieu for the institution narrative. Often content offers (as in the latter instance) a more certain clue to the *Sitz im Leben* than form.

2. The legitimacy of making historical evaluations of the material on the ground of form has frequently been contested, especially by British scholars. The fact is, apart from the parables, form is rarely a decisive criterion for authenticity. In practice (e.g. the christological sayings) the historical verdict is pronounced by the form critics themselves on grounds of content. This does not mean that verdict is wrong.

It means that the verdict is reached not by form but by traditio-historical criticism (see below).

Summary of the History of the Synoptic Tradition

Our study of the history of the synoptic tradition worked backwards from the gospels as finished products. We now summarize that history working forwards. The primary layer of the tradition is the authentic Jesus tradition, his words, work and fate. Next comes the post-Easter recollection of that tradition, coloured by the Easter faith and shaped to serve the practical needs of the community, first Palestinian and then Hellenistic. Next comes the collection of like units of material. Then the primary written (Q, Mk) and unwritten (special Mt and special Lk) collections. Finally the later gospels, Mt and Lk.

The Quest of the Historical Jesus[1]

NT Introduction is concerned with the quest of the historical Jesus only as the identification of the primary stratum in the gospels. In identifying that tradition, the important question is that of the criteria for assigning material in the gospels to that primary tradition, i.e. in the terms of the quest, the criteria of 'authenticity'.

1. The Bultmann school takes its main and often sole criteria from Bultmann's discussion of the similitudes.[2] Here he propounded three criteria of authenticity: (1) a similitude is authentic where its content is opposed to Jewish morality and piety; (2) where it reflects the eschatological temper characteristic of Jesus' proclamation; (3) where such teaching exhibits no specifically Christian traits. Of these, criteria (2) and (3) have played a prominent part in the 'new quest'.

O. Cullmann[3] proposes a modification of these criteria in a positive direction: we may be sure that sayings attributed to

[1] For the history of the 'old quest' and for the so-called 'new quest', see Bibliography.
[2] *History of the Synoptic Tradition*, p. 205.
[3] *Heil als Geschichte*, p. 169.

Jesus are authentic when they differ from contemporary Judaism or from the post-Easter proclamation of the church. Whether applied negatively or positively we call this 'the criterion of distinctiveness'.

2. J. Jeremias,[1] propounds two tests of authenticity. If a saying attributed to Jesus exhibits Aramaic traits (translation Gk, poetic form—synonymous, antithetical, or climactic parallelism;[2] or if it reflects Palestinian conditions (social and domestic customs, agricultural processes, cultus, etc.), its authenticity is assured. These criteria are employed in Jeremias's best known works in English, *The Parables of Jesus* and *The Eucharistic Words of Jesus*. M. Black[3] amplifies the linguistic tests to include mistranslations from Aramaic into Gk, alternative translations of the same saying in two separate lines of transmission, and the occurrence in re-translation into Aramaic of assonance and rhyme.

3. F. C. Burkitt[4] drew up a list of 31 sayings which appear independently in both Mk and Q. This, he argued enables us to trace back the tradition behind those two sources to the forties of the first century. C. H. Dodd[5] later extended this method to the various forms of tradition postulated by the form critics. If a piece of factual information or teaching occurs in more than one form, e.g. in a pronouncement story, a parable and an aphorism, that fact or teaching was not created for the particular forms, but antedates them. The Burkitt-Dodd criterion we call the 'cross-section method'.

C. E. Carlston[6] has proposed what he calls a criterion of consistency. Once the central message of Jesus has been

---

[1] 'Kennzeichen der ipsissima vox Jesu' in *Synoptische Studien* (Wikenhauser Festschrift), 1953, pp. 86–93. Cf. also 'The Present Position in the Controversy concerning the Problem of the Historical Jesus', *Exp. T* 69 (1958), pp. 333–9, esp. p. 337.

[2] On these forms see C. F. Burney, *The Poetry of Our Lord*, 1925.

[3] *An Aramaic Approach to the Gospels and Acts*, 1954².

[4] *The Gospel History and its Transmission*, 1906, pp. 147–68.

[5] *History and the Gospel*, 1938, pp. 91–101. Dr Dodd had already used this method in his Cambridge lectures on 'The Earliest Sources for the Life of Jesus' (1937).

[6] 'A *Positive* Criterion of Authenticity?', *BR* 7 (1962), pp. 33-44.

established, other traditions about Jesus which are consistent
with this central message may be accepted as authentic.

Evaluation of the Criteria

1. *Criterion of Distinctiveness.* The most obvious limitation
of this criterion is that Jesus *may* have agreed with contemporary Judaism or the post-Easter church with him! It
tends to lead to minimal rather than maximal results, and
accounts for the notorious scepticism of the Bultmann school.
O. Cullmann's positive alternative on the other hand deprives
the criterion of its effectiveness. A distinction has to be made
between agreements of Jesus with Judaism and agreements
between Jesus and the early church.

It is obvious that Jesus took over much from the OT and
contemporary Judaism which no one would think of eliminat-
ing (e.g. much in his doctrine of God and his action, salvation
history, the apocalyptic hope, the Torah). Here the right
procedure would seem to be first to apply the criterion in
Cullmann's way, in order to see positively where Jesus differs
from contemporary Judaism, then to apply the criterion of
consistency to the elements of agreement with Judaism. Where
Jesus has transformed an element in Judaism in the light of his
distinctive message, its claims to authenticity are high. Where,
however, Jesus merely repeats the conventional Jewish
teachings without any trace of his own distinctive message,
such a saying is a re-Judaizing of Jesus' teaching by the
church or an erroneous transfer. For instance, a saying like
'The law and the prophets were until John' (Lk 16:16, Q) is
authentic, because it squares with Jesus' message that the
Reign of God has drawn near, whereas the saying, 'Think not
that I have come to abolish the law and the prophets' (Mt
5:17), being inconsistent with Jesus' central message, will be a
re-Judaization of the Jesus tradition.

With regard to agreements between Jesus and the early
church, it is obvious that the early church took over from
Jesus much of his teaching unchanged (nobody e.g. would
say that where the summary of the law appears in Jesus'

mouth it represents an erroneous transference of the early church's teaching to Jesus, simply because the early church also used the summary of the law!). However, where sayings of Jesus reflect the changed eschatological situation in salvation-history as between Jesus and the earliest church which was the result of the Easter event, these sayings have either been created as an expression of the church's post-Easter faith, or are genuine sayings of Jesus transformed in the light of that faith. Thus, e.g., any saying of Jesus in which he employs an explicit christological self-designation will be a post-Easter creation of the church or the transformation of an authentic saying. Thus the criterion of distinctiveness has to be applied rather differently to agreements between Jesus and Judaism on the one hand, and to agreements between Jesus and the early church on the other. The chief justification for its use lies not in an undue scepticism, but in the distinctiveness of the eschatological situation in which Jesus stood as compared with both Judaism on the one hand and with the earliest church on the other. Also, it is not the sole criterion: it has to be employed along with other tests, and at the right stage.

2. *The Linguistic and Environmental Tests.* Obviously if a saying of Jesus is authentic it must have been spoken in Aramaic. But applied by themselves these tests can only take us back to the Palestinian tradition, and therefore only to the earliest Palestinian church.[1] Jeremias's criteria are important at a certain stage of the quest, but cannot be applied in isolation. They can take us back behind the Hellenistic to the Palestinian tradition, but not to Jesus. After the Jeremias-Black tests have been applied, the Bultmann test of incompatibility must be brought in.

3. *The Cross-section Method.* This is highly valuable—again at a certain stage of the process. If the same tradition occurs in

---

[1] Unfortunately this is the case in Jeremias's arguments for the authenticity of the bread and cup words in the eucharistic tradition, *Eucharistic Words*[2], pp. 196–203. He has proven that they go back to the Palestinian Aramaic speaking church, but not that they were spoken by Jesus at the Last Supper.

different primary sources or in different oral forms we can take it back to an earlier stage in the history of the tradition. But by itself, the Burkitt-Dodd method cannot establish authenticity. The traditions still await the application of the linguistic and environmental tests and the test of distinctiveness.

4. *The Criterion of Consistency.* This can be useful *after* the central message of Jesus has been established by the use of all the other criteria. It can also be useful in *confirming* the authenticity of traditions which have been recovered by the other methods. It may occasionally help to recover for the authentic tradition material which had been provisionally rejected on the other tests.

To sum up. The quest of the historical Jesus should be seen as part of and as the end-process of the study of the whole history of the gospel tradition. That study is an attempt to assign to their proper place in the history of the tradition the various strata: first, redaction, then primary sources, then oral tradition, Hellenistic and Palestinian, then finally, the authentic Jesus tradition. The appropriate criteria must be applied at each successive stage.

1. The redaction. This is established from the criteria furnished by source criticism and by the redactio-historical method (K. L. Schmidt).

2. Primary sources. These are established by source criticism.

3. Hellenistic and Palestinian oral tradition. This is established by the cross-section method applied to the primary sources (Burkitt), by form criticism (Bultmann, Dibelius), by the cross-section method applied to the oral forms (Dodd), and by the linguistic and environmental tests (Jeremias, Black).

4. The authentic Jesus tradition. This is established by the criteria of distinctiveness.

5. The criterion of consistency (Carlston) can then be employed to confirm the results at each stage, and to recover for the Jesus tradition some of the material which had been provisionally rejected by the test of distinctiveness.

The Authentic Jesus Tradition: A Representative List of Passages

1. *Narrative*
   (a) Baptism of Jesus, Mk 1:9. Cf. the saying which char-acterizes the ministry of the Baptist as marking the 'shift of the aeons', Mt 11:12 par. Q.
   (b) Galilean Ministry, Mk 1:14. This is redactional, but is confirmed by the Galilean location of many incidents in the body of the pericopes.
   (c) Crisis of the Galilean ministry:
   Feeding, Mk 6:30ff/8:1ff/Jn 6:4ff. We recognize here a factual nucleus no longer recoverable.
   Dismissal of crowd, which sought to make Jesus a Zealot leader, Mk 6:45/Mk 8:9/Jn 6:15.
   Peter's 'confession' (originally expressing agreement with the crowd, and their desire to make Jesus a Zealot leader), Mk 8:29, 32b–33. Cf. Jn 6:66–69 (over-laid with Johannine theology).
   (d) Journey to Jerusalem. The passages which narrate this are redactional, esp. in Luke's 'travel section'. But the shift of scene is indicated by the authentic saying Lk 13:32f, by the Jerusalem location of scenes from the triumphal entry on and independently by Jn.
   (e) The Jerusalem challenge. 'Triumphal' entry (Mk 11:1ff, Jn 12:12ff). The Marcan account is overlaid by Messianic interpretation, but contains an authentic nucleus. Cleansing of the Temple, Mk 11:11, 15–19; Jn 2:13ff.
   (f) Passion narrative. The common outline behind the 3 passion traditions, Mk/Lk/Jn submitted to traditio-historical-tests:
       (i) Jesus' final meal with the disciples, Mk 14:17–18a/Lk 22:14/Jn 13:2a. Cf. 1 Cor 11:23.
       (ii) Retirement to Mt of Olives, Mk 14:26/Lk 22:39a. Cf. Jn 18:1.
       (iii) Betrayal and arrest, Mk 14:43–49/Lk 22:47ff/Jn 18:2ff.
       (iv) Desertion by the disciples, Mk 14:50. Cf. Jn 18:8.

(v) Examination before High priest, Mk 14:53/ Lk 22:54/Jn 18:24. From the title on the cross it may be inferred that at this examination the Jewish authorities decided to hand Jesus over to the Romans for execution as a Messianic pretender.

(vi) Trial before Pilate, Mk 15:1; Lk 23:1/Jn 18:28. From the title on the cross it may be inferred that Pilate condemned Jesus as a political revolutionary.

(vii) Crucifixion at Golgotha, Mk 15:22, 24a, 25/ Lk 23:33/Jn 19:17.

(viii) Title on the cross, Mk 15:26/Lk 23:38/Jn 19:19.

(ix) Burial, Mk 15:26/Lk 23:53/Jn 19:42. Cf. 1 Cor 15:4.

2. *The Words of Jesus*

(i) His eschatological message (the kingdom of God).

(*a*) Future, but imminent
Lk 11:2d Q? Lk 22:18/Mk 14:25; Lk 17:21 (?). Mk 1:15 is redactional, but a fair summary of Jesus' message (cf. Mt. 10:7 Q?)

(*b*) The coming judgment
Mt 5:21f; Mt 7:1f Q; Mk 12:40; Lk 11:31f Q.

(*c*) The promise of future entry into or exclusion from the Kingdom.
Mk 10:15, 23; Mt 5:20; Mk 9:43ff. Inheritance, Mk 10:17.

(*d*) The coming of the Son of man.
Lk 12:8f Q; Mt. 24:44 Q; Lk 17:22–24, 26 Q, 30 Q.

(*e*) Be prepared!
Mk 13:33ff; Mt 24:45ff Q; Lk 12:35ff; Lk 17:34–37 Q.

(*f*) The proleptic presence of the future kingdom.
Lk 6:20ff Q (The Beatitudes); Lk 11:20 Q; Lk 17:21 (?); Mk 4:3–8 (the sower); Mk 4:31f (mustard seed); Mt 13:33 (leaven); Mt 13:24–30 (tares); Lk 12:54–56 Q? (the signs of the weather). Joy at its proleptic presence, Mt 6:16–18; Mk 2:19a. The dispensation of eschatological forgiveness,

Mk 2:5; Mt 18:23-34; Lk 7:47f. Cf. also 3(a) below.

(ii) The demand for radical obedience.

Mt 5:21-48 (the antitheses); Mt 6:19-24 (total obedience); Mk 10:5-9/Mt 5:32, cf. 1 Cor 7:10 (prohibition of divorce); Mk 12:30f (summary of the law); Lk 10:30ff (good Samaritan); Mt 25:31ff (sheep and goats).

(iii) Teaching about God.

Lk 11:2 Q? (Abba) (cf. Mk 14:36—the Gethsemane prayer is built up on the Lord's Prayer); the nearness of his providential care, Mt 6:25-34 Q; God answers the prayer of faith, Lk 17:6 Q; Mk 9:23; Mk 11:22f; Lk 11:9-13 Q; Lk 11:2ff Q?/ Mt 6:9ff (the Lord's Prayer).

3. *Jesus' Activity*

(a) Exorcisms and healings as signs of the proleptic presence of the kingdom.

Mk 3:27; Lk 7:22 Q; Lk 10:23 Q; Lk 10:18; Lk 11:20 Q.

(b) The eschatological meal with the outcast.

Lk 15:4ff Q (lost sheep); Lk 15:8ff (lost coin); Lk 15:11ff (prodigal son); Lk 14:16-24, cf. Mt 22:2ff (great supper); Mt 21:28ff (two sons); Lk 18:9-14 (Pharisee and publican). Also Mk 2:13-17; Mt 11:19 Q; Lk 14:7-14; Lk 13:28f Q.

(c) Call to discipleship.

Mk 1:16ff, 2:14; Lk 5:1ff (Follow me); Lk 14:28-33 (cost of discipleship); Lk 17:33 (Q?); Mk 9:33-37; Mk 10:21; Mt 5:29f; Lk 9:57-60 (Q), 62 (demand for radical decision; cf. Mt 13:44-46 (hidden treasure and pearl).

Reward of discipleship.

Mk 10:29f; Lk 12:8f; Mt 6:19-21 Q.

4. Jesus' fate.

His understanding of his death as the outcome of his eschatological words and works, Lk 13:31-33.

His challenge to the Jerusalem authorities, Mk 11:1ff (entry into Jerusalem); Mk 11:11, 15-19 (cleansing of the temple).

His death as the culmination of Israel's rejection of God's word, Lk 13:34f Q; Lk 11:49ff Q; cf. Mk 12:1ff (Parable of the vineyard, if authentic).

His death as the prelude to the final coming of the kingdom, Mk 14:25/Lk 22:15-18.

Summary of the authentic Jesus Tradition

Jesus of Nazareth emerged out of the Baptist circle and began an independent ministry after the death of the Baptist. This ministry was centred in a message, which like that of the Baptist was couched in apocalyptic terms, but unlike the Baptist's message of imminent judgment, stressed rather the positive side of the imminence of salvation. This eschatological salvation was very near, so near that it was breaking through in advance in the person, word and deed of Jesus himself. It asserted the proleptic presence in Jesus of the future eschatological salvation. To accept Jesus' message was to determine one's acceptance among the elect at the final (imminent) coming of the Kingdom of God in the appearance of the Son of man. Subordinated to Jesus' eschatological message was his assertion of the demand of God for radical obedience, which is assumed to be possible for those who have accepted the message. Here Jesus asserts the ultimate authority of his own word against the Torah and its interpretation in the Rabbinic tradition. Also subordinated to Jesus' eschatological message was his teaching about God as Abba, intimately near, and his providential care.

Coupled with Jesus' words was his conduct. He ate with those who were outcast by the standards of the Torah and interpreted this to be a celebration in advance of the eschatological meal. He called men to follow him as the embodiment of the proleptic presence of the eschatological kingdom, and those who follow him partake prolepticly of that salvation. He performed exorcisms and healings which he interpreted as proleptic operations of the eschatological Reign of God.

The outcome of this activity in Galilee was the final fate of Jesus. He goes up to Jerusalem to issue his eschatological challenge at the heart of Judaism, in full consciousness that it will involve his own suffering and death. He interprets that death as part of the process by which the eschatological Reign of God will come. He is arrested, investigated by the Jewish authorities, and denounced to the Roman occupying power as a zealot revolutionary (this involving a misinterpretation of Jesus' eschatological message) and Messianic pretender, and executed by them as a would-be 'King of the Jews'.

Note on the Scandinavian School

Two Scandinavian scholars, H. Riesenfeld[1] and his pupil B. Gerhardsson,[2] have propounded an alternative to the form critical account of the history of the synoptic tradition. Their thesis is that Jesus deliberately taught his sayings in stereotyped form so as to impress them on the memory of his disciples and to secure their mechanical transmission, after the manner of the Jewish rabbis. This theory (cf. H. Anderson, *Jesus and Christian Origins*, 1964, pp. 99, 309ff) breaks down on the following facts: (1) it assumes in the teeth of all probability that Jesus presumed and catered for an interval between his death and the parousia, whereas this is an adjustment of salvation history to the post-Easter situation; (2) it fails to take into account the determinative influence of the Easter faith in the recollection, shaping, modification, and even in some instances the creation of the tradition; (3) it ignores the part played by the early Christian prophets in creating the Jesus tradition. Many words of the Lord are attributed to the historical Jesus are in fact utterances of the risen Christ transmitted *via* Christian prophets (see above, pp. 92f).

(b) THE GOSPEL OF MARK

We are now concerned not with the traditions behind the

---

[1] *The Gospel Tradition and its Beginnings*, 1957.
[2] *Memory and Manuscript*, 1961; *Tradition and Transmission in Early Christianity*, 1964.

gospels, but with the gospels as finished products. All four of our gospels are products of the sub-apostolic age. They are *primarily* evidence not for the history of Jesus, nor for the theology of apostolic church (though, as we have seen, they contain materials reaching back into both of those phases), but to the theology of the sub-apostolic age. The clue to their theology lies in the evangelists' *redaction* of traditional materials, that is, in the order in which they place the units of material or previous collections of such units, in the links they construct to connect this material, and in their overall shape and structure. It is at this level that we now investigate the gospels.

Date and Authorship of Mark

Questions of date and authorship are relevant in so far as they enable us to form some conception of the milieu in which the evangelists operated, and this in turn will inevitably effect our exegesis of their works. The external evidence for the composition of Mk begins with a statement, quoted by Eusebius from Papias, bishop of Hierapolis, *c.* 140. Papias purports to be quoting an authority whom he designates 'the Elder' (ὁ πρεσβύτερος). The passage reads:

'Mark became Peter's interpreter and wrote accurately all that he remembered, not, indeed, in order, of the things said and done by the Lord. For he had not heard the Lord, nor had he followed him, but later on, as I said, followed Peter, who used to give teaching as necessity demanded, but not making as it were an arrangement of the Lord's oracles, so that Mark did nothing wrong in thus writing down single points as he remembered them. For to one thing he gave attention, to leave nothing out of what he heard and to make no false statements in them.' Eusebius, *H.E.* III. 39 (Tr. K. Lake, Loeb edition).

The value of these statements is much disputed. We will concentrate on four points: (1) the claim that the author of our earliest gospel was Mark; (2) the connection between Mark's gospel and Peter; (3) the statement that Mark was Peter's 'interpreter'; (4) the statement that his gospel was not written 'in order'.

(1) In the second century, apologetic motives led the church wherever possible to ascribe its gospels to apostolic authorship. The fact that Mark was not an apostle would seem to indicate that this attribution (for which there is no internal support)[1] antedates second-century apologetic, and is not a second-century invention. So we must take it very seriously. It is possible to identify this Mark: the John Mark of Acts who belonged to Paul's entourage (Acts 12:12, 25; 15:37, 39; Philem 24; Col 4:10; cf. 2 Tim 4:11).

(2) The connection of Mark's gospel with Peter is much more problematical. The very attempt to connect the gospel with an apostle suggests 2nd cent. apologetic, though that this was done at one remove indicates that the tradition of direct Marcan authorship was already well established. By the second century there was already some tradition of a connection of Mark with Peter (1 Pet 5:13) and this may very well be the source of this second-century apologetic theory. It contradicts almost all that modern critical scholarship has established with regard to Mark. Form criticism has demonstrated that Mark's gospel is the end-result of process of tradition passing through the successive phases of Palestinian and Hellenistic Christianity, not a direct record of immediate eyewitness (see above, pp. 83–93). Attempts have been made to rescue at least part of Mk as Petrine, viz., the scenes at which Peter was the sole or one of few witnesses present (e.g. the healing of Peter's mother-in-law, Mk 1:29–31, the transfiguration, Gethsemane, Peter's denial and the resurrection appearance to Peter (14:28; 16:7). It may well be that some of

[1] It has been claimed that the young man who fled naked in Mk 14:51f is the 'artist's signature in the corner of the picture'. But this identification must be subsequent to the attribution to John Mark, not suggestive of it to a second-century mind. As for its significance, it probably means no more than that the young man was an eyewitness of the arrest. See G. Bornkamm, *Jesus of Nazareth*, p. 163.

these traditions (esp. the healing of the mother-in-law[1]) go back *ultimately* to Petrine witness, but this does not prove that Mark obtained these stories *directly* from Peter. So we discount point number two.

(3) 'Not, indeed in order.' Curiously, this is the one statement to which form criticism has sometimes given credence: it chimes in with the form critical view that Mk is not a chronologically historical account of Jesus' ministry. But it is not at all certain that this is what the Elder meant. It has been suggested that the Elder was comparing the order unfavourably with some other gospel (? Jn). The fact is the meaning of 'not, indeed, in order' is unclear, and therefore nothing can be safely built upon this statement.

(4) 'Interpreter.' This could mean that Mark stood at Peter's side and translated his preaching into Aramaic. It could also mean more generally that Mark simply interpreted Peter's reminiscences. Again, the meaning is quite uncertain. The utmost we can say about Mk in this connection that some of the material, e.g. authentic dominical sayings, is of ultimate Aramaic origin. But it cannot be claimed that Mk is a direct translation of Aramaic.

Date. The Elder gives no clue as to the date, though the phrase 'he remembered' may imply that the gospel was written after Peter was removed from the scene, say after 64. Irenaeus (III, 1.1) says Mk was written after the death of Peter and Paul. Whether this is an intelligent inference from the Elder, or rests upon independent tradition, we have no means of knowing. But since the tendency was to push back the dates of NT writings into the apostolic age (cf. Clement of Alexandria, quoted Eusebius, *H.E.* VI.14), who makes Mark write while Peter was still alive in Rome, Irenaeus' dating may be accepted: Mk was certainly written after 64. This is borne out by internal evidence. The 'Little Apocalypse', Mk 13:5ff, 14, indicates knowledge of events up to the Jewish War (66–70) but no clear knowledge of the fall of Jerusalem. So a date *c.* 68 would be acceptable.

[1] R. H. Fuller, *Interpreting the Miracles*, p. 34.

Provenance

Irenaeus' statement(see above)that Mk was written in Rome has been widely accepted by modern scholars (e.g. Streeter). Attempts have been made to support it by internal evidence (e.g. Latinisms like 'denarius', 'legion'). Such Latinisms, however, are the vocabulary of military occupation and speak as much for Palestinian provenance as for Rome. The connection Mark-Peter-Rome looks like second-century guesswork based on 1 Pet 5:13. Remove the Petrine connection, and the question of provenance becomes wide open. Mk is a Hellenistic gospel. Its language is Gk, and, as we shall see, its traditions, especially in their Christology, contain Hellenistic elements, which Mk qualifies in a Pauline direction. Yet its traditions are also in close touch with Palestinian tradition, not only with earlier tradition as in the miracle stories (Jesus as the eschatological prophet), but in such recent material as parts of the Little Apocalypse. We are drawn to suggest Antioch as the most likely place of origin.

Integrity

Aside from Ur-Markus theories (see above, p. 71) there is little to suggest that Mk has undergone substantial alterations since its composition. The only serious problem is the ending of Mk. The earliest MSS (see RSV and NEB) end at 16:8 with the words 'for they were afraid' (ἐφοβοῦντο γάρ). Later scribes were obviously dissatisfied with this abrupt and defective ending, and added resurrection appearances. The traditional longer ending (AV [KJV] Mk 16:9–20), the gnostic-sounding shorter ending (given at the bottom of the page in RSV) and the 'Freer ending' (an expansion of the longer ending inserted after 16:14) are all later, and as style and content show, non-Marcan.

Mk, then, ends at 16:8. Mk as known to Mt and Lk also ended at 16:8, for at this point both Mt and Lk go their separate ways, altering Mk 16:8 to fit their new material.

Did Mk intend to end at 16:8? Did Mk include material

beyond 16:8 which was lost very early, before it came into the hands of Mt and Lk? Was Mk accidentally left unfinished? Was Mk's ending deliberately cut off by an editor who did not like it? It has been suggested that Mark gave a too 'spiritual' view of the resurrection appearances, which was deemed unsatisfactory at a time when the appearances were becoming increasingly materialized (cf. Lk and Jn). Were there at the time Mk wrote as yet no *narratives* of appearances, but still only the statements that appearances occurred (cf. 1 Cor 15:3ff)? We shall probably never know. All we know for certain is that Mk certainly proclaims the resurrection (cf. the predictions, Mk 8:31; 9:9; 9:31; 10:34; 16:6) and *knows* the tradition of appearances both to Peter and to the Twelve (14:28; 16:7). And we may hazard the feeling (it is no more) that no Gk writer would have ended his work with ἐφοβοῦντο γάρ.

Method, Structure and Theological Intention

As we have seen (above, pp. 84–94), Mark is using two classes of traditional material: a continuous passion narrative, and isolated units (pericopes), some elements of which were probably already collected together according to form or topic. M. Kähler[1] has described the gospels as a 'passion narratives with extended introductions'. This is a profound insight into the character of Mk. (It is less applicable to Mt and Lk.) Mk defines itself as a 'gospel' (1:1)—that is, a proclamation of the saving act of God in Jesus Christ, particularly in His cross and resurrection. A. M. Farrer[2] is making the same point when he treats the episodes in Jesus' ministry as 'prefigurations' of the passion and resurrection.

The gospel or kerygma came to Mark in two forms: the passion narrative, and the pericopes, each of which, as form criticism has taught us, are proclamations of the kerygma

---

[1] *The So-called Historical Jesus and the Historic Biblical Christ*, 1964, p. 80, n 11 (German original 1892). D. E. Nineham similarly once likened Mk to a tadpole with a big head (passion narrative) and a short tail (pericopes), *Theology*, 60 (1957), p. 269.

[2] *A Study in St Mark*, 1951, *passim*, esp. p. 52.

in nuce. Mark combines these two forms of the kerygma together to make a single proclamation or 'gospel'. The clue to Mark's theological stance is to be found in his 'redaction', in the joints which he creates in order to link the pericopes (or collections of pericopes) to one another and to the passion story.

The most striking feature in these links, to which W. Wrede called attention[1] are: (1) the injunction to silence in the exorcisms and healings (to demons, 1:34; 3:12; to the recipients of cures, 1:44, 5:43; 7:36; 8:26; and after revelations to the disciples, 8:30; 9:9); (2) the disciples' misunderstanding of Jesus (esp. 8:16–21); (3) the theory that Jesus' parables were deliberately told in order to provoke misunderstanding (Mk 4:10–12). Wrede showed that the theme of secrecy invariably occurs not in the tradition but in the redaction. Taken together, these redactional passages provide the clue to Mark's theology. Thus these elements cannot be taken directly as historical to Jesus.[2] The fact that in the traditional nucleus of the pericopes these elements are often contradicted (e.g. the command to secrecy is ignored) shows that theme of secrecy is a creation of Mark.

Wrede's explanation of these phenomena was that Mark was seeking to impose a Christology on non-christological material. (Theologically Wrede was an old-fashioned liberal, who believed that Jesus' ministry was un-Messianic, and that the Messianship was purely a creation of the post-Easter church.) It is probably true that Jesus Himself[3] did not make any *explicit* Messianic claim or use any Messianic title as a self-designation. But against Wrede recent scholarship would assert: Jesus' life was implicitly christological through and through; (2) this Christology became explicit with the rise of the Easter faith, and the tradition Mark used was impregnated

---

[1] *Das Messiasgeheimnis in den Evangelien*, 1901.
[2] So, e.g., V. Taylor and C. E. B. Cranfield in their commentaries on Mk.
[3] See R. H. Fuller, *The Foundations of New Testament Christology*, pp. 108ff.

already through and through with this christological interpretation. The Christology occurs in the body of the pericopes.
Hence the Christology is not the creation of Mark. The
Messianic secret motif does not introduce the Christology but
qualifies it.

To understand the nature of this qualification it must be
remembered that Mark was the first to combine the pericopes
with the passion narrative, i.e. two forms of kerygma, the
proclamation of the death and resurrection of Jesus and the
isolated episodes in Jesus' life. The Messianic secret is the
consequence of combining these two forms of kerygma
together. The effect is to correct the view—strongly appealing
to the Hellenistic world—that the isolated episodes, esp. the
miracles were complete manifestations of Jesus as a Hellenistic
wonder-worker of divine man.[1] Jesus was not this kind of
figure, but the crucified One manifested as Messiah after His
resurrection. By his three devices of secrecy Mark tones down
for the reader the impression that the miracles, teaching, and
activity of Jesus are in themselves complete revelations of
Jesus' Messiahship. They are no more than preliminary
unveilings of what was finally manifested only after the
resurrection. In this way the kerygma of the pericopes is
riveted to the kerygma of the passion and resurrection. Thus
Dibelius[2] has aptly called the first part of Mk a book of 'secret
epiphanies'.

Mark's Relationship to Paul

Mk is thus a powerful reassertion, in terms of a 'life of Jesus',
of the Pauline kerygma of the cross. B. W. Bacon[3] raised the
question of the Paulinism of Mk. He found Pauline influence
especially in those passages which speak of the redemptive
significance of Christ's death, esp. 10:45 ('ransom for many')
and 14:24, the cup word at the Supper ('shed for many'). Later

---

[1] See above, p. 50, for this view at Corinth.
[2] M. Dibelius, *From Tradition to Gospel*, p. 232.
[3] B. W. Bacon, *The Gospel of Mark*, 1925, pp. 242ff, 261ff.

scholarship has come to see that these elements are not distinctively Pauline, but are the common stock of apostolic Christianity and go back to the post-Easter interpretation of Christ's death in the early Palestinian community.[1]

Mk is clearly a gospel which emerges out of the Hellenistic church, out of which Paul also emerged. The affinity between Paul and Mk is to be sought in their christological presentation. Mark's favourite christological title is 'Son of God' (Mk 1:1, 11; 3:11; 5:7; 9:7; 15:39). It is also a common title in Paul. Like Paul, Mark seems to presuppose the pre-existence of the Son of God, and his descent into the world,[2] e.g., Mk 1:35ff, 'for this purpose *came I forth*' (ἐξῆλθον, sc. 'from the Father' or 'from heaven'). Mk 12:6 (parable of the vineyard) speaks of God's 'sending' his beloved Son. In addition, the presentation of the miracles as epiphanies implies pre-existence. The transfiguration is an unveiling of the divine 'nature' of Jesus. All this Mark received from the Hellenistic tradition. But like Paul he is concerned to tone down this Hellenistic emphasis. Paul does it by means of the kenosis concept: Phil 2:6ff, a pre-Pauline hymn whose stance Paul fully endorses; 2 Cor 8:9; and by means of his self-understanding as an apostle in terms of the 'cross side' of the kerygma in 2 Cor 10–13 (see above, pp. 49f). Mk is opposing the same type of Hellenistic divine man Christology as Paul in 2 Cor 10–13. Mk does it with the three devices to which Wrede called attention. It is here that the 'Pauline' element in Mk lies.

Structure and Contents of Mk

Mk falls into four main divisions: a Prelude (1:1–13); Jesus' activity in Galilee, etc. (1:14–8:26); Journey to Jerusalem (8:27–10:52); Jerusalem ministry, passion and resurrection (11:1–16:8). These four major divisions are subdivided as follows:

---

[1] H. E. Tödt, *The Son of Man*, pp. 202ff; cf. R. H. Fuller, *The Foundations of New Testament Christology*, pp. 151ff.

[2] For pre-existence Christology in Mk cf. J. Knox, *Christ the Lord*, pp. 96ff.

Part I (Prelude)

1:1–13. The Baptist's preaching, Jesus' baptism and temptation.

Part II (Galilean Ministry)

This is made up of several pre-Marcan collections of material:

1:14–45. A day in Capernaum.

2:1–3:35. Conflict stories (with call of disciples interpolated 3:13–19).

4:1–34. Parables.

4:35–5:43. Miracles.

(Interlude)

6:1–6. Rejection at Nazareth.

6:7–13. The Mission of the Twelve.

6:14–16. Herod and Jesus plus 6:17–29, death of the Baptist.

The climax of the Galilean ministry (duplicated traditions)[1]:

6:30–44. Feeding of 5000.	8:1–10. Feeding of 4000.
6:45–52. Crossing.	8:11–21. Crossing: demand for sign and discourse on loaves.
6:53–56. Generalizing summary.	
7:1–23. Discourse on purity.	
7:24–30. Syro-Phoenician woman.	
7:31–37. Deaf mute.	8:22–26. Blind man of Bethesda.

Part III (Journey to Jerusalem)

8:26–33. Peter's confession and passion prediction No. 1.

8:34–9:1 *The Reward of Discipleship.*

9:2–13. Transfiguration and Elijah discourse.

9:14–29. Epileptic boy.

[1] See V. Taylor, *Mark*, pp. 628ff.

9:30–32. Passion prediction No. 2.

9:33–10:31. Collection of sayings; teaching on marriage, children, and riches.

10:32–45. The Zebedaides' request: Passion prediction No. 3.

10:46–52. Blind Bartimaeus.

Part IV (Jesus in Jerusalem)

(a) Ministry.

11:1–10. Triumphal entry.

11:12–14, 20–25. Cursing of Fig tree.

11:15–19. Cleansing of Temple.

11:24–12:44. Conflict stories.

13. Little Apocalypse.

(b) 14–16:8. Passion and Easter narrative.

(c) THE GOSPEL OF MATTHEW

1. *Authorship*

Like the other gospels Mt is anonymous. The traditional title is a second-century conjecture. The earliest external witness is again Papias, quoting (anonymous) tradition (it is not quite clear whether 'this was said' represents a statement of the Elder, as in the case of Mk):

'. . . and about Matthew this was said, "Matthew collected the oracles in the Hebrew language, and each interpreted them as best he could" ' (Tr. K. Lake, Loeb edition).

This statement raises more problems than it solves. First, the description of Mt's contents as 'logia' (sayings) *could* apply to Mt, but it is an unusual word for a gospel. More enigmatic is the statement that Mt was written in Hebrew or Aramaic. Our Mt is in Gk and uses Gk sources (Mk and Q). Mt could not possibly have existed in Aramaic at any time, though of course it contains authentic sayings of Jesus originally uttered in Aramaic. For this reason it is held by many that (however Papias and Eusebius understood it) this statement originally

applied to something other than Mt. Papias' apparently mis-
taken interpretation has been explained by suggestion that
the statement originally referred to one of Mt's sources, most
plausibly to Q (Harnack); to the Special Matthean material;
or to the OT testimonia used by Mt (Rendell Harris). The
trouble is that all of these elements are themselves the product
of tradition, not the work of a single eyewitness.

The use of sources (Mk, Q, Special Mt material) precludes
apostolic authorship or eyewitness. The name Matthew was
attached to Mt for apologetic reasons in the second century.

K. Standahl[1] has made the interesting suggestion that Mt
was composed not by an individual, but in a kind rabbinic
school. He sees the clue to the composition in Mt 13:52. But
Mt seems more likely the product of an individual thinker,
composing his work for church use.

Date. Mt 22:7 makes it clear that Mt was written after 70. It
is a sub-apostolic work, concerned with the beginnings of
church organization, but without the clear-cut polity of the
Past or Ignatius. A date between 70 and 110 is required:
perhaps about 85. But this date, though widely favoured, is
really no more than a conjecture.

Provenance

It will help to determine the place of authorship if we
consider the sources used. Mk, we have argued, is from
Antioch: Q is Palestinian but not narrowly Judaistic: Special
Mt is narrowly Judaistic, and quite likely from Jerusalem.
These three traditions must have converged after the Jewish
war and the fall of Jerusalem. It was then that the Jerusalem
Christians fled to Pella in Syria. So a place in Syria is
suggested. The affinities between Mt and the Didache also
point to Syria.

It is worth remembering that Mt follows Mk very closely.
It is in fact a revision of Mk. It is therefore attractive to
suppose that Mt like Mk was written at Antioch. It is, we

[1] *The School of St Matthew,* 1954.

suggest, a 2nd edition of the Antiochene gospel resulting from the convergence of other traditions (Q, Special Mt) from Palestine.

For Mk the distinction between tradition and redaction could only be determined by form criticism. It is much easier to identify the redaction of Mt since we possess one of his written sources (Mk) and have some idea of the Q material from Lk. We can thus see how Mt rearranges his sources and traditions, the connecting-links he creates, etc. He follows the outline of Mk quite closely, expanding it at each end with the infancy (chs. 1–2) and resurrection (ch. 28) narratives and with considerable blocks of teaching.

Mt does not, like Mk, describe his work as a 'gospel'.[1] He opens with the words 'The *Book* of the genesis of Jesus Christ'. Does he intend 'book' to refer to the whole book, or merely to the infancy narratives, or to the genealogy? Probably only to the genealogy. Yet the use of the word 'genesis' suggests a parallel with the Pentateuch.

Next, we observe that Mt is at pains to tidy up the Marcan narrative. He has combined the miracles of Mk 2:1–3:6 and 4:35–5:43 into a single block in chs. 8–9. He proceeds similarly with the sayings of Jesus. He found a Great Sermon in the Q material (cf. Lk 6:20–49), and expanded it with sayings derived from other parts of Q[2] and with the special material. He has done the same thing in four other discourses. The basic pattern of Mt is set by these five discourses, each of which concludes with an almost identical formula (7:28; 11:1; 13:53; 19:1; 26:1):

> 1*st Discourse.* Ch. 5–7. The Sermon on the Mount, the New Torah.
>
> 2*nd Discourse.* Ch. 10. The missionary charge (an expanded version of Mk 6).

[1] It has been pointed out that Mt uses the word 'gospel' (εὐαγγέλιον) only where he is following Mk.
[2] This is the chief argument against Lk's use of Mt (Farrer). It involves an unscrambling of the egg with a vengeance!

3rd Discourse. Ch. 13. The parables of the kingdom (an expansion of Mk 4:1–34 with additional parables from Q and Special Mt.

4th Discourse. Ch. 18. Discourse on church discipline (cf. Mk 9:42–50).

5th Discourse. Ch. 23–25. Eschatological discourse, preceded (ch. 23) with a denunciation of the Pharisees—corresponding to the warning against false doctrine as a sign of the last times (see above, p. 48), an adaptation of Mk's Little Apocalypse in ch. 24 and apocalyptic parables in ch. 25. There is precedent for this in the parables at the conclusion of Mk's Little Apocalypse (the fig-tree and the thief at night). Mt gives the parables of the ten virgins, the talents, and the sheep and the goats.

B. W. Bacon[1] suggested that the five discourses correspond to the five books of the Pentateuch. This ties in with the hint about 'genesis', Mt 1:1 (see above, p. 115).

OT quotations. Another notable feature of Mt is the OT quotations, each occurring after the narration of an incident in Jesus' life and introduced with the stereotyped formula, 'This was done that it might be fulfilled which spoken by . . .'. There are 12 of these quotations:

1:22f. Virginal conception, Isa 7:14.

2:5f. Birth at Bethelehem, Mic 5:1, 3.

2:15. Flight and exodus of the Christ Child from Egypt, Hos 11:1.

2:17f. Massacre of the innocents, Jer 31:15.

2:23. Jesus' residence at Nazareth. The quotation, 'He shall be called a Nazarene' is impossible to identify with certainty.

4:14ff. Galilean ministry, Isa 8:23–9:1.

8:17. Jesus' healing ministry, Isa 53:4.

12:17f. Re-interpretation of the Messianic secret as fulfilment of servant prophecy, Isa 42:1–4.

[1] *Studies in Matthew*, 1930.

13:14. Parabolic teaching, Isa 6:9—a re-interpretation of
Mk's parable theory; also, in 13:35, Ps 78:2.

21:4f. Triumphal entry, Zech 9:9.

26:56. Arrest: fulfilment of 'the prophets' (from Mk).

27:9f. The 30 pieces of silver: Zech 11:12f.

Did Mt first find the texts, and create incidents to match
them? Or did he find the incidents in the tradition and match
them with proof texts? Where he introduces them into the
Marcan material it is clear that he does the latter. But he can
allow the text to modify his presentation of the incident, as
when he makes Jesus at the triumphal entry ride on *two*
beasts (!). Mt did not invent the tradition of the virginal conception to square with Isa 7:14 or the birth at Bethlehem to
square with Mic 5:1. For both these traditions are found
independently in Mt and Lk, which proves that they are prior
to both evangelists.[1] It is not certain whether the massacre
of the innocents and the flight into Egypt are traditional, or
whether they are Mt's creation from the prophecies. But the
other instances suggest that there was some precedent in the
pre-Matthean tradition for both of these incidents.

Matthew's Theology. The clue to Mt's theology is the five
discourses. These correspond with the 5 books of the Pentateuch. Jesus is the second Moses, the founder and lawgiver of
the new Israel, the church. The church is becoming institutionalized (early catholicism) with an incipient canon law. This
legislation[2] is closely connected with the function of the
parousia in Mt's teaching. The church will be judged at the
parousia by its observance of the new Torah. This is emphasized repeatedly in the eschatological parables. In the earlier
tradition the final judgment is presented to the crowds as a
challenge to accept Jesus' message.

---

[1] Isa 7:14 has doubtless contributed to the formation of the story
of the conception at an earlier stage in the tradition (see R. H. Fuller,
The Foundations of New Testament Christology, pp. 195f).

[2] G. Bornkamm, G. Barth and H. J. Held, *Tradition and Interpretation
in Matthew*, 1963, pp. 15ff.

Christology. Jesus in his earthly life is the new Moses who gives the Torah. The identification of Jesus with the New Moses is pre-Matthean.[1] But in the earlier tradition the emphasis is primarily on Moses' function as redeemer. Mt has given it a new twist by emphasizing the giving of the Torah. The Mosaic Christology is deeply embedded in the infancy narratives. The parallel between Pharaoh and Herod (the massacre of the infants) is immediately obvious. The supernatural conception of Jesus is also partly rooted in the same type Christology.

In his earthly life Jesus is also the Son of David. This again colours the infancy narratives (birth at Bethlehem). Mt also points out more frequently than Mk that Jesus is hailed as Son of David by those in search of healing (9:27; 15:22; 20:30, 31). And in connection with the healings Mt also brings in the servant prophecies of Dt-Isa. Jesus' Davidic sonship expresses his lowly royalty, his loving concern for his people. Like David he is the ideal shepherd-king. Cf. also the emphasis on Jesus' 'meekness', Mt 11:28ff and the Zech quotation in the triumphal entry (21:5). But from the resurrection on, Jesus reigns as the exalted Son of man who will come again as judge (Mt 28:16–20). This is the two-stage Christology of Hellenistic Jewish Christianity.[2]

(d) THE GOSPEL OF LUKE

Luke is the only evangelist who directly addresses his reader(s) as an author (Lk 1:1–4). Even allowing for a conscious modelling of this preface on those of contemporary historians, and for a certain rhetorical quality in the style, the preface gives valuable information about the author and his procedures.

1. 'Many'—this is a rhetorical feature, and should not be over-pressed. But at least it indicates that Luke is not the earliest evangelist: he had predecessors in the field. Synoptic

---

[1] See R. H. Fuller, *The Foundations of New Testament Christology* pp. 167ff.
[2] Fuller, *op. cit.*, pp. 182ff.

criticism has confirmed this by showing that Luke used sources—Mk, Q material and his own special tradition.

2. Luke distinguishes himself from the eyewitnesses, who handed down their witness in the form of tradition. Whether the eyewitnesses form a group distinct from the 'ministers of the word' is not clear. If they are distinct, Luke stands in a tradition twice removed from the original events of Jesus—the eyewitnesses, the ministers (e.g. Mark), and Luke. Lk is definitely a sub-apostolic work.

3. Luke claims to have been careful about 'order' in which he presents his material. His concept of 'order' is very different from that of Matthew. Matthew conflates his material into tidy discourses and collections of like matter. Luke as a historian seeks to relate matters in the order they were 'said and done'. But his sources were not in this kind of order (cf. Mk above). So his method (rather arbitrary it will seem to the modern historian) is to follow one source at a time. Luke is opposed to rearrangements, and tends to avoid conflation. He follows Mk, Q and Special material in turn.[1]

4. Lk is addressed to one Theophilus. He cannot be identified. The name is Gk, and he is accorded a title, 'most excellent'. This suggests a highly placed imperial official and an educated Gentile. It explains the kind of public Lk was aiming at. It also explains the apologetic motif running through Lk-Acts. Christianity is not a subversive movement. The actions taken by Roman officials against both Jesus and his later followers were due to Roman misunderstandings and Jewish machinations. This suggests that Lk was written when the imperial authorities were beginning to distinguish between Jews and Christians and to refuse to the latter the tolerance they had traditionally shown to the former.[2]

---

[1] Recent treatments of Lk, especially in the Bultmann school, overlook this, particularly H. Conzelmann in his important work on *The Theology of St Luke*, 1960. It is most unlikely, e.g., that Luke deliberately shifted the rejection at Nazareth to the beginning of the ministry for theological purposes.

[2] On this subject see B. S. Easton, *The Purpose of Acts*, 1936, repr. in *Early Christianity* (ed. F. C. Grant), 1954.

E

Luke calls his work not a 'gospel', like Mk, but by implication a 'narrative' (διήγησις). He writes primarily as a historian, not as an evangelist (Mk) or as a scribe of the new Torah (Mt). He looks back upon the history of Jesus as the beginning of the Christian church. The story will continue in Acts. It is the story of 'how we got there'.

He does not, however, write merely as a secular historian, but as the recorder of redemptive history. This accounts for the deliberate imitation of the style of the LXX (see esp. 2:1ff) as well as for the attempt to relate this redemptive history to secular history (*ibid.* and 3:1ff). The thesis of Conzelmann's book (see above, p. 119 n. 1) as indicated by the German title, *Die Mitte der Zeit* ('The Middle of Time'), is that Luke sees salvation history as consisting of three epochs, the OT period of promise, its fulfilment in Jesus, and the subsequent history of the church. Conzelmann's theory involves, however, the further point that Luke is here re-introducing an OT-Jewish conception alien to Jesus and primitive Christianity. For them, salvation history had come to an end in the eschatological preaching and Christ event. Henceforth there was only the ever-repeated point of existential encounter with the Word. This is a misunderstanding of both Lk and of early Christianity. The apocalyptic framework both of Jesus' message and of the preaching of earliest Christianity shows that they too were working with the same basic notion of redemptive history. It is present in Paul (Rom 9–11, see above). Luke does not innovate. He simply adjusts redemptive history to its prolongation through the delay in the parousia. But Conzelmann is right to the extent that this prolongation is characteristic of the sub-apostolic age and represents 'early catholicism'. The postponement of the parousia is an important factor in Lk. Cf. the modification of Mk 1:14f in Lk 4:14f, where all reference to the imminence of the kingdom of God is suppressed. Cf. also Mk 13:7 with Lk 21:9 ('the end is not imminent'), and Mk 14:62 with Lk 22:69, where all reference to the second coming is suppressed in favour of the indefinitely extended rule of the exalted Christ.

Authorship

Luke speaks as if he were known to Theophilus. Attempts have been made to support the traditional identification with Luke, the physician and companion of Paul (Philem 24; Col 4:14; cf. 2 Tim 4:11) by an analysis of Lk's language for signs of medical usage.[1] Unfortunately there was no technical medical language in the ancient world, so this does not prove anything.

External evidence for the authorship is not helpful. Papias has nothing. The earliest information is in the Anti-Marcionite prologue.[2] This reads (Heard's translation):

'Luke is a Syrian of Antioch, a doctor by profession, who was a disciple of the apostles, and later followed Paul until his martyrdom. He served the Lord without distraction, unmarried, childless, and fell asleep at the age of 84 in Boeotia, full of the Holy Spirit.

'He, when the Gospels were already in existence—that according to Matthew written in Judaea, that according to Mark in Italy—impelled by the Holy Spirit wrote this whole Gospel in the regions of Achaea. He shows by means of the preface this very fact, that before him other Gospels had been written, and that it was necessary to set forth, for those of the Gentiles who believed, the accurate narrative of the dispensation, that they should not be distracted by Jewish fables nor miss the truth by the heretical and vain fantasies. So we have received as most necessary at the beginning the birth of John, who is the beginning of the Gospel, in that he was the forerunner of the Lord and a sharer both in the preparation of the Gospel and the fellowship of the Spirit. This dispensation a prophet among the Twelve calls to mind.

'And afterwards the same Luke wrote the Acts of the Apostles.'

What value can be placed on all this? Most of it could have been inferred from the NT writings, though some biographical facts

[1] W. K. Hobart, *The Medical Language of St Luke*, 1882.
[2] On these see R. G. Heard, 'The Old Gospel Prologues' *JTS* n.s. 6 (1955), pp. 1–16.

(Luke's virginity, age and place of death) may, according to Heard, rest on genuine tradition.

If we can convince ourselves that a companion of Paul wrote Acts, the traditional identification of that companion with Luke the physician is as good as any. The anti-Marcionite prologue gives no hint as to date, except that it rightly places Mk and (probably correctly) Mt also earlier than Lk (but perhaps this was a mere conjecture due to the traditional order of the gospels). For Lk is more clearly 'early catholic' than Mk or even Mt; *c*. 90 would be a good date. As for the place of origin, the statement of the prologue that it was written in Boeotia is intriguing, since it is nowhere suggested in the NT. Heard thinks it is an inference from the place of Luke's death (Achaea). Could it however have been written at Rome? Acts reaches its climax with Paul's preaching at Rome. Also, Marcion used Lk as his only gospel while at Rome. It is not difficult to imagine Mk finding its way from Antioch to Rome, and the Q and special Lucan material coming from Palestine *via* Hellenistic Christianity to Rome.

(e) THE ACTS OF THE APOSTLES

Like the other traditional titles of the NT books, 'The Acts of the Apostles' is not what the author called his work. Probably, had he given it a title, he would have called it 'the second word' (ὁ δεύτερος λόγος), since he refers to his gospel as 'the first word' (τὸν πρῶτον λόγον, Acts 1:1). Indeed, he would hardly have called his second word 'the Acts of the Apostles', since for him it is (*ibid.*) by implication the acts and teaching of Jesus continued in His church, or the acts of the Holy Spirit in the church. Again and again, in each significant movement in the story it is the exalted Jesus or the Spirit who takes the initiative.

In the opening chapter the author sets out the plan of his work. In v. 8 he says: 'But you shall receive power when the Holy Spirit has come upon you; and you shall be my witnesses in Jerusalem and in all Judea and Samaria and to the end of the earth'. This is what he covers so far as his sources permit. He is very meagre on Judea, gives only one or two stories about Samaria, and 'the end of the earth' is covered by Paul's journey to Rome (with nothing about the prior foundation of the church there).

Structure. It is generally agreed that Acts falls into two halves, though there is some disagreement as to where the division comes. Often, it has been placed at the end of ch. 15. Probably this view is unconsciously based on the apparent change of sources in ch. 16 where (v. 10) the 'we sections' begin (see below). Marxsen,[1] however, puts the division at the end of ch. 12. There is something to be said for this. In chs. 1–12 Peter is the central figure, whereas in chs. 13–28 it is Paul. However, this division is not clear-cut either, for Paul's conversion is narrated in ch. 9, in the Petrine half of the book, while the Jerusalem council where Peter is prominent occurs in the second half. Perhaps the reason for this overlapping is the author's desire to weld the two parts together (the Cornelius episode achieves the same end) by putting Paul's commission under the aegis of Peter.

Sources. The synoptic gospels exhibit literary parallels which enable us to track down the sources. There are no such parallels to Acts. The presumption is that since the author used sources for his 'first word' he followed the same method in his second word. Yet not only was the Acts the first product of its kind, but the conditions for writing anything like the history of the church or even for keeping archives were lacking in the apostolic age, when the parousia was believed to be imminent: the church never suspected that it would have a history. Nor were the units of material in Acts handed down in preaching: the church preached Jesus, not the Apostles.[2]

There is however one internal phenomenon which points to a source, namely the 'we sections'. The narrative is normally in

---

[1] *Einleitung*, following E. Haenchen, *Die Apostelgeschichte* (Meyer Comm.), 1961.

[2] See M. Dibelius, *Studies in the Acts of the Apostles* (ET 1956), pp. 1–25, esp. p. 4.

the 3rd person, but at certain places it switches to the 1st person plural. The first occurrence of this switch (in the usual text) is at 16:10. Paul is at Troas, and as a result of a vision sets out for Macedonia. At this point the account continues: '*we* sought to go on to Macedonia'. The 'we'-style continues to 16:17 (at Philippi), where it is dropped. Then it is resumed at 20:5 to continue as far as the arrival at Miletus (20:15). It fades out during the speech to the Ephesian elders, to be resumed at the departure from Miletus (21:1) and continued through 21:18 when the party arrives at Jerusalem. Finally the 'we'-style reappears in 27:1, where Paul leaves Caesarea for Rome, and continues through the rest of the voyage until the arrival in Rome (28:16). In the 'Western' text of Acts (see below, pp. 131f) there is an earlier 'we' at 11:28, which may be original.

There are three possible explanations of the 'we sections': (1) the traditional view is they represent the reminiscences of the author himself (whether taken from a diary or recorded from memory), who was therefore a companion of Paul; (2) the 'we sections' are incorporated by the author from a diary of a companion of Paul; (3) the 'we sections' are the artificial creation of the author of Acts in order to claim for himself eyewitness for part of the story.

Of these explanations No. 3 is least likely. For in that case one would have expected the 'we' to be kept up much longer. Moreover, as a historian Luke attaches more importance to the use of sources than to personal eyewitness (Lk 1:1–4). The remarkable circumstance that the 'we' is both dropped and resumed at Philippi (16:17, 20:5) strongly suggests the abandonment and resumption of a source rather than artificial insertion.

The traditionalist arguments against No. 2 are: First, that any conscientious author would have carefully removed the 'we' when incorporating the material into his gospel; and second, stylistic analysis fails to reveal any difference of style between the 'we sections' and the rest of Acts. Neither of these arguments, however, is cast-iron. There are literary precedents in antiquity for such a procedure as the retention of the 'we' from a source.[1] The author of Acts, as is shown by his treatment of sources in Lk, consciously impregnates his sources with his own style.

In favour of (1), it may be urged the identity of the diarist and the author of Acts is after all the most natural explanation. Whether we accept it or not will depend on whether on other grounds we deem it possible that Acts could have been written by a companion of Paul. A final answer must wait until we have investigated the portrait of Paul in Acts compared with the epistles.

Any further attempt to postulate sources amounts to little more than a classification of the material. M. Dibelius[2] suggested that in addition to the 'we sections' the source for 13–21 is an *itinerary* of Paul, i.e. a list of places visited and people encountered on those visits.

If however, as we are inclined to think, the first missionary journey (chs. 13–14) is a duplication of the second (see above, pp. 9, 26) there is no need to postulate an itinerary over and above the 'we sections' for chs. 13–28. Outside of the 'we sections' the author must have used a number of local traditions for the intervening gaps, esp. between 16:17 and 20:5. But these traditions are defective.[3] The speech to the Ephesian elders is a Lucan composition reflecting the polity and theology of the sub-apostolic church.

The three accounts of the conversion of Paul (chs. 9, 22 and 26) constitute a special problem. It seems unlikely that the author would have composed three different accounts on the same subject. Of the three, that in the speech before Agrippa (ch. 26) tallies most closely with the data of the epistles, and it has been thought to come from the diarist author of the 'we sections'. The narrative in ch. 9 is related from the point of

[1] See H. Windisch in *The Beginnings of Christianity*, ed. K. Lake and F. Jackson. II, ii, 1922, p. 343, who cites Ezra 7:27–8:34; Neh 1:1–7:5; 12:31; 13:6–31 as examples.

[2] M. Dibelius, *op. cit.*, pp. 5ff.

[3] We have seen how defective Acts is on the Ephesian ministry and on the problems in Galatia and Corinth (above, pp. 23ff, 40ff).

view of Damascus, and would seem to come from the tradition
of that church. The version in ch. 22 combines features of the
other two accounts, and is probably an entirely Lucan
composition.

The speeches of Paul in 14:15–18 (Lystra) and 17:22–31
(Areopagus) reflect the apologetic of the sub-apostolic age and
are probably Lucan compositions.[1]

The question of Aramaic sources for chs. 1–12 has been
much discussed. C. C. Torrey maintained that they were
directly translations from Aramaic. J. de Zwaan[2] held an intermediate position, viz., an Aramaic origin for parts of these
chapters, including the kerygmatic speeches in chs. 2, 3 and 10.
H. F. D. Sparks[3] showed that most of supposed translation
Greek in these chapters can be explained as due to conscious modelling on the style of LXX. But his argument did
not affect the kerygmatic speeches. While these speeches, in
their finished form are like all the speeches in Acts, the products of the author, they nevertheless can be safely regarded
as enshrining primitive liturgical and kerygmatic formulae[4] as
well as traditional testimonia or proof texts. Stephen's speech
(Acts 7) is an exception. It appears to be based on a pre-Lucan
and perhaps pre-Christian Hellenistic Jewish summary of OT
history. For the rest, the author seems to have used separate
units of material: cycles of tradition connected with key people
in the Christian community, esp. Peter, and oral information
obtained from various Christian centers such as Jerusalem,
Samaria, Damascus and Antioch.

Recent study of Acts, especially that of Haenchen, detects
Lucan composition in the generalizing summaries (e.g. Acts
2:42–47; 4:32–35; 5:12–16).

[1] M. Dibelius, 'Paul on the Areopagus' in *Studies in the Acts of the
Apostles*, pp. 26–77.
[2] J. de Zwaan in *The Beginnings of Christianity*, II, ii, pp. 30–65,
followed by C. H. Dodd, *The Apostolic Preaching and its Developments*,
1949, pp. 19f.
[3] 'The Semitisms of Acts', *JTS* n.s. 1 (1950), pp. 16–28.
[4] E. Schweizer, 'Concerning the Speeches in Acts' in: *Studies in Luke-
Acts*, ed. L. E. Keck and J. L. Martin, 1966, pp. 208–216. This will apply
also to Paul's speech in ch. 13.

Acts and the History of the Early Church (chs. 1–12)

It follows from all this that Acts cannot be used as a continuous history for the early church any more than the gospels can be so used for the life of Jesus. It is as impossible to write a connected history of the early church as it is to write a connected story of Jesus' ministry.

As with the life of Jesus we may however say that the broadest outline of Acts is correct. Much of the following is confirmed by the data of the epistles. The Christian proclamation and the earliest community began at Jerusalem. Its leaders were the apostles (from Acts 1–12 we would gather that only the 12 were apostles, whereas we know from Paul that the apostles were a wider group, of which the 12 were an inner nucleus). Peter was their leader and spokesman. The Jerusalem church was in close connection with the Jewish community, yet it had a distinctive eschatological self-understanding indicated by its self-designation 'ecclesia'. There emerged in time a different form of Christianity which was Greek-speaking ('Hellenists'), and more liberal in its attitude to the law and the temple than the original Aramaic speaking Christians. This led to the persecution and dispersal of the Hellenists, while the Aramaic-speaking Christians remained immune. Peter and the Twelve finally left Jerusalem, and James and the elders constituting a kind of Christian sanhedrin then took over the management of the Jerusalem church.

In addition, some of the details probably rest on earlier tradition. These include the replacement of Judas by Matthias, the surrender of his goods by Barnabas and the partial surrender by Ananias and Sapphira (made by the summaries of Acts into a general rule of the community). Stephen's murder was probably a lynching, transformed by Acts into a judicial sentence. Philip was the founder of the Samaritan mission. The earliest church protested at the admission of uncircumcised Gentiles. James bar Zebedee was executed by Herod Agrippa I in c. 44.[1]

---

[1] The foregoing is based on Haenchen.

To this we should add the story of the Ascension, Acts 1:9–11. This rests upon primitive tradition, for it reflects the Christology of the earliest Aramaic speaking community,[1] according to which Jesus is assumed into heaven (not enthroned) after the resurrection, and remains inactive until the parousia (cf. Acts 3:20f). Despite the heavy overlay of theological symbolism in the Pentecost narrative, it too contains a nucleus of fact: the beginning of the kerygma, and its probable accompaniment by an outburst of ecstatic speech. Finally, although the summary in Acts 2:42–47 is probably the composition of the author, it contains valuable information about the primitive community meal.

The 'Paulinism' of Acts

Acts views the history of the apostolic church from the standpoint of the sub-apostolic age. It is much more a direct source for sub-apostolic theology than it is for the history of the apostolic age. This comes out clearly in Acts 13–28, where a comparison with the Pauline epistles is possible. We have already noted factual differences between Acts and the Pauline letters, and the existence of lacunae in Acts. More significant is the contrast between Paul's understanding of his apostleship and the way it is presented in Acts. Paul emphatically insists that he is an apostle by a direct commission from the risen Lord, identical in form and content with the commissioning of the first apostles (Gal 1:1, 15ff; 1 Cor 9:1; 15:8ff). In Acts, Paul is never called an apostle except at Acts 14:4, 14. But here the title is shared with Barnabas, and probably means envoys commissioned by the Antioch community, not apostles of Jesus Christ. In Acts Paul's conversion is not the commissioning of an apostle; it is precisely a conversion vision, indistinguishable from other visions Paul received. Paul's mission to the Gentiles is communicated not from the risen Lord directly, but through Ananias (9:15) or

[1] See R. H. Fuller, *The Foundations of New Testament Christology*, pp. 154, 184f.

through a subsequent vision (22:21). Paul is actually ordained for this mission by the prophets at Antioch (13:1ff). In fact, he stands in a kind of apostolic succession from Peter *via* Barnabas and the Antioch community.

The distinctive features of Pauline theology are ironed out, and the speeches attributed to him Paul becomes the mouth-piece of sub-apostolic theology (Acts 13, 14, 17), with its positive natural theology and natural law.[1] He provides his missions with a sub-apostolic form of polity, with presbyter-bishops (Acts 14:23, 20:17, 28), whereas the historical Paul left his churches in the hands of charismatic ministers (1 Cor 12–14; Rom 12—Phil 1:1 is probably no real exception).

Finally, Paul's leading role in the Gentile mission is played down in the interests of Peter's (chs. 10, 11, 15) and James's leadership.

Authorship

We are now in a position to draw tentative conclusions on the question of authorship.

The earliest external evidence, furnished by Irenaeus, *Adv. Haer* III, 14, 1, states that Acts was written by Luke the companion of Paul. The Muratorian Fragment (*c.* 200) says:

'Moreover the Acts of all the Apostles are included in one book. Luke addresses them to the most excellent Theophilus because several events took place when he was present, and he makes this claim about the . . . journey of Peter and the journey of Paul.'

It is clear that by the end of the second century the traditional view that Acts was the work of Luke, the companion of Paul is well established. This tradition still commands wide assent today and is well supported by internal evidence (the 'we sections').

[1] P. Vielhauer, 'On the "Paulinism" of Acts', *Studies in Luke-Acts*, pp. 33-50.

But it is not without its difficulties.[1] The chief of these is the portrait of Paul. Could a companion of Paul, especially one who in his preface to his 'first word' professedly aims at historical accuracy, have so radically re-interpreted the portrait of Paul and his theology? Any attempt to save the traditional authorship by harmonizing Acts and the epistles blocks the way to a true understanding of Acts, and must be rigorously avoided. Secondly, could a companion of Paul have produced a work so clearly sub-apostolic and early catholic in its theology and polity?

Thirdly, would a companion of Paul have inserted into the body of the 'we sections' such obviously legendary material as the highly improbable account of the earthquake in the gaol at Philippi (Acts 16:26ff)?

Dibelius was impressed by all of these difficulties, and in fact was the first to call attention to them in their full seriousness. Yet he could still accept the traditional authorship. We may follow suit provided we do not allow it to control our understanding of Acts and blind us to its sub-apostolic, early catholic character. In that case we must assume that Luke was writing from a distance of the events he narrates, and that his own theology had developed since he was a companion of Paul.

Summary of Contents

Part I (The Foundation of the Church)

Ch. 1. The Ascension and the choice of Matthias.

Ch. 2. The Pentecost event and the beginning of the kerygma.

Ch. 3–5. The Jerusalem community.

Ch. 6–8:3. The rise of Hellenistic Jewish Christianity under Stephen and the seven; the martyrdom of Stephen and the persecution of the church.

---

[1] See esp. H. Windisch, 'The Case against the Tradition', *Beginnings*, II, ii, pp. 298–348; John Knox, *Chapters in a Life of Paul*, 1950; Haenchen, *op. cit.*; P. Vielhauer, *op. cit.*

Ch. 8:4–12:25. The transition to the Gentile mission through
    Judea to Samaria, the conversion of Paul, the Cornelius
    episode and the foundation of the church at Antioch.

Part II (The Mission of Paul)

13:1–14:28. The 1st missionary journey.

15:1–35. The Apostolic Council.

15:36–18:22. The 2nd Missionary journey.

18:23–21:14. The 3rd Missionary journey.

Paul in captivity: Jerusalem, 21:15–23:22.
                    in Caesarea, 23:23–26:32.
                    journey to Rome, 27:1–28:15.
                    in Rome, 28:16–31.

Note on the Western Text

The old Latin texts and the bilingual MS, Codex Bezae
(Cambridge University Library) exhibit in Acts a form of
text which amounts to more than a number of variant
readings of the usual kind. This family of MSS, called the
Western text, is characterized by a wholesale series of
expansions compared with (both the earlier Alexandrian
texts and the later Byzantine standardized text). The
expansions consist of picturesque details and embellishments,
as well as theological modifications.

Westcott and Hort maintained that the Western text was
in its entirety an inferior second-century revision.

Some textual critics have taken a different view. F. Blass
and T. Zahn held that both forms of text were the work of Luke
himself: he wrote a rough draft which was circulated in the
west, and a polished final version, which became the normal
text. A. C. Clark,[1] reversing Westcott and Hort, believed that
the Western text was original and the normal text a second-
century revision (and therefore a corruption).

The trend today is to avoid being dogmatic, and to judge

[1] *The Primitive Text of the Gospels and Acts*, 1914.

each Western reading on its merits. Westcott and Hort were
in the main right, and the text of Acts clearly underwent
editorial expansion in the second century. But occasionally
the Western text has preserved readings which merit serious
consideration. One such instance is the 'we' passage in Acts
11:28. Cf. also Acts 12:10, 19:9.

IV.—THE DEUTERO-PAULINE LITERATURE

(a) THE PASTORAL EPISTLES (1, 2 TIMOTHY and TITUS)

Past might have been included among the 'disputed letters' of Paul (pp. 57–68) since there are some reputable scholars, notably J. Jeremias[1] and J. N. D. Kelly[2] who still maintain their Pauline authenticity. But the overwhelming majority of critical scholars, the English-speaking world included, regard them as deutero-Pauline. The name Past was first given to these letters by a German Lutheran divine, Paul Anton (1753). They are purportedly written by Paul to Timothy and Titus as pastors to instruct them about their pastoral duties. But this designation does not entirely cover the contents, since they lay down rules for the congregations as well as for their ministers. They are more like Church Orders than letters of advice to young clergymen.

There are many reasons for questioning the authenticity of Past p 46, the earliest MS containing the Pauline letters, does not have them (it ends with 1 Thess). It could be argued that the end of p 46 has been lost so this argument is not conclusive.

Marcion (c. 150) did not include Past in his canon. Marcion of course was capable of excluding them if they did not suit his purpose. But there is less OT matter in Past than, e.g., in Rom. So it is more probable that Marcion either did not know them, or did not accept them as Pauline.

The Muratorian fragment (c. 200) places Past after Philem. This suggests that Past were only just beginning to find their way into the Pauline corpus, and were still treated as a kind of appendix to it.

Other reasons for questioning the authenticity of Past are

---

[1] *Die Briefe an Timotheus und Titus*, NTD 9, 1954[7].
[2] *A Commentary on the Pastoral Epistles*, 1963.

well set out by B. S. Easton in his commentary.[1] He says, 'Paul
was inspired, the Pastor is orthodox'. The religious and theological atmosphere of Past is palpably different from those of
the genuine Pauline writings. E.g., Paul normally uses 'faith'
(πίστις) in the sense of personal trust in the saving act of God
in Christ, whereas in Past 'faith' is normally 'the faith', a body
of truths requiring intellectual assent (fides quae creditur, as
opposed to fides qua creditur). The necessity of good works is
strongly emphasized in Past, e.g. 1 Tim 2:10; 5:10; 6:18;
2 Tim 2:21; Tit 3:14. Easton tends, however, to exaggerate this
difference. Paul himself also undoubtedly attaches importance
to good works as such, but they are not instrumental to
justification, but rather its outcome. They are the fruit of the
Spirit. Note too the frequency of ethical exhortation in the
genuine Paulines. But Past tend to combine good works with
faith: both are instrumental to justification. According to
Easton, the 'Pastor' picked up some elements of Paul's
teaching which served his purpose and left out much else, thus
creating a different overall impression.

Some maintain that the Christology of Past is on a more
elementary level than in Paul. They contain nothing, e.g. about
Christ's pre-existence or his agency in creation. This may be
questioned. The hymn 1 Tim 3:16 certainly implies the
incarnational Christology of the Hellenistic mission.[2] In any
case the christological statements of Past occur mostly in
traditional formulae. They have no distinctive Christology of
their own. This is also true of Paul, but in a different way: Paul
also draws on traditional formulae, and cannot be said to
develop them. Rather, he re-interprets them in terms of
Christian existence.[3]There is nothing of the kind in Past. It is
quite wrong to argue as Easton does that whereas for Paul
justification is by faith, for Past it is through the sacrament of
baptism. Such an antithesis is entirely false.

[1] The Pastoral Epistles, 1948.
[2] See R. H. Fuller, The Foundations of New Testament Christology,
pp. 216ff. Cf. also 2 Tim 1:9f.
[3] Cf. above, pp. 54f. on Rom 1:3ff compared with Rom 1:17.

The absence of key Pauline concepts and phrases from Past is striking, e.g. ἐν Χριστῷ ('in Christ') and ἐν πνεύματι ('in the Spirit'). True, the Spirit plays an important role in the charismata as in Paul, but the charismata are canalized in the ministerial succession, rather than diffused through the whole body (indeed, the concept of σῶμα Χριστοῦ, the body of Christ, is absent from Past).

According to pre-computer calculation, there are 306 words in Past which are not in Paul. Some of these are key terms, replacing a very different series of Pauline key terms. E.g. εὐσέβεια ('piety'), ὑγιαίνουσα διδαχή ('sound doctrine') σωφροσύνη ('sobriety'). These words seem typical of the sub-apostolic age, when the church is no longer creative but conservative.

Jeremias puts up the best case for the Pauline authorship of Past (and is followed largely by Kelly). First, he submits the beginnings and endings of all the Pauline letters, including Past, to a minute analysis, and finds a progressive development of formulae from 1 Thess through Col to Past. Past continue the development where Col leaves off. Then Jeremias refers to the 'personal testimony' of Paul, i.e. passages where Paul speaks autobiographically and especially of his spiritual life: 1 Tim 1:12–16; 2 Tim 3:10–12, 4:6–8. But the proper assessment of these passages is uncertain. 1 Tim 1:12ff has been used, with even more justification, as an argument for non-Pauline authorship. Would Paul really have excused himself by saying that he persecuted the church in 'ignorance'? 2 Tim 3:10ff could just as well have been lifted from the data of Acts 13–14 to create an air of authenticity. 2 Tim 4:6–8 could have been suggested by Phil 2:17, though it is also one of the passages which has given rise to the fragment theory (see below).

The positive doctrine of the state in 1 Tim 2:1ff is for Jeremias a further indication of a date in Paul's lifetime (cf. Rom 13:1ff and contrast Rev 13). There is no indication of state persecution as would be expected between 90 and 110. But the passages exhorting to obedience to the state are commonplace catechetical teaching, found also in 1 Pet 2:13ff, a document which (see below, pp. 157f) almost certainly emanates from 90–110, and which despite persecution continues to maintain the positive doctrine of the state. Moreover, all persecutions at this time were sporadic and local.

Jeremias maintains that gnosticism is at the same stage of development in Past as in Col, i.e. it still is a movement within the church. But need we suppose a synchronized development of gnosticism everywhere? This argument is irrelevant.

Jeremias contends that in Past the ministry (bishop-presbyters and deacons) has reached the same point of development as in Phil 1:1. As we shall see, the ministry is characteristically sub-apostolic, despite Phil 1:1.

The portrait of Timothy is not flattering. 2 Tim 2:3, 12, 22 gives the picture of a youthful, headstrong and ambitious personality. So far from arguing authenticity this points in the opposite direction. The historical Timothy was entrusted with responsible missions, and his gifts ungrudgingly recognized by Paul (1 Cor 4:17; Phil 2:20–22). The 'Timothy' of Past is clearly a personified symbol of the nascent ministry of the sub-apostolic age.

The strongest argument for authenticity, Jeremias claims, is furnished by the concrete situations and details of Past, esp. Paul's farewell, 2 Tim 4:9–21, also parts of chs. 1–3 and Tit 3:12–14. Much of 2 Tim, we shall argue, is from a genuine farewell letter of Paul, which the 'Pastor' has utilized as the basis of his own letter. On Tit 3:12ff see below, pp. 139f.

Finally, Jeremias accounts for the palpable differences of style and vocabulary by the secretary hypothesis, which we have employed for Col. This is not in principle untenable, but the non-Pauline elements are so far removed from the genuine Paul, and appear to reflect rather the outlook of the sub-apostolic age to a degree which is not the case in Col.

P. N. Harrison[1] made a brilliant attempt to rescue from Past a series of fragments, which he conceives to be genuinely

---

[1] *The Problem of the Pastoral Epistles*, 1921. Cf. now also his *Paulines and Pastorals*, 1964, for a later treatment of the same subject.

Pauline, and fits into situations in the period of Paul's life
covered by Acts and the genuine Paulines.

The passages are as follows:

Tit 3:12–15. Paul is writing from W. Macedonia in the
period between 2 Cor 10–13 and 2 Cor 1–9. There are
affinities of diction with 1 Cor 16.

2 Tim 4:13–15, 20, 21a. Written about the same time as
the Tit fragment. Paul had left his cloak etc. at Troas, and
needed them with the approach of winter, also the books
and parchments for writing Rom. There are affinities of
diction with the Tit fragment, and with 2 Cor 1–9 and Rom.

2 Tim 4:16–18a (?18b). Situation: imprisonment of
Paul at Caesarea. The 'first defence' is that at Jerusalem
(Acts 22:1ff).

2 Tim 4:9–12, 22b. Situation: at Rome, after Phil (which
Harrison places in the Roman captivity). There are
affinities of diction with the epistles of the captivity.

The last fragment is Paul's farewell letter, just before his
martyrdom at the end of the 2 years of Acts 28:30. It is more
difficult to construct, as it is the basis of 2 Tim. Harrison
includes in it: 1:16–18; 3:10f; 4:1–2a; 5b–8, 19, 21b.

It is noticeable that there are many fragments in 2 Tim, only
one in Tit and none in 1 Tim. This is one of Easton's arguments
for placing the composition of Past in that order. He employs
two other arguments for this order. (1) The church order
undergoes a development from 2 Tim through Tit to 1 Tim.
In 2 Tim 'faithful men' are to be appointed as tradition bearers
(2:2). In Tit elders are to be appointed in every place (1:5). In
1 Tim the existence of an ordered ministry of bishop, presbyters and deacons is taken for granted, and rules are established for their payment and discipline. (2) There is a pro-
gression in the treatment of heretics. In 2 Tim 2:17–20 the
heretics Hymenaeus and Philetus are still in the church. In
Tit 3:10 heretics are to be excommunicated if obdurate.
In 1 Tim 1:20 Hymenaeus and Alexander have now been
'delivered to Satan'.

There are three possible views: the traditional view of Pauline authenticity (Jeremias-Kelly), the fragment theory of Harrison, and the critical view of Easton (and many Germans) that Past are entirely deutero-Pauline. Jeremias's arguments and counter-arguments all collapse on investigation. Harrison's fragment theory is ingenious, but too complicated. Easton best accounts for the facts, except that he is inclined to overstress some of the differences between Past and Paul. His proposed order of composition is convincing, and will be accepted here. However, we should leave open the possibility that the 'Pastor' used in 2 Tim a genuine farewell letter of Paul, covering at least 2 Tim 4:6–8, 16–18. We must assume that he filled out Past with details from Acts and the genuine Paulines in order to create an appearance of Pauline authorship. He did the same to a much lesser degree in Tit and by the time of 1 Tim he felt able to stand on his own feet (Harrison would say he had exhausted the available fragments).

Date, Authorship and Provenance

The use of Acts and the Paulines points to a date later than 90.[1] The development of the ministry has reached about the same point as in Acts, but probably not the point it has reached in Ignatius. The dates proposed by Easton, 2 Tim—95, Tit—100, 1 Tim—105, are as good as any, but no more than conjectural.

Past are written by one who claims to speak with the authority of the apostle Paul, i.e. by one who understands himself to be in the apostolic succession. He has an authority which permits him to write to the leadership of local churches from outside those churches. He stands therefore between the apostles of the first age and the second century bishop, who is also a successor of the apostles, but whose authority unlike the Pastor's, is confined to a local church.

---

[1] For other affinities with Acts see C. F. D. Moule, *The Birth of the New Testament*, 1962, pp. 220f.

The churches over which the author claims authority are those of the Pauline mission in the E. Mediterranean (Crete, Ephesus, etc.).

2 *Timothy*

The situation devised by the Pastor is this: Paul is in prison in Rome (1:17), and in severe confinement (2:9). He has already had a hearing which went favourably (4:16f), but expects things to go worse next time (4:6–8). He writes to Timothy (at Ephesus?) asking him to come to Rome, bringing from Troas a cloak, parchments, etc., the latter presumably needed for his second defence. Prior to this second imprisonment Paul has been in Troas, Corinth and Miletus. It is very difficult to fit these data into Acts, even at the end of the imprisonment of Acts 28:30, because by then the 3rd missionary journey was several years past. The Pastor must assume that after release at the end of that period Paul went on a 4th missionary journey to the East. The statement in Acts 20:25 (cf. v. 38) seems to indicate that the 4th journey is pure fiction. The Pastor's desire is to allow Paul to provide for the continuity of the church after his departure. For that the narrative of Acts left no space.

The author has created the situation from a (?) genuine farewell letter of Paul plus material from Acts (2 Tim ch. 1; 2:1–13; 3:10f; ch. 4). Using this material as a skeleton framework, he has inserted two sections dealing with his real concern, 2:2, the preservation of the apostolic tradition through ministerial succession, then 2:14–3:17 (minus 3:10f), directed against the false teaching of the heretics.

Titus

The situation devised by the Pastor is this: Paul and Titus have been working at Crete. Paul left Titus behind and is now at Nicopolis (3:12), whence he writes directions to Titus for the completion of the work in Crete, before rejoining him at

Nicopolis. The situation has probably been constructed by the Pastor from Acts 20:3.[1]

The real situation is this: the Pastor follows up 2 Tim with a second, more considered attack on the heresy and a more systematized church order.

After an opening greeting, 1:1–4, he proceeds to church order, 1:5–9. In vv. 10–16 he attacks the heresy, and in the same anti-heretical context he sets forth teaching on Christian ethics (2:1–3:7). Then in 3:8–11 he returns to the attack on the heresy. 3:12–15 forms the epistolary conclusion.

1 *Timothy*

The situation devised by the Pastor: Paul and Timothy have been working together at Ephesus. Paul has left for Macedonia. He writes 1 Tim to give interim instructions to Timothy prior to his return to Ephesus (3:14; 4:13). The situation is a variant of that devised in Tit. It appears to be constructed from the data of Acts 19 and 20, but since the data do not entirely correspond, the Pastor evidently intends to imply a 4th missionary journey.

This letter contains the Pastor's most developed attack on the heresy, and his most developed church order. The structure is very neat. The opening greeting, 1:1f is followed by 1:3–20, an attack on the false doctrine of the heretics; chs. 2–3, church order, part I; 4:1–11, an attack on the ethics of the heretics; 4:12–6:19, church order, part II, the duties of 'Timothy'. Epistolary conclusion: 6:20f.

The Heresy combated by the Pastorals (2 Tim 2:14–3:17; Tit 1:10–16; 2 Tim 1:3–20; 4:1–11)

The heresy involved genealogical speculations (1 Tim 1:4; Tit 3:9). Two explanations of this have been offered: (1) rabbinical fables and legends about the OT genealogies; (2) gnostic-mythological cosmic heirarchies (like the second-

---

[1] So Dibelius-Conzelmann *ad loc.*

century systems of the Valentinians, etc.). Other data point clearly in a gnostic direction, rather than to rabbinic concerns. Hymenaeus and Philetus, who have been shipwrecked on the matter of faith, assert that 'the resurrection', i.e. of believers, has already taken place (2 Tim 2:18). Here is an over-realized eschatology, which ignores the proleptic character of present participation in the eschatological salvation. It extracts the kerygma from its original context in Jewish apocalyptic[1] and transposes it into an alien framework such as we have already observed in the gnosticism of the Corinthian community (see above, pp. 43–45). Tit 1:16 says, 'they say they *know* God', a typical gnostic claim (cf. 1 Cor 8:1ff, etc.; it will also recur in 1 Jn). In 1 Tim 6:20 there is a warning against 'empty talk and the antitheses of *knowledge*, falsely so-called'.

The false doctrine has typically gnostic ethical consequences (cf. Gal, 1 Cor, Phil, Col). 'They say they know God, but deny it by their works' (Tit 1:16). On the one hand there is libertinism, Tit 1:10ff. On the other hand in 1 Tim 4:3 there is a reference to various kinds of asceticism: prohibition of marriage, abstinence from certain kinds of foods. Both libertinism and asceticism arise from a false dualism. Note the Pastor's stress on the doctrine of creation, 4:4f in opposition to the dualism.

There are certain Jewish elements in the false teaching. In Tit 1:10 the Pastor denounces 'especially those of the circumcision party'. In Tit 1:14f 'Titus' has to warn against 'Jewish fables', and in Tit 3:9 is enjoined to 'avoid foolish questionings and strife about the law'. In 2 Tim 3:15–17 the heretics misuse the OT scriptures. In view of the gnostic elements and false dualism which appear elsewhere, it would be wrong to conclude from these passages that the Pastor's

---

[1] In that context the resurrection of Jesus is the first and determinative occurrence of entrance into the life of the age to come. The resurrection of Christians, to whatever degree it is anticipated in baptism (Rom 6: 3f; Col 3:1), still awaits consummation (1 Thess 4: 13ff; 1 Cor 15:12ff; Phil 3:21).

opponents were Judaizers such as Paul had had to contend with in Antioch and at the Jerusalem council. Clearly, it is some kind of syncretism, which in addition to gnostic features included Jewish elements, especially circumcision as in Galatia.

There are hints that in conformity with their dualism false teachers held a docetic Christology. The Past stress the incarnation in such a way as to suggest that the heretics denied the true humanity of Jesus (2 Tim 2:8; 1 Tim 3:16).

It can hardly be said that the Pastor's attempt to combat this heresy is creative (contrast Paul in Gal, 1 and 2 Cor, where the Apostle combats his opponents by taking the argument to the heart of the kerygma of the cross). The Pastor's method, mainly, is to reassert the apostolic tradition, and to tighten up the ministerial organization in order to guard that tradition.

The Ministry

The relevant passages are:

2 Tim 1:6, which refers to 'Timothy's' ordination by the laying on of the apostles' hands.

2 Tim 2:1ff, where the Pastor instructs Timothy to hand over the tradition which he has received from Paul to 'faithful men' who will be able to teach 'others' also. Here are four links in the apostolic succession: Paul—'Timothy'—'faithful men'—'others'.

2 Tim 2:15. The function of Timothy is not only to guard the 'word of truth' but to 'divide it'—i.e. apply it to the changed situation of the sub-apostolic age.

2 Tim 2:25. 'Timothy' is responsible for the discipline of those who oppose, i.e. the heretics.

Tit 1:5. 'Titus' is instructed to appoint 'elders' in every city, and qualifications are laid down for these elders. In listing the qualifications, the Pastor shifts from elders in the plural to 'bishop' ($\epsilon\pi\iota\sigma\kappa\sigma\pi\varsigma$) in the singular (v. 7). The same shift will be found in 1 Tim (on this see below).

1 Tim gives the most complete ministerial order.

1 Tim 3:1–8, the Pastor lays down the qualifications for the bishop (note the singular again). Stress is laid on the

bishop's functions as the community's representative to the outside world. Then, qualifications for the deacons are listed, with particular stress on their financial integrity, suggesting that it was their function to distribute charitable relief. For presbyters see 5:1, 2, 17, 19.

The interpretation of this evidence is not easy. There is first the Pastor himself, speaking in the name of Paul. The Pastor's own position (see above, pp. 138f) is by implication that of an intermediate functionary between the apostolate (now died out) and the local ministries. Since 'Timothy' and 'Titus' are not the historical personages named, but symbolic figures, we may assume that it is the Pastor himself carrying out the functions specified for them, i.e. it is *he* who is organizing the local ministries. And in doing so he understands himself to be carrying out in the changed conditions of the sub-apostolic age the intentions of the Apostle himself. We may (following Bp. Gore, who however thought the Past authentic, and applied the description to the historical Timothy and Titus) call the Pastor an 'apostolic man'. It is men of this type who write the literature of the sub-apostolic age. They are concerned with the problem of how to be apostolic now that the apostles are removed from the scene (cf. the authors of Heb, 1 Pet, James, Jude, 1, 2, 3 Jn).

In the local churches the spontaneous charismatic ministries of the Pauline churches are disappearing. In their place there is being established an institutionalized ministry, receiving its charisma through the laying on of hands with prayer. This ministry consists of 'elders' and 'deacons'. The term 'elder' is derived from the Jewish synagogue, and first entered the Christian church at Jerusalem (Acts 11:30 and ch. 15). There were no presbyters in the Pauline churches during the Apostle's lifetime. The thing, though not the name, is present in 2 Tim. The name first occurs in Tit. But it is being coalesced with the Pauline title *episcopos* (Phil 1:1, where the term probably refers not to an institutionalized ministry, but to individuals who have assumed the charismatic function of *episcope*, 'oversight.) At first (Acts 20:17, 28) the two titles

were used synonymously, but already in Tit and 2 Tim one
episcopos appears to be emerging out of the body of the *presbyteroi*. By the time of Ignatius the term *episcopos* has become
confined to the president of the presbyteroi. Thus Past represent
a situation midway between Acts and Ignatius. In 1 Clem 44 a
similar distinction is beginning to emerge. But whereas in Past
the *episcopos* is the guardian of the apostolic tradition, in
1 Clem his functions are liturgical. Ignatius again sees the
bishop in mystical terms as the centre of the church's unity.
Organizationally, though not theologically, Ignatius marks the
culmination of the sub-apostolic development. The claim of
Past and 1 Clem 44 that this development had direct apostolic
sanction is of course unhistorical. But in a profound theological sense it is true: the apostolic witness could only be
preserved after the apostles were gone by the crystallization of
the apostolic tradition and by the emergence of accredited
persons to guard it.

It is thus a distinct gain, both exegetically and dogmatically,
that criticism has discovered the sub-apostolic character of
the Past. Conservative defenders of their Pauline authenticity
do a disservice to the understanding of 'early catholicism' as
the church's normative response to the apostolic age.

(b) The Epistle to the Hebrews

Heb is not properly speaking an 'epistle': it is not by Paul,
and it was not written to the 'Hebrews'.

Date

The *terminus ad quem* is 96, for parts of Heb are quoted
verbatim in 1 Clem 36. The older conservative view, revived
in critical scholarship by W. Manson[1] and T. W. Manson,[2]
was that Heb assumes that the priesthood and Jewish sacrifices
are still functioning in the temple and that therefore the date

[1] W. Manson, *The Epistle to the Hebrews*, 1951.
[2] T. W. Manson, *Studies in the Gospels and Acts*, pp. 242–58.

must be prior to 70. This is an exegetical fallacy. Heb is not talking about the third temple at Jerusalem, but about the tabernacle in the wilderness during the post-exodus wanderings. His argument is purely scriptural (see below).

Heb 10:32f refers to a severe persecution 'in the former days' in terms recalling ($\theta\epsilon\alpha\tau\rho\iota\zeta\delta\mu\epsilon\nu\omega\iota$, 'made a gazing stock') the Neronian persecution in Rome, A.D. 64. This identification cannot be proved but it would make a date *c*. 85 suitable.

Heb 2:3 indicates that both the author and his addressees belong to the sub-apostolic age. He mentions three links in a chain of succession: (1) Jesus; (2) the original eyewitnesses; (3) the author and his readers.

Like the Pastor in Past, the author writes with a quasi-apostolic authority enabling him to address his readers over the heads of its local leaders (Heb 13:17).

Authorship

Its sub-apostolic situation (above) throws doubt on the Pauline authorship (and Paul did not depend for his faith upon the original eyewitnesses, Gal 1). The linguistic phenomena and theological content substantiates these doubts. Also, in the early church its Pauline authorship was long contested. True, the Eastern church as a whole accepted it as Pauline, but with two notable exceptions: Clement of Alexandria (†*c*. 215) and Origen (†*c*. 254). Trained as they were in the Alexandrian school of literary criticism, they were as conscious as any modern scholar of its non-Pauline character. Clement suggested Luke as the author, while Origen thought it might have been by Clement of Rome.

In the west the Pauline authorship of Heb was consistently questioned, not on scholarly grounds, but because of its unpalatable theological content: Heb 6:4ff, cf. 10:26f, denies the possibility of a second repentance. These rigoristic passages provided ammunition for the later Novatianists and Donatists against the Catholic position that apostates in persecutions should be permitted to work their passage home. The Western church, without the scholarly scruples of the Alexandrians, cut short the argument by denying Pauline authorship. But it must have had some traditional ground for doing so, which suggests that Heb probably had never been accepted in the west as Pauline (cf. Tertullian). The position of Heb in the canon, as an appendix to the Pauline corpus after Philem, instead of in a position where its length would entitle it to be placed (e.g. after 2 Cor) still reflects these earlier doubts.

The Alexandrian objections still hold good. Attempts have been made to ascribe Heb to some other figure of the apostolic age (Tertullian suggested Barnabas, Luther and recent British scholars since T. W. Manson have favoured Apollos).[1] But Origen spoke the last word on the subject, when, despite his suggestion that is written by Clement of Rome, he concluded, 'Who wrote it, God knows'.

Literary Character

There is no opening address, as in normal epistolary style. Heb plunges *in medias res* (1:1). But there *is* an epistolary conclusion, 13:23–25, which appears to associate the letter with the Pauline circle (Timothy). This conclusion could be explained in four ways: (1) it is genuine and shows that the author belonged to the Pauline circle (T. W. Manson, etc.); (2) it is added by the author like the fragments in Past to create the impression of Pauline authorship; (3) it was added later by another hand to dress up the document as a Pauline letter; (4) the ending is genuine, but is not intended to claim Pauline authorship: the writer is connected with the Pauline circle, and Timothy is still alive c. 85. We prefer the last of these views.

There are other features which suggest that Heb was not originally a letter. In 13:22 the document styles itself as 'a

---

[1] Cf, esp. Montefiore, pp. 23–7. This conjecture would fit the description of Apollos in Acts as 'mighty in the scriptures', and Heb's allegorical exegesis of the OT. The element of truth in this plausible suggestion is that it was probably written by an early Alexandrian Christian. The major objection is the sub-apostolic character of Heb.

word of exhortation' (τοῦ λόγου τῆς παρακλήσεως). *Paraklesis*
is a destinctive form of preaching,[1] viz., pastoral preaching to
an established community. Like a preacher, the author of Heb
quotes a text at length, then expounds it verse by verse (e.g.
Ps 95:7–11 in 3:7ff). He frequently refers to himself as 'speaking' rather than as writing (2:5; 8:1; 9:5). The final doxology
(13:20f) would be a fitting conclusion to a sermon.

The Addressees and the Occasion

The traditional view that Heb was addressed to Jewish
Christians in danger of relapsing into temple worship rests on
several fallacies: (1) the title, 'To the Hebrews' is of course not
original, but a later conjecture; (2) it assumes that temple
worship was a live option for first-century Jews, whereas only
the synagogue was; (3) it assumes that the writer is talking
about the temple, and not the tabernacle of the wilderness,
and that the temple is therefore still standing; (4) it mis-
construes the situation of the addressees (see below); (5) it
ignores the syncretistic elements in their beliefs and practices
(see below).

There is much to be said for the view[2] that the addressees
were not a whole congregation, but a group within it. In 13:24
the author bids them 'greet all your leaders *and all the saints*'.
From 10:25 it is evident that they are absenting themselves
from the Christian assembly. In 5:12ff he reproaches them for
having stagnated instead of becoming qualified to serve as
teachers.

Heb 13:24 gives some hint as to their geographical location:
'those who *come from Italy* send you greetings'. The word
from (ἀπό) clearly indicates (despite the hesitations of Bruce
and others) that the people who send their greetings are *away
from* Italy, not there at the moment. This suggests that the
addressees were themselves resident in Italy. Some confirmation of this may be obtained from the possible reference to the

[1] R. H. Fuller, *What is Liturgical Preaching?*, p. 22.
[2] A. A. Nairne, *The Epistle of Priesthood*, 1915, pp. 10ff.

Neronian persecution in 10:33 and from the fact that Heb
is first quoted in 1 Clem, which was written from Rome in
96.

The clue to the purpose of Heb is to be found in the hortatory
parts of the letter. The addressees have been Christians for a
long time and are growing weary (2:1–4; 3:12ff; 5:11–6:8;
10:35f; 12:12ff). Their situation is aggravated not by violent
persecution but by constant petty pinpricks (10:32ff; 12:3ff).
Significantly the author draws a parallel between his addressees and Israel in the wilderness. It is a constant feature of the
OT wilderness story that Israel 'murmured'. Between the
exodus and the entry to the promised land Israel exists
'between the times' precisely like the Christian church
between the first and second comings of Christ (9:28). Meanwhile, as Israel neglected its salvation, and did not enter into
the rest which God promised, so these Christians are in danger
of forgetting the eschatological salvation in which they
proleptically participate through their baptism.

There is further indication that the addressees were not
simply lapsing *away* from Christianity but *into* certain questionable practices: 'Do not be led away by diverse and strange
teachings; for it is well that the heart be strengthened by
grace, not by foods' (13:9). The following verse seems to hint
that these practices had some Judaistic connection for it goes
on to contrast the Christian altar at which the Christian
sacrifice is offered (v. 15) with the tabernacle of the Levitical
cultus. The mention of 'foods' accords ill with the traditional
interpretation that the addressees were lapsing into temple
worship. It suggests rather some kind of syncretism in which
dietary asceticism was combined with elements from the
Jewish cultus[1] (cf. 1 Tim 1:6f; Tit 1:13ff; Col 2:16, 21ff). But
there is not enough evidence to warrant the suggestion (so
E. Käsemann, *Das wandernde Gottesvolk*, 1957) that their
syncreticism were specifically gnostic, as in 1 Cor and Past.

[1] G. Bornkamm, 'Das Taufbekenntnis im Hebräerbrief', 1942,
reprinted in *Studien zu Antike und Urchristentum*, 1959, pp. 188–203,
esp. p. 195.

In reply, the author takes his start by recalling the addressees to their baptismal confession (ὁμολογία)[1] 3:1; 4:14; 10:23; of Jesus as the 'Son of God' (Heb 1:1–4, 5ff; 5:5). But instead of merely repeating these 'first principles' (5:12) and 'elementary doctrines' (6:1) the author moves on to 'solid food' (5:12). This advanced teaching is an exposition of Christ as high priest, i.e. the new function upon which as Son of God he enters at his exaltation. Following the tradition, Heb connects Ps 2:7 with Ps 110:1 but then connects these passages with Ps 110:4, a verse which had not previously been applied to Christ, but which was suggested by the author's Alexandrian environment (see below). Having announced this doctrine in 4:14, 5:10, and having prepared the ground for it in ch. 7, he expounds it by a series of comparisons and contrasts with the Levitical high priesthood in 8:1–10:18. This doctrine is not expounded for its own sake, but in order to establish the finality of the Christian redemption and to reinforce the exhortation against backsliding.

The Author's Religious and Intellectual Milieu

The affinities of the author with the Alexandrian Hellenistic Judaism of Philo have frequently been noted. Both use the LXX. There is a considerable amount of Philonic language in Heb (e.g. cf. the wisdom Christology of 1:3 with Philo's language about the Logos, and the passage about the Word of God in 4:12f). In Philo also the Logos is high priest. Even more reminiscent of Philo is the language Heb uses about the two tabernacles, the earthly and heavenly (8:5f; 9:1–5; 11, 23).

But there is an important difference. Philo uses this language cosmologically (all earthly entities have their heavenly counterparts). Heb applies it within an apocalyptic and redemptive-historical framework, and restricts it to earthly tabernacle and the redemptive work of Christ. There is some confusion as to whether the OT cultus points *forward* to the Christ event in history, or *upward* to Christ's work in

---

[1] G. Bornkamm, *op. cit.* This important essay is unnoticed by F. F. Bruce and H. W. Montefiore in their recent commentaries.

heaven. The same kind of confusion between the two ages and the two worlds is found in apocalyptic. The milieu of the author is therefore Alexandrian Hellenistic Judaism modified by early Christian redemptive history and its apocalyptic setting.[1]

Summary of Contents

Chs. 1–4 form an introduction, where the author sets out his starting-point in the baptismal confession of Christ's sonship, and exhorts his addressees to hold fast to this confession. Chs. 5–6 form a preparation for the central argument. Advancing from a Christology in terms of Sonship to one of high priesthood, the author enunciates his thesis: 'Thou art a priest forever, after the order of Melchizedek'. This thesis is elaborated by a series of comparisons and contrasts with the Levitical high priesthood in 7:1–10:18. 10:19–13:21 is the concluding exhortation (note ch. 11, the roll call of the OT heroes of faith), and 13:22-end the epistolary conclusion.

The Importance of Hebrews

Heb makes the chief NT contribution to that part of Christology which concerns the heavenly work of Christ between his exaltation and the parousia, viz., as a priestly work in which his once-for-all sacrifice is the ground of his continued intercession and appearance before God for the faithful on earth (7:25; 9:24).

As a writing of the sub-apostolic age, it testifies to the growth of liturgy as one of the institutional structures which perpetuate the apostolic witness after the apostles have died (13:10, 15,[2] see Bornkamm, *op. cit.*, pp. 193–200).

It is probably the earliest literary production of Christianity at Alexandria.

---

[1] The recognition of this combination is the contribution of E. Käsemann, *op. cit.* We prefer however to speak of Alexandrian Hellenistic Judaism rather than 'gnosticism'.

[2] The eucharistic reference of these passages have frequently been denied by exegetes. The recognition of the post-Pauline, sub-apostolic dating of Heb should free us to recognize this element of 'early catholicism' in Heb.

V.—THE CATHOLIC EPISTLES

THERE are seven non-Pauline letters in the NT—Jas; 1, 2 Pet; 1, 2, 3 Jn; and Jude—which go by the name of the 'Catholic Epistles'. 'Catholic' is here used in the sense of universal, general, i.e. not written to by a specific church, but presumably to the church as a whole.

The title 'catholic' is not altogether accurate. 2 Jn was almost certainly written to a particular church, and 3 Jn to an individual member of a particular church. Even 1 Pet does not altogether suit the description, for it was written to a regional group of churches. Eusebius, *H.E.* II 24, is the first witness to *seven* Catholic Epistles. Earlier writers had given the title to one or more of these letters. But 'Catholic' is the traditional title.

Yet despite its inaccuracy, the title does justice to a common element in all of these letters. Compared with the Paulines, they are far less specific or concrete. They tend to deal with general themes in a general way. As will be argued, they are all pseudonymous products of the sub-apostolic age.

The doubts about the apostolic authorship of these writings are not only modern and critical, but were shared to a considerable degree by the early church. Some of these writings long hovered on the fringe of the canon.

(a) JAMES

The external attestation of Jas is late and weak. Origen is the first Church Father to recognize it, but admits that it is not generally recognized (*Comm. on John* 19, 23). Eusebius classes it among the 'antilegomena' or controverted writings.

The writer claims to be James ('Jakobos'). He describes himself simply as 'a servant of God and of the Lord Jesus Christ'. There are several Jameses in the NT. Obviously, this is not

F

James bar Zebedee, for he was martyred in 44. Traditionally, the author is identified with James, the brother of the Lord (Mk 6:3 par.; Acts 12:17; 15:13; 21:18; 1 Cor 15:7; Gal 1:19; 2:9, 12). This James suffered martyrdom in 62 (Eusebius, *H.E.* II 18, from Hegesippus). If Jas is by this James, its date must be prior to 62. But there are reasons for thinking it must have been written much later, and therefore could not have been the work of James the brother of the Lord (see below). Either it is by some unknown James, or the name James has been deliberately adopted to claim apostolic authorship.

The epistle is addressed to 'the twelve tribes of the dispersion'. This is a theological designation of the Christian church, the New Israel, existing in the midst of the world as a dispersion (cf. 1 Pet 1:1).

Significantly, the writer, alone of NT authors, refers to the local Christian congregation as a 'synagogue' (2:2). This indicates pretty certainly that he is a Jewish Christian, writing for a Jewish Christian community. Thus far, everything would fit the traditional authorship. But James as he appears both in Paul and in Acts was a protagonist of the Jewish *ceremonial* law. Even if he was not an out and out circumcisionist (he accepted the 'gentlemen's agreement' at the apostolic conference, Gal 2:9), his major concern was with the maintenance of the Jewish food laws in mixed communities (Gal 2:12; cf. Acts 21:21). Jas, on the other hand, is concerned with practical morality.

There is very little kerygmatic or dogmatic concern in Jas. Its ethical teaching is derived from various sources. There are parallels with the Q and the special Mt material. There are further parallels with the ethical parts of the Pauline and deutero-Pauline letters and with 1 Pet. More remotely, there are parallels with Hellenistic Jewish ethical teaching, which (cf. the later wisdom literature) was itself already coloured by Stoicism, as is the teaching of Jas. All told, it would seem that this epistle draws upon a great deal of the pattern of catechetical teaching which was the common stock of the Hellenistic congregations, both Jewish and Gentile.

A suggestion was made in 1930 by A. Meyer.[1] He accounts for the apparent disorder of the ethical injunctions by the theory that Jas consists of twelve exhortations, each based on the name of one of the twelve patriarchs. This theory can be tied in with another theory, that of F. Spitta, who maintained[2] that Jas is a Christianized version of an originally Jewish document. This theory in turn may explain the paucity of references to specifically Christian doctrines.

W. Marxsen[3] has carried these theories a stage further. He suggests that in the original Jewish document the name 'Jakobos' stood for the patriarch Jacob. The Christian editor of the document let 'James' stand, thus producing (whether consciously or not) a claim that it was by James the brother of Lord. The allusion to the twelve tribes will similarly have been re-interpreted in a Christian sense.

The other major problem, which is also connected with the date of Jas, is its relation to Paul. Jas 2:14-26 treats the great Pauline themes of justification, faith and works in a way entirely opposed to Paul's treatment of them in Gal 3 and Rom 4. Jas also uses Abraham as Paul does, but to prove a very different position, and actually quotes Paul's key text in 2:23 (Gen 15:6; cf. Gal 3:6; Rom 4:3). It is hard to believe that there is no relationship between Paul and Jas. But what is that relationship? Did James (as the traditionalists would argue— and there are modern critical defenders of this tradition[4]) first put forward his position, to be countered by Paul in Gal and Rom? Was Paul first, and is James deliberately combating him? Or is the author of Jas a sub-apostolic writer faced with an ultra-Paulinism which was a misunderstanding of the Apostle's teaching?

[1] *Das Rätsel des Jakobusbriefes*, 1930. So far as I am aware, only A. Farrer, among English-speaking scholars (*A Study in St Mark*, p. 320) has noted this work with approval.

[2] F. Spitta, 'Der Brief des Jakobus', in *Zur Geschichte und Litteratur des Urchristentums*, II, 1896, pp. 1ff.

[3] *Einleitung*, p. 198.

[4] R. G. Heard, *Introduction*, 1950, pp. 164–6; G. Kittel, 'Der geschichtliche Ort des Jakobusbriefes', in *ZNW* 41, (1942), pp. 71–105.

Everything points to the third of these solutions. Consider the meaning of 'faith' in Jas. 'You believe that God is one' (2:18). 'Faith' here has the characteristic sub-apostolic sense, i.e. propositional faith. 'Faith' here is the πίστις of Past carried to the extreme of a moribund orthodoxy divorced from ethical concern. In its solution Jas comes pretty close to contradicting Paul: 'A man is justified by works, and not by faith alone' (contrast Rom 3:28, where Luther by inserting 'alone' made the apparent contradiction complete). In the last resort, however, Paul and James are really not in conflict. Paul would agree that good works are the necessary fruit of justification. James by implication ('not by faith alone') also makes faith instrumental in justification. But they use the same key words differently. Paul's doctrine of justification sprang from his realized (but not over-realized) eschatology. In justification we are proleptically acquitted as we shall be finally acquitted at the parousia, an acquittal which releases the dynamic creative of Christian obedience. For James, justification is purely future-eschatological, our acquittal at the day of judgment. (For James's futuristic eschatology cf. 5:7.)

We must therefore locate Jas in Hellenistic Jewish Christianity and in the sub-apostolic age. It is unlikely that Jas is directly dependent on Gal or Rom, otherwise he would be exposed to the charge of deliberate caricature. Thus Jas probably antedates the publication of the Pauline corpus (see below, p. 192). Jas is combating a corrupt Paulinism as a practical phenomenon. A date towards the end of the 1st cent. would be in order.

Contents

Following A. Meyer, we divide Jas into twelve exhortations without, however, following his specific connections with the 12 patriarchs.

The Importance of Jas

It is important that Jas is in the NT canon. It serves as an important corrective to the ever-present danger of misinterpreting Paul in an antinomian sense. Luther's famous devaluation of Jas as a 'right strawy epistle' was legitimate in so far as Jas is very little informed by kerygma. But Jas has a legitimate concern for a right response to the kerygma which, by its place in the Canon, if not in the author's own understanding, it presumes.

In the last resort, the relation of Jas to the kerygma is analogous to that of the Q logia. By preserving the teachings of Jesus Q implicitly affirms the death and resurrection of Jesus (see below). Jas certainly calls Jesus Lord (1:1; 2:1) and affirms his parousia (5:7, 9). Jesus' words have authority because of his vindication at the resurrection, a vindication which will be made public at the parousia.

(b) 1 PETER

1 Pet claims (1:1) to be written by 'Peter, an apostle of Jesus Christ'. The author also says (5:1) that he was 'an eyewitness of the sufferings of Christ and a partaker of the glory that is to be revealed'. It is not quite certain how this statement is intended. It could mean that the author is claiming to have been present

at the passion. But in the Gospels (Mk 14:72 par.) Peter dis-
appears from the passion narrative after his denial. If 1 Pet is
pseudonymous it could refer to Peter's martyrdom in Rome.

The claim to Petrine authorship is modified in 5:12, which
states that the letter was written 'by Silvanus, a faithful
brother'. Here is the secretary hypothesis explicitly alleged.
Silvanus is probably intended to be Paul's companion, and co-
author of the Thessalonian letters (1 Thess 1:1; 2 Thess 1:1;
cf. 'Silas', Acts 15:22).

From 5:13 it would appear that 1 Pet was written from
'Babylon'. Sometimes this has been taken literally.[1] But Babylon is frequently used as a cryptogram for Rome in contemporary writings, e.g. Rev 14:8, etc.; 2 Esdras 3:1ff, etc. Also,
there is no other evidence whatever for connecting Peter with
Babylon, whereas there is plenty of evidence for his connection
with Rome from 1 Clem 5 (probably) on.

Mark is mentioned in 5:13 as 'my son'. This ties in with the
second century tradition that Mark was Peter's interpreter and
compiled his gospel at Rome from Peter's reminiscences (see
above, p. 104).

It appears that a case is being built up in 1 Pet for its having
been written at Rome with Peter's *imprimatur*. If this claim is
true, a date between Paul's arrival at Rome and Peter's
martyrdom is required, i.e. a date between 57 and 64. Can this
claim be substantiated?

External Testimony

The external testimony is quite good. In the second century
there was a strong tradition that 1 Pet was a genuine letter of
Peter. Polycarp (†156) quotes from it several times (Pol, Phil
1:3; 2:1; 8:1; 10:2). But probably the oldest reference to 1 Pet is
2 Pet 3:1, 'This is the second letter that I have written to you',
and 2 Pet is to be dated *c.* 125 (see below, p. 162). By the time
of Irenaeus (*c.* 180) the tradition is firmly established.

---

[1] R. G. Heard, *Introduction*, p. 171. On the subject see esp. O.
Cullmann, *Peter*, 1953, pp. 83–6.

Indirect Internal Evidence

It is when we look at the indirect implications of the letter
that difficulties begin to arise. 1 Pet contains some of the best
Gk in the NT. It has often been asked whether such Gk is
credible for a Galilean fisherman. Also, 1 Pet uses the LXX.
These two points could be accounted for by the secretary
hypothesis (Silvanus).

1 Pet is allegedly full of Paulinisms (e.g. 1:14/Rom 12:2
3:9/Rom 12:17; 4:10f/Rom 12:6ff). It has been said that but for
the name 'Peter' in the opening address, 1 Pet would have been
regarded as a deutero-Pauline letter. In fact, it is much more
Pauline than the Past. Again, the Paulinisms could be attributed to Silvanus.

More serious is the objection that Peter by the terms of the
'gentleman's agreement' (Gal 2:9) headed the mission to the
Jews. What was he doing, writing to churches in the Pauline
area (1:1)? Did Peter take over Paul's missionary area after
Paul's death? All these questions are speculative.

Perhaps most pertinent question is the persecution envisaged in 1 Pet. From 4:12 onwards that persecution is actual,
and impending for the church in Asia Minor. It is a deliberate
policy of the state directed against 'Christians' as such (4:14,
16). We know of Nero's persecution in Rome in 64, but for Asia
Minor only later, probably in the reign of Domitian (81–96)
(cf. Rev), and certainly under Trajan (98–117) in Bithynia
(Pliny the Younger, Ep X, 96). A close correspondence has
been detected between Pliny's description of his experiences
and 1 Pet 4:12–16.[1]

Integrity of 1 Peter

The situation with regard to persecution differs from 4:12
on, compared with the first part of the letter. In the first part

---

[1] F. W. Beare, *The First Epistle of Peter*, 1947, p. 14. This book
provides the best modern arguments for dating 1 Pet *c.* 112, the year of
Pliny's letter to Trajan.

(1:6; 3:13–17) it is hypothetical and contingent, and appears to
result from the petty pinpricks from pagan neighbours (4:4). It
is local, sporadic and unofficial—the sort of thing that
Christians had to encounter any time from the beginnings of
the Christian mission down the reign of Domitian. After 4:12 it
is an impending certainty, a new departure of policy, 'something strange' and due to the very fact of their being Christian.
It is also very severe (4:18). The use of Babylon as a cryptogram points likewise to a period of official state persecution.
Clearly a different situation is envisaged from 4:12 onwards.
Those who maintain the integrity of the letter would minimize
the difference or argue that fresh news came in. But is that type
of persecution conceivable for Asia Minor prior to 90–95?

Another striking feature of 1 Pet 1:3–4:11 is its wealth of
baptismal allusions (1:3, 18, 22f; 2:2, 10, 21; 3:21).[1] There are
further allusions to the church as a liturgical community into
which Christians are admitted through baptism (2:5, 9). Also
the author draws upon a traditional pattern of catechetical
teaching[2] (1:13; 2:1, 11f, 13–17) and the household code (cf.
Col, Eph, and Past). These features should not be regarded as
Paulinisms, although the pattern appears in the Pauline
letters. But the household codes become more common in sub-
apostolic writings (Eph, Past). The best explanation of 1 Pet is
that it was a baptismal homily (1:3–4:11) adapted as an
encyclical letter to the churches of Asia Minor by the addition
of 1:1–3; 4:12–5:14 at a time when state persecution was impending (i.e. in the reign either of Domitian or of Trajan). In
view of the deutero-Pauline character of the letter, it is surprising that it claims Petrine authorship. But this claim clearly
has some connection with the development of the tradition of
the connection between Mk and Peter (cf. the Papias fragment)
and of the tradition of Peter as the founder of the church in
Rome. It also reflects the later rejudaization of Paulinism,

---

[1] F. L. Cross has argued that 1 Pet is a baptismal *liturgy*, intended
for use as such on Easter even. This is probably going too far. But
there are certainly many baptismal allusions, and also liturgical fragments in 1 Pet 1:3–4:11. It is more like a baptismal homily.
[2] Cf. P. Carrington, *op. cit.*, pp. 31ff.

manifested in the moralism and institutionalization of the deutero-Pauline writings.

The Importance of 1 Peter

Like Heb, 1 Pet is an important document of early catholicism showing the crystallization of liturgy in the early subapostolic age as one of the institutions through which the apostolic tradition was perpetuated after the death of the apostles.

Summary of Contents

1:1f. Epistolary opening.

Part I 1:3–4:11 (Baptismal Homily)

1:3–12. First doctrinal section

> 1:3–5. Thanksgiving for resurrection of Christ and for new life through baptism.
>
> 1:6–9. Christian joy in time of trial.
>
> 1:10–12. Testimony of OT to the universality of the church, now being realized through missionary expansion.

1:13–2:3. First exhortation.

> 1:13–16. Holiness of Church corresponding to:
>
> 1:17–21. Holiness of Christ as paschal lamb.
>
> 1:22–25. New birth leading to agape in the Christian community.
>
> 2:1–3. Renunciation of evil (in baptism) and perseverence in the life of grace.

2:4–10. Second doctrinal section.

> 2:4f. The Church as the true temple.
>
> 2:6–8. The Church's relation to Christ.
>
> 2:9f. The Church as the New Israel.

2:11–3:12. Second exhortation (embodying household code).

2:11f. Importance of good behaviour towards the outside world.

2:13–17. Obedience to the state.

2:18–25. Duty of Christian slaves to follow Christ as the Servant of Yahweh.

3:1–6. Duty of wives.

3:7. Duty of husbands.

3:8–12. Summary of Christian ethics with citation from Ps 34.

3:13–22. Third doctrinal section.

Cosmic significance of death and resurrection of Christ as victory over the evil powers and typological fulfilment of Noah's flood.

4:1–11. Third exhortation.

4:1–6. Avoidance of pagan vices.

4:7–11. Agape in the life of the church, with the last judgment as the sanction for Christian behaviour.

Part II. The impending persecution.

4:12–19. Reward of persecution: joy now through the Spirit and vindication by Christ at the parousia.

5:1–5. Closing injunctions.

5:12–14. Epistolary conclusion.

(*c*) JUDE

Jude is treated before 2 Pet since the latter incorporates Jude (see below) so that Jude must be the earlier document.

Literary Character

Jude is really a tract. The epistolary beginning and conclusion are merely a conventional device. It has an apocalyptic character, but is not exactly an apocalypse like Rev.

Circumstances and Purpose

Jude is directed against false teachers, apparently gnostics of the libertinist variety (vv. 8, 12f, 16, 18, 23). They hold a dualism which denies the importance of the flesh as God's creation, and deduces as a consequence that deeds done in the flesh are morally indifferent. To call them gnostics appears justified from the term ψυχικοί (RSV 'worldy') (v. 19). This was one of three gnostic categories: 'pneumatic', 'psychic' and 'sarkic'. The concept of gnosis, however, does not figure in the discussion.

Jude's method of dealing with the false teaching is the least creative in the NT. He does not argue with them on fundamental kerygmatic principles, like Paul, or provide a constructive creative restatement of kerygma in the gnostics' own language as does 1 Jn. Like Past, Jude does show a little concern to maintain the apostolic tradition (vv. 3, 17, 20), but none about a ministerial organization as a means to perpetuate it. For the most part, he delivers a long tirade against the false teachers and their morality, descending to name-calling (vv. 12f, 16) and threatening them with dire examples of OT and pseudepigraphal punishments (vv. 6f, 9, 11) and eschatological punishment foretold in Enoch (14f).

Authorship

The author calls himself 'Jude, a slave of Jesus Christ and the brother of James'. Presumably the James intended is the Lord's brother (cf. Mk 6:3), and reputed author of Jas, with which the writer wishes to associate himself (cf. Jas 3:15, which Jude may have thought was a reference to the type of gnosticism with which he himself was contending). Verse 17 seems to put it beyond all doubt that Jude is post-apostolic: 'Remember the words which were *formerly* spoken by the apostles . . .'. So too does the reference to the 'faith once delivered to the saints' (v. 3). The author stands at some remove from the apostolic age.

The type of gnosticism envisaged (libertinism) is hardly conceivable in a Palestinian milieu, such as would be expected for the historical Jude. The familiarity with pseudepigrapha suggests a Hellenistic Jewish Christian environment.

External Testimony

Church tradition on Jude is not so weak as one might expect. 2 Pet is the first evidence for its acceptance. Clement of Alexandria wrote a commentary on it. Tertullian mentions it and the Muratorian Canon accepts it as canonical. Origen, however, is doubtful about it and Eusebius includes it among the 'antilegomena'. The Syrian church has never accepted it.

Date

Jude is later than Jas (see above) but earlier than 2 Pet. The quotation from Enoch does not help in dating. A date between 100 and 125 is probable, but no further certainty is attainable.

(d) 2 PETER

Direct Internal Testimony

2 Pet makes a strong and sustained claim to be by the apostle Peter. In the opening address the Aramaic name 'Symeon' is used as well as the Gk surname, Peter. In 1:16 the author claims to have been present at the transfiguration (cf. Mk 9:2ff par.). He alludes almost certainly to 1 Pet in 3:1 ('this is the *second* epistle I am writing to you'). In 3:15 he calls Paul his 'brother'.

External Attestation

2 Pet is badly attested in church tradition—a fact which has encouraged even such conservative critics as Bishop Gore to reject its Petrine authorship. It is unknown until Origen, who first mentions it, but says its authenticity is doubted, while Eusebius classifies it among the 'antilegomena'. Jerome says

most people do not regard it as the work of Peter. Only in the
fifth century did it become generally accepted. The Syrian
church has never regarded it as canonical.

Indirect Internal Evidence

Chapter 2 is lifted almost *verbatim* from Jude. But Jude's
denunciations and eschatological threats are applied to a
different situation. 2 Pet's opponents are not libertinist
gnostics (see below).

In some ways this is theologically the most Hellenistic of all
the NT writings. Note the phrase, 'partakers of the divine
nature' (θείας φύσεως, 1:4), a Greek rather than Biblical
concept.

2 Pet is written at a time when the NT Canon is taking shape,
both in idea (3:16, γραφαί) and in fact. He shows knowledge of a
Pauline corpus (3:15ff, contents not specified) and other 'scriptures'. He probably knows the synoptic accounts of the baptism[1] and transfiguration (1:17f). He appears to allude to
Jn 21:18f in 1:14 (martyrdom of Peter). He knows Jude (ch. 2).
He regards the church as the authoritative guardian and
interpreter of scripture (1:20).

All these factors indicate a date well into the second century.
Its *terminus a quo* is 100 (Jude), and a date *c.* 125 would appear
to fit the case.

The Opponents in 2 Peter[2]

The author is confronted by 'scoffers' who ask (3:3): 'Where
is the promise of his coming?' (3:4). They deny the parousia
hope. The common view is that they were simply ordinary
Christians who were concerned at the delay in the parousia,
and therefore eliminated it from their faith. But this is to over-

---

[1] The heavenly voice combines the voices at the baptism and transfiguration.
[2] Cf. the treatment in E. Käsemann, 'Eine Apologie der urchrist-
lichen Eschatologie' (1952), repr. in *Exegetische Versuche und Besinnungen*, I, 1960, pp. 135–57.

look the importance of ch. 2. Here the author takes over Jude's diatribe against the libertinist gnostics, and carefully re-edits it to apply its denunciations and threats to his opponents. It is unlikely that 2 Pet would have retained such strong language against harmless Christians concerned with a legitimate problem. They are clearly 'false teachers . . . bringing in destructive heresies' (2:1). They celebrate their own (sectarian) agape (2:13). They follow the way of Balaam (2:15)—the same accusation levelled against heretics in Rev 2:14. We begin to suspect some kind of gnosticism, albeit a different kind from that combatted in Jude. The denial of the parousia suggests an over-emphasis on the 'already' of Christian experience like that which led to a denial of the future resurrection by the gnostics at Corinth and in 2 Tim 2:18. The reference to 'cleverly devised myths' (1:16) reminds us again of the gnostics in Past. The matter appears to be clinched where the author holds out against them the true 'knowledge' (ἐπεγνωκέναι) (2:21) and says it would have been better for them never to have *known* the way of righteousness than after knowing it to turn back (to a false gnosis); cf. 1:2, 3, 8.

The Author's Reply

In ch. 2 the author repeats the denunciations, threats and name-calling of Jude, with the modifications which have thrown light on the distinctive nature of his opponents as compared with those of Jude. But he also develops in reply an element only briefly touched upon in Jude namely the assertion, over against the gnostic 'myths', of the authentic apostolic tradition ('faith', 1:1; 'the truth that you have', 1:12; 'the holy commandment *delivered*' (παραδοθείσης, i.e. tradition, 2:21). This tradition takes its origin in the eyewitness of the apostles (1:12ff, the transfiguration). The device of Petrine pseudonymity serves the same purpose. Unlike the gnostics, the author does not intend to innovate, but to allow Peter and the authentic apostolic tradition to be heard in the post-apostolic age.

This tradition is enshrined in an incipient canon of scripture which includes the OT (1:20) plus a nucleus of NT scriptures (3:15f). But it is not enough to have a canon, for the scriptures can be 'twisted' (3:16) by 'private interpretation' (1:20, RV), which is precisely what the gnostics were doing to St Paul (by isolating the 'already' from the 'not yet'?) 2 Pet is concerned to reassert the 'not yet' by re-affirming the parousia hope in language derived from some primitive Christian apocalypse (3:7, 10, 12f), but removing from it the imminence of the final catastrophe. The latter he does by appealing to Ps 90:4 (for God 1 day = 1000 years, and 1000 years = 1 day, 3:8). This removal of the element of imminence radically distinguishes the author's position from that of the apostolic age; cf the treatment of futurist eschatology in Lk-Acts, see above, p. 120. The function of the parousia is also markedly different. The parousia simply serves to reward the godly and punish the heretics (cf. 2 Thess, see above, p. 58). Despite 3:13 there is little emphasis on the final cosmic triumph of God in Christ (contrast 1 Cor 15). The reward is conceived in characteristically Hellenistic terms as participation in the divine nature (1:4). Meanwhile, in order to attain that reward the faithful are exhorted to a bourgeois morality reminiscent of Past (1:5ff; 3:11). Note again the word εὐσέβεια (piety), 1:3, 6, 7; 3:11, characteristic of Past, and ἀρετή, 'virtue', used by Paul only where he is deliberately quoting a list of Stoic virtues (Phil 4:8).

Summary of Contents

Ch. 2. Attack on the false teachers. The credibility of their false teaching destroyed. Jude is incorporated almost *in toto*.

Ch. 3. An apology for the church's traditional futurist eschatology, incorporating a little apocalypse (3:10ff).

3:17f. Concluding exhortation and doxology.

The Importance of 2 *Peter*

Its patent unauthenticity and the unbiblical, Hellenistic elements in its thought have led to the relegation of 2 Pet to the fringe of the NT Canon and to its widespread neglect. This is unjustified. 2 Pet is the clearest example in the Canon of 'early catholicism', and as such it is of great importance both historically and theologically. Historically it shows how two of the main features of early catholicism: (1) the formation of the NT Canon as the norm of Christian faith; (2) the concept of the church as its guardian and authorized expositor, took shape in response to the challenge of gnosticism, with its claim to fresh revelations additional to the once-for-all revelation in the Christ event attested by the apostolic witnesses.

Theologically, it poses (together with the other 'early catholic' writings in the NT, viz. Lk-Acts, Past, Heb, Jas, 1 Pet, and Jude), by its very place in the Canon, the question of authority of early catholicism in the continuing life of the church. Early catholicism was faced with the problem, how does the church continue the apostolic witness in the post-apostolic age? It answered this question by the development of four institutional structures: (1) the Canon of scripture, including both the OT and Christian writings (2 Pet); (2) the creeds or confessions of faith (the creedal hymns); (3) the baptismal (1 Pet) and eucharistic (Heb) liturgies; (4) a ministry in apostolic succession as the guardians and interpreters of apostolic tradition (Lk-Acts, Past). The fact that all of these developments are beginning within the NT indicates that the institutional structures of early catholicism are not to be dismissed as a sad declension from the amorphous freedom and spontaneity of the apostolic age, but are the normative response to that age by the post-apostolic church. The church continues to be post-apostolic today, and is faced by the same basic problem, how can it continue to be apostolic now that the apostles have gone? These four institutional structures remain the normative answer to that question.

Not all aspects of early catholicism are salutary, e.g. its conventional bourgeois morality, its propositional understanding of faith, its relegation of the eschatological hope to the last chapter of dogmatics and the consequent loss of its existential relevance, the total suppression of the charismata. But these writings are balanced by the presence of earlier, apostolic writings in the NT, viz., the gospel tradition, the kerygmatic traditions in Acts and the genuine Pauline letters. Without the institutional forms of early catholicism, these apostolic elements would have evaporated in the speculative mythology, the dualistic asceticism and libertinism, and the false spiritual enthusiasm of gnosticism.

CHAPTER

VI.—THE JOHANNINE LITERATURE

THE Johannine writings (Jn; 1, 2, 3 Jn) demand a chapter to themselves. The fourth gospel is so different from the synoptics in structure, contents and theological outlook that it cannot be treated with them. And although the letters belong to the sub-apostolic period, they differ so markedly from the 'early catholic' outlook of the deutero-Pauline and non-Pauline writings that they too require separate treatment.

True, Johannine Christianity was wrestling with many of the same problems which confronted the other sub-apostolic writers. It too was faced with the same basic question, how to be apostolic now that the apostles have been removed from the scene. It too was confronted with a heresy, which as, we shall see, was a particular kind of gnosticism. It too had to come to terms with the delay in the parousia. But the answers it came up with were very different, so different as to form a new and creative type of Christianity. Johannine Christianity in some ways revived the essential features both of Jesus' message and (without direct dependence upon it) of the Pauline kerygma, though it presented both in a markedly different idiom. Above all, Johannine Christianity does not fit into the neat patterns of early catholicism, with its institutional structures. It has even been suggested[1] that it was formulated in conscious opposition to early catholicism. It is better perhaps to see in it an independent creative achievement which served whether intentionally or not as a much needed corrective to the less salutary tendencies in early catholicism. Johannine Christianity is thus a unique phenomenon in the NT.

[1] E. Käsemann, 'Ketzer und Zeuge' (1951), repr. in *Exegetische Versuche und Besinnungen*, I, pp. 168–87.

THE GOSPEL OF JOHN

The history of Johannine criticism down to 1960 has been
sketched in the present writer's *The New Testament in Current
Study*, 1963, to which the reader is referred. The discussion
here will be devoted to the question of (1) sources; (2) the
Johannine composition; (3) Redaction and Displacement
Theories; (4) authorship, date, provenance, and purpose.

(1) *Sources:* (i) *Narrative*

Since the appearance of *The New Testament in Current Study*,
Dr C. H. Dodd has published *Historical Tradition in the Fourth
Gospel*, 1963. This great work has reinforced the trend there
noted, viz., the view that Jn is independent of the synoptists,
including Mk.

Jn's resemblances to Mk are confined to three stretches: the
Baptist's preaching and the baptism of Jesus (Jn 1:19–34); the
central crisis (Jn 6:1–21, 66–71); and the passion narrative with
its prelude (2:13–22; 12:1–8, 12–15; 13:1f, 21–38; 18; 19;
20:1–10). We agree with P. Gardner Smith, R. Bultmann and
C. H. Dodd that in none of these three stretches is there
sufficient verbal similarity to justify a theory of the literary
dependence of Jn upon Mk. Instead, we conclude that Mk and
Jn are drawing upon a tradition which was ultimately from the
same source but which has been transmitted by different
channels. This suggests that all three of these complexes
(Baptist's ministry, central crisis, and passion narrative) took
shape quite early in the history of the tradition. At certain
points the Johannine version represents a better tradition than
that found in Mk, thus enabling us to correct Mk by Jn. The
following material may be assigned to these three complexes[1]:

(i) Baptist Complex:

1:19–51.

3:22–30.

---

[1] Allowance must be made throughout for growth in the tradition,
and for Johannine redaction.

(ii) Central crisis:

    6:1–24.

    6:66–71.

(iii) Passion narrative:

    12:1–19. Anointing and entry.

    2:13–22. Cleansing of Temple.

    11:47–53. Plot of Sanhedrin.[1]

    13. The supper: the meal, the footwashing, the un-masking of Judas and prediction of Peter's denial.

    18–20. The arrest, examination, trial, crucifixion, and resurrection narratives.

Secondly, following Bultmann, we postulate a collection of signs[2] containing:

    2:1–11. Cana of Galilee.

    4:46–54. The Official's son.

    5:1–16. The Bethesda healing.

    9:1ff. The man born blind.

    11:1ff. The raising of Lazarus.

Thirdly, it is possible that the evangelist had further traditions of the pronouncement story type, now no longer recoverable in their original form:

    3:1ff. The visit of Nicodemus.

    4:1ff. The Samaritan woman.

    7:1ff. Jesus at the Tabernacles.

    10:22ff. Jesus at the Hanukkah.

    12:20ff. The Greeks at the Passover.

Either the evangelist has a series of episodes connected with

---

[1] The evangelist has clearly rearranged this material. For Jn the Cleansing of the Temple serves as a programmatic preface to the ministry, while the plot of the sanhedrin has been attached to the raising of Lazarus, so that the latter becomes the immediate cause of the arrest.

[2] The evidence for this is set out in *Interpreting the Miracles*, pp. 88ff, and the separation of the tradition from the reaction, *ibid.*

Jesus at various feasts at Jerusalem,[1] or he has himself constructed these connections with Jewish feasts for symbolic
reasons.[2] On the whole, however, it does not appear that the
evangelist invents narrative incidents, but takes them from
the tradition.

The narrative tradition used by the evangelist appears to be
of varying antiquity and historical value. Some of it is of high
value and enables us to supplement or correct the synoptic
accounts, e.g. the attempt of the crowd after the feeding to put
Jesus at the head of a Zealot movement (6:15), or the dating of
the last supper on the eve of the passover (13:29; 18:28; 19:14).
Often, the narrative material shows remarkable familiarity
with Jerusalem topography (e.g. the pool of Bethesda, 5:2;
Siloam, 9:7, 11; Kidron, 18:1; Gabbatha, 19:13). Often too, the
language shows a high degree of semitic colouring. On the other
hand, the miracle tradition is far more developed in a Hellenistic direction than the synoptic miracles[3] and surpasses Mk in
presenting Jesus as a Hellenistic 'divine man'. The narrative
tradition in the fourth gospel has passed through a long history.

At certain points (where the narrative tradition passes the
tests of authenticity), it may be used in the quest of the
historical Jesus. It is no longer legitimate to leave the Johannine material completely aside in historical reconstruction.
Thus we can employ the data in the Baptist complex to yield
the information (not obtainable from the synoptists) that
Jesus and some of his later disciples began their career as
disciples of John the Baptist, and that only after the latter's
imprisonment did Jesus begin an independent ministry.

We have already used the Johannine data to elucidate the
central crisis (above, p. 82n2).

[1] Historically there is something to be said for John's extension of the
Jerusalem ministry backwards from the final Passover to the previous
Tabernacles. These are hints in the synoptists of a longer Jerusalem
ministry, esp. Lk 13:34 par. (Q).
[2] It has sometimes been suggested that the Evangelist arranged his
teaching material according to the Jewish liturgical calendar. Cf. e.g.
A. Guilding, *The Fourth Gospel and Jewish Worship*, 1960.
[3] See *Interpreting the Miracles*, pp. 92–6.

Finally, we have used the Johannine passion narrative in the attempt to establish a common nucleus and the earliest form of the passion tradition (above, pp. 89–91), and have indicated that Jn helps us to elucidate the chronology and topography of the passion story.

(ii) *The Logia Tradition in John*

The Johannine discourse material enshrines logia which are couched in the same forms (parabolic sayings and poetic aphorisms) as the synoptic material and cover a similar content.[1]

   (i) Sayings (often poetic in form and in content, with parallels in the Synoptics):

      3:3, 8; 5:30; 6:38; 10:15; 12:25, 26; 13:16, 17, 20; 14:13f; 16:23f.

   (ii) Parables and parabolic sayings:

      3:29; 4:35–38; 8:35; 10:1–5; 11:9f; 12:24; 16:21.

   (iii) 'Son of man' sayings:

      1:51; 3:13–15; 5:27–29; 6:27, 53, 62; 8:28; 12:23, 34; 13:31f.

   (iv) 'Son' sayings (= later development of Son of man sayings):

      3:16, 35f; 5:19–23; 25f.

   (v) Paraklete sayings:

      14:15–17, 25f; 15:26; 16:4b–11, 12–15.

   (vi) OT testimonia in discourses:

      6:31 = Ps 78:24; 6:45 = Isa 54:13; 7:42 = Mic 5:1; 12:38 = Isa 53:1; 12:40 = Isa 6:9f; 13: 18 = Ps 41:10; 15:25 = Ps 69:5.

---

[1] See C. H. Dodd, *Historical Tradition*, pp. 315–420. The criteria for distinguishing between tradition and redaction in the discourses are provided by form—and style—criticism. The characteristics of Johannine style are ascertainable from features common to the letters and the discourses in the gospel.

(2) *The Johannine Composition*

Like the synoptists, John has provided editorial links for his pericopes and blocks of material. Such links are: 2:12f; 4:1–4, 43–46; 5:1; 6:1f; 7:1; 10:40; 11:54; 12:1, 9–11. Characteristic of the Johannine links are the cross references. There are also generalizing summaries, similar to those in the synoptic gospels: e.g. 2:23–25; 3:22–24; 10:19–21, 41f.

But the most important feature of the Johannine composition is the discourse material. This includes: the Prologue (1:1–18); the Nicodemus dialogue (3:4–21); the Baptist's testimony (3:27–36); the dialogue with the Samaritan woman (4:9–26); dialogue with the disciples in Samaria (4:31–38); the discourse appended to the healing at Bethesda (5:17–47); the bread discourse (6:26–58); discourse and dialogue at the Tabernacles (7:16–36, 37–52; 8:12–58); the discourse on the Good Shepherd (10:1–18); dialogue at the Dedication (10:24–38); discourse to the Greeks at the Feast (12:23–36); evangelist's concluding comment on the signs (12:37–43); Jesus' concluding words on the signs (12:44–50); farewell discourses (chs. 14–16); high priestly prayer (ch. 17). In addition, certain narratives, which do not have full-length dialogues or discourses appended to them, have received Johannine touches (the Cana miracle (2:1–11); the official's Son (4:4:46–54); the raising of Lazarus (11:1–44)[1]; the feet-washing (ch. 13).

Two questions arise in connection with this Johannine material. First, to what extent did the evangelist use sources? Bultmann[2] believes that the bulk of this material is derived from an earlier source consisting of 'revelation discourses'. This is highly uncertain, and has not found general acceptance, even within the Bultmann school.[3] Only the Prologue may with some probability be assigned to a source, perhaps a pre-Johannine hymn to the Logos derived from Baptist sources.[4]

---

[1] See *Interpreting the Miracles*, pp. 96ff.
[2] *Das Evangelium des Johannes*, Meyer Commentary 1959[16].
[3] See *The New Testament in Current Study*, p. 125 (U.S. Ed. p. 113).
[4] See *The Foundations of New Testament Christology*, pp. 222ff.

But the discourses are not entirely the free composition of the evangelist. It has already been shown that there are embedded in them many tradition logia and parabolic sayings (see above, p. 172). The Johannine discourse material gives the impression of being the result of prolonged mediation upon these sayings, couched in the evangelist's own thought and language. This thought is based upon a dualistic conception of light/darkness, truth/falsehood, life/death, love/hatred, world/Christian fellowship. But it is a 'dualism of decision' (Bultmann), not a metaphysical dualism. Jesus is the Revealer who brings the eschatological revelation of light, truth, life, faith and love. Men are confronted with a decision to receive it: if they reject it they choose darkness, falsehood, death, unbelief, hatred.

The evangelist provides an important clue to his composition of the discourses in the Paraklete sayings of the farewell discourses where Jesus is made to affirm that the revelation he brought will be continued by the Paraklete: 'he will glorify me, for he will take what is mine and show it to you' (16:14); 'when he (sc. the Spirit of truth) comes he will guide you into all the truth; for he will not speak of himself' (16:13); 'he will bear witness of me' (15:26). The evangelist claims that in his discourses the Paraklete is doing precisely this, taking the sayings of Jesus as they have come down in the tradition and expounding them in the later situation of the church.

If we reject Bultmann's theory of the gnostic revelation discourses as the source for the Johannine discourse material, we are still left with the problem of the origin of Johannine thought. The affinities of Johannine thought with the dualism of the Dead Sea Scrolls suggests that there is some connection.[1] The best explanation seems to be that Johannine thought springs from early Palestinian Jesus tradition, which, unaffected by the Pauline-Marcan tradition, coalesced with Jewish heterodox traditions of a dualistic character which in turn as the prologue suggests, reached Christianity *via* Baptist circles.

[1] *New Testament in Current Study*, pp. 137–41 (U.S. Ed. pp. 125–9).

(3) Redaction and Displacement Theories

The story of the woman taken in adultery (*pericope de adultera*), Jn 7:53–8:11, is a later, non-Johannine interpolation, as the MS evidence and considerations of form and style show.

Chapter 21 is widely considered to be a later addition. The style, vocabulary and content are thoroughly Johannine, but 20:30f looks like the concluding summary of the gospel. Jn 21 begins a completely new series of resurrection narratives located in Galilee and unrelated to the Jerusalem series in ch. 20. At the very least, 21:24f is an editorial addition. More likely it indicates that ch. 21 as a whole is an appendix added by the Johannine school. Its purpose is to identify the beloved disciple with the writer of the gospel.

Bultmann has carried the theory of redaction much further. He holds that an 'ecclesiastical redactor' added the passages concerning futurist eschatology (5:25–29; 6:39, 40, 44, 54) and concerning the sacraments (3:5; 6:51c–58). He holds that the radical theological re-interpretation of the evangelist left no room either for futurist eschatology or for the sacraments. There is no MS evidence whatever for these omissions, and their effect is to reduce the Johannine theology to what Bultmann thinks it ought to be. Although the evangelist has practically equated the parousia with the coming of the Paraklete, he still leaves open the recognition that present salvation is an anticipation of the end, and awaits consummation (cf. 1 Jn). And although he concentrates on the continuation of Jesus' revelation through the church's preaching of the word through the Paraklete, this word is concretely actualized in the sacraments.

There are a number of dislocations and bad connections in the narrative and discourses. This has led to widespread theories of displacement. The most plausible are:

> 3:22–30 to after 2:12.
> Ch. 5, 6, 7 to the order: Ch. 6, 5, 7.
> 7:15–24 to after 5:47.

10:19–29 to after 9:41.

14:31 to after the farewell discourses.

Bultmann has proposed far more extensive rearrangements, too numerous to be listed here.[1] Some advocates of displacement theories have sought objective support from the fact that the displaced sections are often of the same length, thus suggesting the accidental rearrangement of leaves of a codex. But there is no MS evidence for these theories. Probably the apparent dislocations are due to (1) the 'spiral' nature of Johannine thought (see below, p. 178); (2) the unfinished nature of the gospel. Some of the discourse material has not been thoroughly assimilated into the discourse form (e.g. 3:31–36). The evangelist seems to have been toying with two versions of the farewell discourse (chs. 14, and 15–16). Rearrangement theories (esp. Bultmann's) are, like Bultmann's redaction theory, in danger of making Jn say what we think he ought to say. The task of exegesis is to make sense of the text before us. The reconstruction of the text is solely the task of legitimate textual criticism.

(4) *Authorship, Date, Provenance and Purpose*

Since the evangelist stands at the end of a process of tradition, Palestinian, Hellenistic, and Jewish-heterodox-Baptist, it is impossible to accept the traditonal (Irenaeus, *Adv. Haer* III, 1, 1) ascription of this gospel to John bar Zebedee. The alternative, John the Elder, is a shadowy figure, and does not help us very much. In any case, speculations about the relation of the two Johns have no basis in the evidence. The gospel remains anonymous. The traditional authorship is once more a second century attempt to secure apostolic authorship for a work it wanted to include in the Canon. Already the redaction of 21:24 identified the author with the 'Beloved Disciple' of 13:23; 19:26 (? 18:1f); cf. 19:35. The 'Beloved Disciple' is

---

[1] They are listed on pp. 5*–8* of his commentary, and the whole gospel as rearranged by Bultmann is set out by R. M. Grant, *A Historical Introduction to the New Testament*, 1963, pp. 160–2.

probably the eyewitness behind the passion narrative, hardly an 'ideal figure' (so Bultmann).

The date is certainly not later than 100, as the Roberts fragment shows.[1] Jn's probable independence of the synoptists removes the date of the latter as a *terminus a quo*. The appendix was clearly added later than Peter's martyrdom (21:19), but this does not help us to date chs. 1–20. The long development of the tradition apparent in Jn makes a date 90–100 still the most probable.

As for the provenance, a location which will do justice to the tradition-history behind Jn is required: a Palestinian narrative and logia tradition independent of the synoptists and overlaid by Hellenistic Gentile material, together with heterodox Jewish-Baptist thought. Wherever we locate Jn, the riddle remains of Jn's independence both of Paul and of Mk. The traditional assignment of Jn to Ephesus, dating from Ireneaus, satisfies most of the requirements. The Baptist movement is evidenced for Ephesus (Acts 19:1–7). But it cannot explain the absence of Pauline influence. W. Bauer's[2] suggestion that the gospel emanated from East Syria appears to be gaining favour among German scholars, especially in the Bultmann School. The problem with a Syrian provenance is again the absence of Pauline, Marcan (and Matthean) influence. It is more important to ascertain the place of Jn in the history of tradition than to assign it to a definite provenance.

The evangelist's purpose in writing is succinctly stated in 20:31. It is to contend against unbelief and to evoke the decision of faith in Jesus as the bearer of God's final revelation. There is an element of apologetic in the early chapter against the acceptance in Baptist circles of John the Baptist as the bearer of God's final revelation. Some have discovered an anti-docetic purpose in the emphasis on Jesus' humanity (e.g. 4:6f; 11:35). But these traits occur in the tradition, rather than in the Johannine composition, and take the human emotions of Jesus for granted rather than stress them theologically.

[1] See *The New Testament in Current Study*, p. 122 (U.S. Ed. p. 110).
[2] *Das Johannes-Evangelium*, HNT 6, 1925[2].

The absence of anti-docetic polemic is the most important difference between Jn and 1 Jn.

The Johannine Epistles

Together with the Fourth Gospel, 1, 2, 3 Jn form a distinct group in the NT. The theology, vocabulary and style of the epistles is remarkably similar to that of the discourse material in the gospel. For the most part, there is the same religious terminology, the same dualism between light/darkness, truth/falsehood, life/death, faith/unbelief, love/hatred, world/Christian fellowship. The thought of 1 Jn exhibits the same 'spiral structure' (esp. in 1 Jn; 2, 3 Jn by the nature of their material are more concise). The author states a thought, contemplates it from every angle, and apparently finishes up where he started. Yet there is a slight but perceptible movement to another thought, and the process is repeated.

On the other hand there are some differences between the thought of 1 Jn and that of the gospel. These differences were stated very forcibly by C. H. Dodd.[1] He notes a poverty of style in 1 Jn—the author works to death a few favourite constructions and expressions, and his vocabulary is more limited than that of the gospel. Some of these differences are due to the fact that Jn is using traditional sources (see above, pp. 169–172), whereas 1 Jn is mainly writing on his own account, and only occasionally drawing upon traditional formulae. Hence the absence of Semitisms and of OT testimonia (there is only one OT allusion, 3:12) from 1 Jn. The differences are accentuated if we follow Bultmann's theory about the ecclesiastical redactor of Jn (see above, p. 175), for then the futurist eschatological and sacramentalism allegedly absent from Jn are strongly marked in 1 Jn (futurist eschatology: 2:17, 18, 28; 3:2, 3a; 4:17; sacramentalism: 2:12, 20, 27; 3:9; 5:1, 6). Those who follow Bultmann (e.g. Marxsen, *Einleitung*, p. 221) make the interesting suggestion that there was an affinity between the hypothetical ecclesiastical redactor of Jn and the author of 1 Jn.

[1] *The Johannine Epistles* (Moffatt Commentary), 1946, pp. xlvii-lvi.

Both belong to the more ecclesiastical, traditionalist wing of
the Johannine school. Marxsen calls 1 Jn 'deutero-Johannine'.
Rejecting the redactor hypothesis, we see in this a confirmation
that Johannine theology has integrated the new elements with
traditional formulae, both in Jn and in 1 Jn.

There is a difference of purpose between Jn and 1 Jn. Jn is
directed against unbelief, and seeks to establish faith (see
above, p. 177). For Jn the opponent is unbelief, symbolized by
the 'Jews'. 1 Jn is directed against a heresy (see below).

Author. 2 and 3 John are without question by the same
author (cf. 2 Jn 1 and 3 Jn 1, and the cross-reference to 2 Jn
in 3 Jn 9). He calls himself *'the* Elder'. The use of the article
indicates that he is an Elder in a special sense, not just one of a
group of elders of a local church. He clearly claims a quasi-
apostolic authority. He addresses a local church over the heads
of its leaders (2 Jn) and addresses a leading member of the
church (3 Jn). He writes, like the author of Past or the author of
Heb and 1 Pet, as an apostolic delgate.[1]

While it is possible that 1 Jn is by a different author from
2, 3 Jn, there is no clear case against their identity.

The strong statements of 1 Jn 1:1–4 must not be taken to
imply apostolic authorship or eyewitness of the historical
Jesus. To 'see' (cf. 3:6) is the common experience of the whole
Christian fellowship, resting as it does on the work of the
Paraklete in transmitting the words and works of Jesus to later
generations (see Dodd, *ad loc.*).

There is no clear evidence for the dates of these three documents. It is not quite certain whether they were written before
or after Jn, though 1 Jn 5:8 appears to presuppose Jn 19:34.
2 Jn seems to have been written after 1 Jn, for the docetists
have now left the church and have organized a counter-
mission. Also 2 Jn 7 presupposes 1 Jn 2:18; 4:3. 3 Jn was clearly
written shortly after 2 Jn (3 Jn 9).

1 Jn was known to Papias (according to Eusebius, *H.E.* III,
39). The first clear attestation of 2 Jn is in Irenaeus. 3 Jn is not

---

[1] On the identification of the Elder of 2, 3 Jn with Papias' John the
Elder see above, p. 176.

clearly attested until Origen (first half of third century).
Eusebius places 1 Jn among the 'unquestioned books', 2 and 3
Jn among the 'antilegomena' (*H.E.* III, 25). 1 Jn was firmly
included in the canon by the end of the second century
(Muratorian Canon). 2 and 3 Jn were not finally included until
Athanasius (367).

1 JOHN

Occasion

The clue to the purpose of 1 Jn lies in 2:19. The author is
faced with a '1662 situation'. An influential group has left the
church. From the polemics of 1 Jn we gather that they were
gnostics. In 2:4 there is an attack on those who say 'I know
him', and against them 1 Jn develops the theses that orthodoxy
is the true gnosis (cf. 2:3, etc.). They appear to hold a docetic
Chritology: they denied the coming of Jesus in the flesh (1 Jn
2:22f; 4:2f; 5:6). The author's emphasis on the *blood* of Jesus
(1:7; 5:6; cf. 2:2) suggests that their docetism led to a denial of
the atoning significance of the cross. Coupled with their doctrinal heresies was a neglect of ethics. There is no indication
that they were libertinists (contrast Jude). Rather, their emphasis on an esoteric experience of gnosis leads them to despise
those ordinary church members who did not share this experience (cf. the pneumatics at Corinth). Hence the author's
insistence that true gnosis demands love of the brethren
(chs. 2, 3, 4 *passim*).

The departure of the gnostics was clearly a shock to the
continuing membership. So the author undertakes to re-
establish their confidence in Christian orthodoxy.

To begin with, the author identifies the gnostics with the
antichrist (2:18–22; 4:3). This is not mere name calling as in
Tit or Jude, but an attempt to place them in their proper
context in salvation history so as to reassure the faithful that
this is the last hour (2:18); at the same time it demythologizes
the concept (contrast 2 Thess 2:8ff). But the author is not
content with this. He goes on to make a constructive, creative

theological reply (contrast Past, Jude) by taking up the language of the gnostics and restating Christian orthodoxy in its terms. He transforms their metaphysical dualism (which gave rise to docetism and exclusiveness) into a dualism of decision, like that of Jn (1:5ff and *passim*). This Christian gnosticism preserves the reality of the incarnation (2:1, 23; 3:23; 4:1–6; 5:5–8) and atonement (1:7; 2:2; 3:16; 4:10; 5:8) and does justice to the ethical seriousness of the Christian faith (1:5–2:17; 2:28–3:24; 4:7–5:4a).

Literary Character

In form 1 Jn is not a letter, for it has no epistolary introduction or conclusion. Yet in content it is undoubtedly a letter. It envisages a very concrete situation (see above). And in 1:4; 2:1, 12ff; 5:13 the author refers to himself as 'writing' (contrast Heb). It seems that the author is really writing a letter, but that allows his theological concern to dispense him from the epistolary form, and to substitute a theological exordium (1:1–4) and conclusion (5:13–21) for the usual epistolary beginning and ending.

At the same time his work shows a homiletic pattern (cf. Heb) of alternating theological exposition and ethical exhortation:

1:5–2:17. Ethical exhortation. Right behaviour is consequence of true gnosis.

2:18–27. Christological exposition (against docetism).

2:28–3:24. Exhortation: 'abide in him'.

4:1–6. Christological exposition.

4:7–5:4a. Exhortation: What it means to be 'of God'.

5:4b–13. Christological exposition.

Appendix: 'The Three Heavenly Witnesses'

The modern critical texts of 5:8 read: 'There are three who bear witness, the Spirit, and the water, and the blood; and these three (literally) are into one', i.e. they converge upon one point, make the identical witness. AV (KJV) reads: 'There are three who bear witness on earth, the Spirit, and the water, and the blood, and these three are one, and there are three that bear witness in heaven, the Father, the Word, and the Spirit'.

This interesting reading, the clearest statement of the doctrine of the Trinity anywhere in the NT, is beyond all doubt a later insertion. It occurs in no Gk MS earlier than the fourteenth century, in no early Church Father, in no Old Latin text, and is absent even from the earlier texts of the Latin Vulgate. It is first quoted by Priscillian (†385, Spain). For the history of the reading after the printing of the first Gk NT see Dodd, *op. cit.*, pp. 127f, note 1.

2 JOHN

2 Jn is a real letter, both in form and content, written by 'the Elder' to 'the elect lady'. The content of the letter makes it obvious that 'lady' is a personification of a local congregation (vv. 1, 5, 6). Cf. 3 Jn 9, which is a cross-reference to 2 Jn.

2 Jn presupposes the same general situation as 1 Jn: docetists who have left the church (v. 7), and are stigmatized as antichrists. But the situation has a new feature: these docetic heretics are appearing as wandering preachers to pervert continuing Christians (v. 10). The letter is written to instruct the church what to do when such emissaries arrive (*ibid.*).

The readers have received the true teaching (vv. 1, 4, 6, 8) and so have the doctrinal and ethical criteria by which to judge the false teaching. The emissaries are to be tested by their acceptance of the incarnation, the reality of Jesus' coming in the flesh. If they deny that, they are to be refused hospitality.

3 JOHN

3 Jn, like 2 Jn, is definitely a letter, addressed by the Elder not to a church but to an individual, one Gaius (v. 1). He cannot be identified, but is clearly a prominent member of the local church to which 2 Jn is addressed (v. 9).

The letter is occasioned by a concrete situation. Travelling missionaries have turned up in the church (v. 5f). They are not however the gnostic-docetic missionaries of 2 Jn, but orthodox missionaries sent by the Elder himself (vv. 5, 9). Gaius is praised for having received them (v. 5). But another member of the church, one Diotrephes, has refused to accept them (v. 9) and has thwarted those who were all ready to do so (v. 10).

Does the question of orthodoxy *versus* heresy play any part in the contest between Diotrephes and Gaius? The only clear accusation against Diotrephes is that he was an ambitious demagogue (v. 9). Some (Dodd, Käsemann) have suggested that Diotrephes was aspiring to the monarchical episcopate, and that the author of 1 Jn is resisting this development. But there is perhaps some suggestion that Diotrephes was sympathetic towards gnosticism in (vv. 11f). The phrase 'has not seen God' suggests the gnostic claim to visions. The reference to 'evil' may be an allusion to heresy and the emphasis on 'truth' in vv. 1, 3, 4, 8 and 12 suggests that doctrinal error was involved. So we cannot rule out the possibility of a gnostic background to the controversy between Diotrephes and Gaius. The Demetrius mentioned in v. 12 is probably an emissary of the Elder.

3 Jn is written in order to encourage Gaius to stand firm until the Elder himself arrives (v. 14).

G

VII.—THE APOCALYPSE

Apocalyptic as a Literary Genre

After the Babylonian exile there was a decay of prophecy in Israel. Its place was taken by the wisdom literature, and by apocalyptic. Like prophecy, apocalyptic takes for granted Israel's election and redemptive history. Like prophecy, too, it is concerned with the future, especially with the culmination of history. But unlike prophecy, apocalyptic portrays that culmination not in this-worldly terms, but in a new heaven and a new earth. It envisages two ages, this age and the age to come. It is this transcendental element which marks the salient difference betqeen prophecy and apocalyptic. A second difference is apocalyptic's use of the most fantastic imagery to describe both historical and transcendental events. This imagery, like the basic concept of the two ages, appears to have been derived originally from Persian (Zoroastrian) sources.

Apocalyptic writing takes the form of a series of visions purportedly delivered to some patriarch or prophet of old and sealed up (Dan 12:4; Rev 22:10) until their 'discovery' at the real date of writing. The reason for this device is that, with the decay of prophecy, this was the only way the apocalyptist could put across his message as the word of the Lord. The visions convey first, the history of the 'future' (actually, the past up to the time of writing), and then the real future at the time of writing. This real feature again is divided into two parts: first, future events in history, then the final cosmic catastrophe issuing in a new heaven and new earth. Each of the periods is described in different sets of imagery. The imagery which describes past events up to the time of writing is thinly veiled and easily decoded. That which describes future events on the historical plane is vague and imprecise,

and that which describes future cosmic events is bizarre and
fantastic. It is the point at which the shift occurs from the
easily decoded to the vague imagery that marks the date of the
apocalypse.

The first complete apocalypse which we have is the Book of
Daniel (though parts of Isa and Zech 9–14 include apocalyptic
material). The other Jewish apocalypses are found in the
apocrypha (2 Esdras) and pseudepigrapha (Enoch, Sibylline
Oracles etc.).

The purpose of all apocalyptic writing is to reassure the
elect that their present tribulation will be short-lived and will
soon issue in the final triumph God's purpose in the advent of
the age to come. Apocalyptic thus tends to appear in times of
crisis. At certain crises of Israel's post-exilic history, e.g. the
Maccabean Revolt, the Roman conquest, the Jewish War of
66–70, apocalyptic flares up, only to die down when the crisis
is past.

The Apocalypse

Unlike the Jewish apocalypses, Rev is not attributed to a
patriarch or prophet of the remote past. The author simply
gives his own name ('John', 1:1, 4, 9; 22:8). He is not John
the Apostle (cf. 18:20 and 21:14 where the apostles are a closed
group of which he himself is not a member), nor is he using the
name John as a pseudonym in order to suggest apostolic
authorship, for nowhere does he assert the claim of eyewitness
to the historical Jesus. This is significant. In the early church
there was a revival of genuine prophecy as a charisma (cf. 1 Cor
11–14), and a prophet could once more speak with the authority of 'Thus saith the Lord'. There was no longer any need to
adopt the pseudonym of a bearer of revelation in the remote
past of salvation history. To his readers (though not to us)
John was well known. He writes to seven churches in Asia
Minor. He is one of themselves, but exiled on the island of
Patmos not far from Ephesus on the mainland. The fact that
the seven churches begin at Ephesus and continue in a circle
from there indicates that John came from Ephesus.

In Direct Evidence

The author can hardly be identical with the author(s) of the Johannine writings, despite the long tradition in favour of their identity. There are too many differences between Rev and the Johannine writings. For instance, the seer uses Johannine words in an un-Johannine sense (e.g. ἀλήθεια, truth). He also uses different words for the same concept, e.g. 'Lamb' as a christological term in Rev is ἀρνίον (5:6, etc.) and in Jn ἀμνός (Jn 1:29, 36). But still more striking is the difference in the Gk. Rev contains the worst Gk in the NT. The author translates Semitic idioms literally (e.g. 1:5; 2:27; 3:8; 12:6). He makes grammatical mistakes (1:4, 15f; 2:13f; 3:12). Sometimes this could be explained as a translation Gk. More often it is the writing of one who thought in Hebrew (or more likely in Aramaic), and who, having come to use Gk late in life never really mastered it. Perhaps he was an elderly refugee from Palestine who settled in Ephesus after 70. At the same time, there is some indisputable connection between the Johannine literature and Rev. The same phrases occur, e.g. Rev 2:2/Jn 16:12; Rev 20:6/Jn 13:8; Rev 22:15/Jn 3:21; Rev 22:17/Jn 7:37. Note also the same departure from LXX in the citation of Zech 12:10f in Rev 1:7/Jn 19:37.

R. H. Charles[1] explained these facts by suggesting that both writers were members of the same religious circle in Ephesus. But they are poles apart in theology. Jn is the least apocalyptic of all NT writings (see above, p. 175). Perhaps the facts can be sufficiently accounted for by assuming that the Jewish heterodox-Baptist tradition in Jn grew out of apocalyptic.[2] It seems difficult to postulate any *direct* contact between the author of Rev and the Johannine school.

---

[1] *The Revelation of St John*, Vol. I (ICC), 1920, p. xxxiii.
[2] Some of the phrases common to Jn and Rev occur in the Dead Sea Scrolls—e.g. 'do the truth/falsehood'. Dr R. M. Grant has suggested that 'gnosticism is apocalyptic run to seed' (*Gnosticism and Early Christianity*, 1959). While his genetic theory is untenable in the form in which he has propounded it, there is something to be said that the dualism of the Dead Sea Scrolls which found its way into later Jewish heterodoxy was grafted on to an originally apocalyptic tradition.

Date

Irenaeus, writing *c.* 180 (*Adv. Haer.* V, 30, 3), quotes a statement (probably from Papias) to the effect that 'the Revelation
was seen not long ago, but almost in our generation at the end
of Domitian's reign (i.e. *c.* 96)'. 'Not long ago' will refer to a date
not shortly before 180, but shortly before Papias' time (140).
There is internal support for this dating.

Rev knows the earlier NT writings: Mt and Lk, the Pauline
epistles (except Past). There is, it is true, some internal
evidence for an earlier date. On the most likely interpretation
of Rev 13:18, the number 666 refers to Nero (54–68). In 17:10f
five kings (Roman Emperors) are said to have fallen, and the
sixth to be still alive, which takes us down to Galba (68–69).
The 'ten diadems' of 13:1 is probably a reference to ten
Emperors, which brings us down to Titus (79–81). These
passages may however have been incorporated from earlier
apocalyptic material. According to Charles (*op. cit.*, pp. scv, ff)
the Nero *redivivus* myth developed in two stages. At first it was
believed that Nero had not actually died (cf. Kitchener,
Hitler) but had gone to Parthia, whence he would return at
the head of an army to attack the empire. This is the form of
the myth in Rev 17:11–18. By the 90s it was accepted that
Nero had actually died, but expected he would be resurrected
in the form of the Great Beast. This form of the myth occurs
in Rev 13:11–17. Thus Rev contains material of various dates,
the latest of which points to a date in the 90s.

It is often argued that the persecution in Rev (1:9; 2:13;
6:9; 12:7f; 17:6) indicates a date towards the end of Domitian's
reign. Domitian was the first emperor actively to encourage
the imperial cultus in the East. He banished his niece,
Domitilla for 'atheism' (i.e. refusal to participate in the
imperial cultus) and executed her husband, Flavius Clemens.
It is almost certain that Domitilla was a Christian. But there is
otherwise no evidence for the persecution of Christians in Asia
Minor. We must be careful not to argue in a circle, by saying:
Rev shows that there were persecutions in Asia Minor in the

reign of Domitian, Rev was written in a period of persecution,
therefore it was written in the reign of Domitian. But the
'persecution' in Rev need not be a systematic attempt to
extirpate Christianity, as in the persecutions of the third
century. All that has actually taken place in Rev is one
martyrdom (2:13) and one banishment (1:9). It is not clear
that the martyrdoms of 6:9 have already occurred. This is
consistent with the policy of Domitian at the end of his reign.
It was one of 'capricious terrorism rather than systematic
persecution' (H. M. Gwatkin). Thus far, we may say that
Rev which *on other grounds* appears to have been written in
the 90s, is consistent with a date *c.* 95 in its references to
persecution.

The Occasion and Purpose of Revelation

John the Seer was in exile on the isle of Patmos 'for the word
of God', i.e. for refusal to participate in the imperial cultus.
There he receives a vision, which he is instructed to convey to
the seven churches of Asia Minor (1:11). The purpose of this
vision, as of all apocalyptic writing, is to encourage the elect
to hold firm in tribulation. This tribulation is caused partly
by the state persecution, partly by (?) Jewish antagonism[1]
(2:9; 3:9) and partly by internal heresies (2:2, 6, 14, 20ff). The
name-calling here suggests some type of libertinist gnosticism.

The Plan of the Apocalypse

There have been many attempts to analyse the structure of
Rev. The overall plan is simple enough: (1) Prologue, 1:1–8;
(2) Opening Vision, 1:9–20; (3) Letters to the seven churches;
chs. 2–3; (4) Visions, 4:1–22:5; (5) Epilogue, 22:6–21. The
difficulties lie with (4), the long central section which forms the
bulk of the book, and this is where the analyses differ. The
most plausible is that of E. Lohmeyer, reproduced by Bishop
Lilje in his commentary.[2] Its basis is that the author is working

[1] It is possible that 'synagogue of Satan' may also refer to a syncretistic gnosticism containing Jewish features.
[2] H. Lilje, *The Last Book of the Bible*, 1957.

VII] THE APOCALYPSE

with an unfolding series of sevens, the last of which unfolds
into the next series of seven. 'The series of visions open like a
seven-leaved flower, or a rocket in the night sky throwing out
more and more graceful forms in showers of sparks' (Lilje,
p. 24f). So we get:

4:1–5:14. The sevenfold prophecy.

6:1–7:17. The seven seals.

8:1–11:14. The seventh seal: the seven trumpets.

11:15–13:18. The seventh trumpet: the seven dragon visions.

14:1–20. The seven visions of the Son of man.

15:1–16:21. The seven bowls of the wrath of God.

17:1–19:10. The seven visions of the fall of Babylon.

19:11–21:5a. The seven visions of fulfilment.

The series of visions are then rounded off with:

21:5b–22:7. The promise.

22:8–19. The final scene.

22:20f. Conclusion and blessing.

Interpretation

Rev is written for a concrete situation. The church is in
tribulation, and the end of the world is imminent. Rev is not a
prophecy of later events in world history: its crisis is not some
contemporary crisis of our day. This is the sectarian misunderstanding of Rev.

The permanent value of Rev lies elsewhere. It provides
insights into the Christian understanding of history. History
is seen as the arena in which God works out His purpose. This
purpose embraces both the church and the unbelieving world.
History is a conflict between evil, which is cosmic on its scale,
though it uses historical powers as its instruments. The purpose
of God is to create a new heaven and a new earth in which the
elect will be vindicated.

There has been much discussion as to whether Rev should
be in the NT Canon. It is said, e.g., that the attitude towards the

church's enemies is sub-Christian (contrast, e.g., 6:10 with the Sermon on the Mount). Rev has been criticized for its emphasis on the wrath rather than on the love of God. But this is only to say that Rev does not contain the whole gospel. It is only one book in the Canon, and its partial insights can be balanced and corrected by the other books. The book is certainly Christian in the sense that, despite its concentration on futurist eschatology, the decisive event of redemption has taken place already (1:5; 5:6, 9; 11:8; 13:8).

VIII.—THE CANON OF THE NEW TESTAMENT

(a) THE FORMATION OF THE CANON

We have investigated the rise of the individual documents of the NT. All that remains is to trace the collection of these 27 books into a single volume. To do this in detail would require a book in itself, and all we shall attempt is to take soundings from various periods down to 367, when the Canon as we know it was complete. In so doing we shall concern ourselves not so much with the details of the story as with the motives which led to the collection of the NT books, and the criteria for acceptance or rejection of particular writings.

Period I—The Apostolic Age (30–70)

As yet even the OT Canon had not been finally fixed. But the Pharisaic school accepted the Pentateuch ('Moses') the historical books and the twelve prophets ('the Prophets'), the psalms and the OT wisdom literature (the 'writings').[1]

The apostolic kerygma proclaimed that the Christ event, to which the apostles bore witness, had happened 'according to the scriptures' (1 Cor 15:3f) that is, in fulfilment of God's future eschatological promises in the OT. Thus from the beginning the church took over ready made from old Israel the *idea* of a Canon of scriptures, but reinterpreted these writings in the light of the Christ event. Luke 24:44 shows exactly what the early church did: 'everything written about me in the law of Moses and the prophets and the psalms must be fulfilled'. The 'Canon' of this period consisted of the OT plus the living voice of the apostolic witnesses. Paul's 'Canon' has very little Jesus tradition. As part of this living voice the tradition containing the words and works of Jesus began to take shape side by side

---

[1] On the OT Canon see Anderson, pp. 10–11.

with the kerygma itself, as one of the means of perpetuating
the testimony to the Christ event. The earlier church continued Jesus' proclamation of the kingdom side by side with
its own. In this same period also, Paul wrote his letters. They
were a kind of extension of his own apostolic witness, given in
his missionary preaching. But they were written, as we have
seen, for concrete situations. Paul had no thought of creating a
new body of canonical writings. The fact that there was a
'living voice', then, was the primary reason why during period
I there was as yet no NT Canon or any idea of one. Secondly,
the early church believed that the parousia would occur within
the lifetime of the 'living voice', the apostolic witnesses to the
Christ event.

Period II—The Sub-Apostolic Age to the Apolojists (70–150)

The dying out of the apostles as the bearers of the living
testimony to Jesus Christ as the saving act of God together
with the non-arrival of the parousia and the consequent re-
adjustment to the continuation of salvation history made it
necessary for the church during the sub-apostolic period to
wrestle with the problem: how to be apostolic now that the
apostles were removed from the scene. The sub-apostolic
church coped with this problem by developing certain
institutional structures, which, as we have seen, are characteristic of 'early catholicism' (see above, pp. 166f). Of these
structures the idea of a Canon of normative Christian writings
was one. We can see this idea, like the other institutional
structures, already taking shape in the later writings of the NT.

2 Pet is the probably earliest and certainly the clearest
witness to the beginnings of a NT Canon (see above, pp. 163,
166). This document testifies (3:16) to the existence of a corpus
of Pauline writings (though its components are not specified).
These it recognizes explicitly as 'scriptures', together with
'other' such writings (*ibid.*). Again, the exact content of these
'others' is not specified. But the author clearly knows one or
more of the gospels (see above, p. 163) and 1 Pet (2 Pet 3:1).

Also, he knows Jude, but since he undertakes an extensive revision of that work, the author clearly does not regard it as authoritative. 2 Pet also witnesses indirectly to a decision with regard to the OT Canon, because it excludes Jude's quotations from the pseudepigraphical writings (Enoch).

Papias and Justin belong to roughly the same period as 2 Pet. Papias still prefers the 'living voice', i.e. unwritten tradition, as the source of knowledge about Jesus Christ.[1] But this source is running dry, and he cannot get much from it. Hence his further concern with Mk and Mt. He seeks to establish their apostolic authority by showing that Mt was written by the apostle Matthew and that Mk was dependent on the testimony of Peter (see above, pp. 113 and 104). The drying up of oral tradition is another of the motives which led to the idea of a body of apostolic writings as the norm of the church's faith.

Justin Martyr (Apology I, 67, 3) tells us that the 'memoirs' (ἀπομνημονεύματα) of the apostles', i.e. the gospels, were read at the liturgical assemblies of the church. He thus witnesses not only like 2 Pet and Papias to the *fact* of an incipient collection of writings (the precise constituents of which he again does not specify) but to another motive leading to the growth of the Canon. 'Canonical' means among the things 'accepted for liturgical use'.

Period III—To the End of the Second Century

Before the last half of the second century the church had developed the *concept* of a Canon, but had not found it necessary to come to any decision as to precisely what books were to be included in it. It is generally recognized that the heretic Marcion (Rome, c. 140) forced the churches to come to a decision on this question. In the interests of his own particular heresy Marcion set up a precise Canon of NT writings. He rejected the whole OT, and accepted among the Christian writings only: (1) 'The Gospel': Lk; (2) 'the Apostle', ten Pauline writings in the order: Gal, 1, 2 Cor, Rom, 1, 2 Thess,

[1] Eusebius, *H.E.* 39, 4.

Eph (which he called 'Laodiceans'), Col, Phil, Philem. He expurgated these writings of nearly all of their OT quotations.

The church perceived in Marcion's Canon a serious reduction of the number of those books which (without being very specific about it) it had regarded as canonical. So it had to come to grips with the question, what books it accepted in its Canon. Marcion did not create the *idea* of the Canon. He forced the church to make up its mind what was to be included in it, to produce a precise list of canonical books.

The earliest surviving list is the so-called Muratorian Canon.[1] The list contains: Mk (probably), Lk, Jn, Acts, 1, (?2) Cor, Eph, Phil, Col, Gal, 1, (?2) Thess, Philem, Tit, 1, 2 Tim, Jude, 1 and (?)2 Jn, Rev. It mentions two Pauline Epp, which were Marcionite forgeries, Laodiceans and Alexandrians, plus 'many others which cannot be received into the Catholic Church'. It also accepts an Apocalypse of Peter but with the qualification 'which some of us refuse to read in the Church'. Finally it mentions the Shepherd of Hermas, which it says ought not to be read because it was 'written very recently in our time'.

The Muratorian Canon indicates its criteria for admission not systematically, but incidentally. The criteria are: (1) apostolic authorship, whether direct, or mediate as in the case of Mk and Lk-Acts; (2) orthodoxy; (3) antiquity (which is another aspect of the criterion of apostolic authorship), cf. its attitude to Hermas; (4) use in the liturgical assembly (cf. Justin).

By now the Canon, both in idea and in content, has taken firm shape. The essential core consisting of the four gospels,[2] the Pauline epistles,[3] the Catholic epistles and less certainly

[1] This document is a Latin fragment contained in an eighth century MS. This MS was discovered in the library at Milan in 1740 by the librarian, Muratori, thence its name. A tr. will be found in H. Bettenson, *Documents of the Christian Church*, 1943, pp. 40f.

[2] The Muratorian Canon probably began with Mt. But the beginning has been lost. Mk is not named, but the incomplete opening sentence almost certainly refers to Mk. Lk is called the 'third gospel'.

[3] It is most likely that 1,2 Cor and 1,2 Thess are referred to as single epistles.

Rev is established. Some writings were later accepted but are not as yet included or even mentioned (Heb, Jas, 1, 2 Pet and one of the Johannine Epistles). Other writings are hovering on the edge of the Canon, either in it or out of it, like Hermas, and surprisingly, the Book of Wisdom.

Period IV—200–367

After 200 the fringe writings (Heb, 2 Pet, 2, 3 Jn, Jude, Jas, Rev) continued to be disputed being accepted by Rome churches and rejected by others. The Paschal letter of Athanasius (367) gives a list identical with our own 27 books, and in their present order. Doubts still lingered about some of the fringe writings, but the Canon of Athanasius came to be almost universally accepted.

(*b*) PROBLEMS OF THE CANON

The concept of the Canon raises a number of problems which belong to the prolegomena of Systematic Theology ('the sources of Christian Doctrine') rather than to NT Introduction. Such problems are: the nature of the Biblical norm for Christian doctrine and preaching, and the relation between scripture and tradition. Nevertheless, NT Introduction does have a bearing on these problems, and to this extent they are relevant here.

Modern critical study has in the first place made it impossible to regard the NT as a norm in any propositional sense. The NT contains not a single dogmatic system, but many different proclamations of the Christian faith (kerygmata) adapted to successive environments (earliest Palestinian Christianity, the Hellenistic Jewish congregations, the Gentile mission, and the sub-apostolic Hellenistic churches), and ranging over 75 years (50–125). Consequently there are as many variations in the kerygma as there are NT writers, and even within Paul there are variations between his earliest kerygma and his latest (cf. 1 Thess with Rom, and Col if genuine). This is a problem for Biblical theology rather than for NT Introduction.

Its solution must be found by inquiring into the basic unity which underlies all these varieties of kerygma. That unity will be found to lie in the proclamation of Jesus Christ as God's eschatological act, as the one in whom God has acted redemptively in anticipation of his final redemptive act in the end of history. This underlying kerygma gives a criterion for judging the variations of the kerygma. How far are these true to the basic kerygma as applications of that kerygma to each new situation?

A particularly acute form of the problem occasioned by the variations in the kerygma has come to the fore in the recent recognition of the presence of 'early catholicism' in several writings included in the NT Canon. The Bultmann school, to whom this recognition is due,[1] incline to relegate these writings to a subordinate position, if not to their practical exclusion from the Canon. For Käsemann, the Pauline doctrine of justification by faith alone is postulated as the true 'Canon within the Canon' (cf. Luther), and all other NT writings are measured by this norm. The early catholic writings esp. Lk-Acts, Past and 2 Pet) are seen as a sad declension from the Pauline heights. Their institutional structures are seen as unwarrantable restrictions of Pauline freedom and as a recrudescence of unevangelical Judaistic legalism. H. Küng has rightly criticised this kind of à la carte treatment of the Canon,[2] with its arbitrary selection of the Pauline doctrine of justification as the norm of canonicity. As we have implied in our discussion of the variations in the kerygma the idea of a Canon within the Canon is not in itself illegitimate, and in fact is necessary. But the inner Canon must lie at the heart of the NT message, in all its forms. The Pauline doctrine of justification is but one application of the core kerygma (see above, p. 56). Early Catholicism has to be accepted as an integral part of the Canon. It is the church's normative response to the apostolic age. Since the church in subsequent ages is always

---

[1] See esp. E. Käsemann, *Essays on New Testament Themes*, 1964.
[2] H. Küng, 'Early Catholicism in the New Testament', *The Council in Action*, 1963, pp. 159–95.

inevitably post-apostolic, it too is faced with the problem, how to be apostolic after the passing of the apostles. The response of the sub-apostolic church to this problem has normative significance for all succeeding ages. Early Catholicism is not the whole of the Canon. Its defects, when taken alone, we have freely admitted (see above, p. 167). Early catholicism stands open to balance and correction from other parts of the Canon, including the Pauline writings themselves. Above all, the institutional structures of early catholicism, viz., Canon, creed, baptismal and eucharistic liturgy, and ministry of bishops-in-presbytery standing in apostolic succession have their justification not in themselves, but precisely because and in so far as they are the providential means where by the apostolic testimony to Jesus Christ as the saving act of God was maintained in the sub-apostolic age and is still mediated to the church today.

A third problem raised by modern Biblical criticism for the concept of the Canon is that the criterion for canonicity is broken down today. Of the 27 books of the NT only the authentic Pauline epistles are, strictly speaking, the testimony of an apostolic witness. And even Paul (though his claim to be commissioned by the risen Lord as an apostle must be accepted by us as it was by the original apostles) was not a witness of the historical Jesus, so that to that extent his capacity as a witness is limited. Since the earliest witnesses wrote nothing (modern critical scholarship rejects the traditional apostolic authorship of Mt, 1 and 2 Pet and the Johannine writings), there is not a single book in the NT which is the direct work of an eyewitness of the historical Jesus. This would seem at first sight to destroy the whole notion of canonicity, as the preservation of the normative apostolic witness to the Christ event. In facing this difficulty, we have to recall that the earliest church also admitted Mk and Lk, which it confessedly regarded as apostolic only in a mediate sense. Therefore the Canon itself already recognizes the principle of mediate apostolic testimony. It is now necessary to extend this principle to all of the NT writings, save for the genuine Pauline epistles. And even here the principle of mediacy applies in part, since Paul is not a witness of the historical Jesus. See, e.g., 1 Cor 11:23ff, 15:3ff. It is precisely the concept of the 'Canon within the Canon' which we need again. Behind all the mediate apostolic witness lies the testimony of the first witnesses and what that testimony presupposes: the authentic memories of the words, works, and fate of Jesus, and the Easter encounters. Between them these memories and the Easter encounters created the basic kerygma, which underlies all the variations of the kerygma in the mediate witnesses. The NT may be accepted in a mediate sense as the record of this apostolic testimony. Of all the NT writers, in varying degrees, it may be said, as E. C. Hoskyns said of the author of the Fourth Gospel, that they, 'though belonging to a later generation, have been so completely created by apostolic witness and formed by apostolic obedience that they are veritably carried across into the company of the original disciples of Jesus and invested with the authority of their mission' (*The Fourth Gospel*, 1940, pp. 100f).

The final problem of the NT Canon set by modern criticism is that it has broken down the hard and fast distinction between scripture and tradition. Form criticism and traditio-historical criticism generally have shown that the NT is the tradition of the church between 30 and 125. Further, the NT is only a selection of the available traditions of that period: we know, e.g., that there were other Pauline epistles now lost (1 Cor 5:9; Col 4:16 [if Col. be genuine]). There were other remembered words and deeds of Jesus (Jn 20:30). There were the lost sources of the synoptic gospels, especially the Q source. And is there any distinction in principle today between the latest NT writings and such works as, say, 1 Clem, the Didache or Ignatius' letters? Unless we are to fall back upon some arbitrary theory of inspiration,[1] we are, it appears, hard

---

[1] On the unsatisfactory nature of this term for modern discussion see R. P. C. Hanson, 'The Inspiration of Holy Scripture', *ATR*, 43 (1961), pp. 145–52. Hanson proposes to substitute 'unique and indispensable witness' (p. 151).

put to it to justify the selection of this particular part of the tradition from 30 to 125 and the pronouncement of this and none other to be normative. Our answer again lies in the concept of the 'Canon within the Canon'. If we establish the basic kerygma behind its variations, it can be shown that the writings included within the NT stand relatively close to this basic kerygma, in a way which cannot be asserted of works outside the NT. The early church may not have been consciously aware of our concept of 'basic kerygma', but it showed a sure instinct in sifting out what was truly kerygmatic from what was not (faith would say this was divine providence). Of course there are rough edges. We might feel that 2 Pet and Jude or Rev are less close to the kerygma than Rom, Mk or Jn. We might equally feel that 1 Clem or the letters of Ignatius stand closer to the kerygma than the moralism of the Epistle of James. But this only shows that the concept of the Canon is not a legalistic one. The canonical writings shade off into the non-canonical ones. 'We might describe the Canon as a circle of light, with dazzling light at the centre and twilight at the edges.'[1] The dazzling light is the basic kerygma, the proclamation of Jesus Christ as the eschatological act of God, the Canon within the Canon.

[1] R. P. C. Hanson, *Tradition in the Early Church*, 1962, p. 246.

SELECT BIBLIOGRAPHY

The following list is limited to works in English and does not include commentaries.

1. GENERAL INTRODUCTIONS

The best short works are:

A. M. Hunter, *Introducing the New Testament* (S.C.M. Press, 1957²). Simple, lucid and reliable, from the British critical-conservative point of view.

E. J. Goodspeed, *An Introduction to the New Testament* (Chicago University Press, 1937). A standard work by one of the greatest American New Testament scholars.

The following are not technically introductions, but perform many of the functions of an introduction:

E. C. Hoskyns and F. N. Davey, *The Riddle of the New Testament* (Faber, 1931).

C. F. D. Moule, *The Birth of the New Testament* (A. and C. Black, 1962).

Of medium size:

A. H. McNeile, *Introduction to the Study of the New Testament*, rev. by C. S. C. Williams (Oxford University Press, 1953).

Full-scale works:

J. Moffatt, *An Introduction to the Literature of the New Testament* (T. & T. Clark, 1911). Still of great value as a history of criticism down to its date.

T. Zahn, *Introduction to the New Testament*, 3 vols. (T. & T. Clark, 1917²). A standard conservative introduction, of massive learning.

2. Special Subjects

A. *The Gospels*

B. H. Streeter, *The Four Gospels* (Macmillan, London, 1924).

M. Dibelius, *From Tradition to Gospel* (Nicholson and Watson, 1934).

R. Bultmann, *History of the Synoptic Tradition* (Blackwell, 1963).

H. Anderson, *Jesus and Christian Origins* (O.U.P., 1964). The best account in English of the 'new quest' of the historical Jesus and its literature.

P. Gardner Smith, *St John and the Synoptic Gospels* (C.U.P., 1938).

W. F. Howard, *The Fourth Gospel in Recent Criticism and Interpretation* (Epworth, 1955), rev. by C. K. Barrett.

Sherman Johnson, *The Theology of the Gospels* (Duckworth, 1966).

B. *The Acts*

F. J. Foakes Jackson and K. Lake, *The Beginnings of Christianity*, Part I, Vol. 2 (Macmillan, London, 1922). Definitive for the criticism of Acts in the pre-Dibelian era.

M. Dibelius, *Studies in the Acts of the Apostles* (S.C.M. Press, 1956). These essays, published at intervals from 1923, mark the shift from the source- to the form-critical study of Acts.

C. K. Barrett, *Luke the Historian in Recent Study* (Epworth, 1961).

C. *Paul*

A. Schweitzer, *Paul and His Interpreters* (A. & C. Black, 1912). The standard history of Pauline criticism through the first decade of the twentieth century.

J. Knox, *Chapters in a Life of Paul* (A. & C. Black, 1950). Recognizes the priority of the Epistles over Acts for the life and chronology of Paul.

F. W. Beare, *St Paul and His Letters* (A. & C. Black, 1962). Popular broadcast talks by an outstanding Canadian New Testament scholar.

D. *The Later New Testament Writings*

P. Carrington, *The Primitive Christian Catechism* (Cambridge, 1940). Form-critical method applied to the paraenetic sections of the epistles.

B. H. Streeter, *The Primitive Church* (Macmillan, London, 1929).

E. Käsemann, *Essays on New Testament Themes* (S.C.M. Press, 1964). Chapters III, IV and VIII. Käsemann inaugurated the discussion of 'early catholicism' in the later New Testament writings.

E. *The Canon*

A. Souter, *The Text and Canon of the New Testament* (Duckworth, 1960), rev. by C. S. C. Williams.

R. P. C. Hanson, *Tradition in the Early Church* (S.C.M. Press, 1962).

See also the essay, 'The History of the New Testament Canon' by W. Schneemelcher in E. Hennecke, *New Testament Apocrypha*, ed. by W. Schneemelcher (Lutterworth, 1963), vol. 1, pp. 28–60.

INDEX OF SCRIPTURE REFERENCES

INDEX OF AUTHORS

ANCIENT AUTHORS

MODERN AUTHORS

INDEX OF SUBJECTS